Rational Foundations of Democratic Politics

Democracy is widely accepted today as the most suitable form of government. But what is democracy, and does it always produce good government? Democracy is often associated with the existence of competitive elections. But theory and experience suggest that these are not sufficient for democracy to function reasonably well. In this book, a number of experts from North America and Europe use a rational choice approach to understand the foundations of democracy – what makes democracy successful, and why. They consider diverse problems of democratic governance such as the importance of morals or virtue in political life, negative advertising, the role of social capital and civil society in sustaining democracy, the constitutional and cultural prerequisites of democracy, and the interaction of democracy and markets.

Albert Breton is Professor of Economics Emeritus at the University of Toronto. He is author of *Competitive Governments* (1996) and *The Economic Theory of Representative Government* (1974), as well as numerous articles in professional and scholarly journals. Professor Breton has served as president of the Canadian Economic Association and is an officer of the Order of Canada.

Gianluigi Galeotti is Professor of Public Finance at the Universitá di Roma (La Sapienza), coeditor of several books, and author of numerous articles in professional and scholarly journals. He has previously taught at the Universities of Pisa and Perugia.

Pierre Salmon is Professor of Economics at the Université de Bourgogne. He is the author of numerous articles and coauthor of *Méthodologie Economique* (1985). He formerly taught at the Universitiés of Rennes and Paris and at the European University in Florence.

Ronald Wintrobe is Professor of Economics at the University of Western Ontario. He coauthored with Albert Breton *The Logic of Bureaucratic Conduct* (1982), and he is the author of *The Political Economy of Dictatorship* (1998), as well as numerous articles in professional and scholarly journals.

Professors Breton, Galeotti, Salmon, and Wintrobe previously coedited *The Competitive State* (1991), *Preferences and Democracy* (1993), *Nationalism and Rationality* (1995), *Understanding Democracy* (1997), and *Political Extremism and Rationality* (2002). Professors Galeotti, Salmon, and Wintrobe also coedited *Competition and Structure: The Political Economy of Collective Decision: Essays in Honor of Albert Breton* (2000).

Rational Foundations of Democratic Politics

Edited by

ALBERT BRETON

University of Toronto

GIANLUIGI GALEOTTI

Università di Roma (La Sapienza)

PIERRE SALMON

Université de Bourgogne

RONALD WINTROBE

University of Western Ontario

PUBLISHED BY THE PRESS SYNDICATE OF THE UNIVERSITY OF CAMBRIDGE
The Pitt Building, Trumpington Street, Cambridge, United Kingdom

CAMBRIDGE UNIVERSITY PRESS
The Edinburgh Building, Cambridge CB2 2RU, UK
40 West 20th Street, New York, NY 10011-4211, USA
477 Williamstown Road, Port Melbourne, VIC 3207, Australia
Ruiz de Alarcón 13, 28014 Madrid, Spain
Dock House, The Waterfront, Cape Town 8001, South Africa

http://www.cambridge.org

First published 2003

Printed in the United States of America

Typeface Times New Roman 10/12 pt.   *System* LATEX 2_ε [TB]

A catalog record for this book is available from the British Library.

Library of Congress Cataloging in Publication data

Rational foundations of democratic politics / edited by Albert Breton . . . [et al.].
p. cm.
Includes bibliographical references and index.
ISBN 0-521-82254-8
1. Democracy. I. Breton, Albert.
JC423 .R3234 2003
321.8–dc21   2002191145

ISBN 0 521 82254 8 hardback

Contents

Contributors

Albert Breton, Department of Economics, University of Toronto

Frédérique Chaumont-Chancelier, Centre d'Analyse Economique, Université d'Aix-Marseille III

Roger D. Congleton, Center for Public Choice, George Mason University

Gianluigi Galeotti, Università di Roma, La Sapienza

Alan Hamlin, Department of Economics, University of Southampton

Michael C. Munger, Department of Political Science, Duke University

Pierre Salmon, Faculté de Science Economique, Université de Bourgogne

Stergios Skaperdas, Department of Economics, University of California at Irvine

Viktor J. Vanberg, Department of Economics, University of Freiburg

Stefan Voigt, Department of Economics, University of Kassel

Ronald Wintrobe, Department of Economics, University of Western Ontario

Donald Wittman, University of California at Santa Cruz

1

Introduction

Albert Breton, Gianluigi Galeotti, Pierre Salmon,
and Ronald Wintrobe

Democracy is widely accepted today, perhaps as never before, as the most suitable form of government. But what is democracy, and does it always produce
good government? There is a tradition in popular thinking and in political science that associates democracy with the existence of competitive elections. This
follows the tradition of Schumpeter (1950) and Downs (1957) in public choice.
Competitive elections are undoubtedly a necessary condition for democracy.
But they are not sufficient for true democracy or for democracy to function reasonably well. For example, the fathers of the American Constitution expressed
their fear of factions and of mob sentiments. One problem with competitive
elections is that they provide no protection for minorities. A second is that they
may not express the long-term interests of the electorate itself, or their attitudes
in sober second thought. Yet a third is the well-known Arrow problem of cycli-
cal majorities – perhaps one of the central discoveries of modern public choice.
A fourth is the recurring tension between the two principles of government by
majority on the one hand and the rule of law on the other.

Contemplating the failures of democracy in theory, one early tradition in
public choice theorizing was based on the idea that, whatever its failings in
theory, democracy works well in practice. This puzzle arose early in public
choice theory,[1] and the question, "Why so much stability?" that is, specifically,
"Why do democracies appear so much more stable in practice than in theory?"
became an early preoccupation of public choice theory.

More recently, the notion of "civil society" has been advanced to explain
why some democracies seem to function fairly well, while others do not. The
experience of the Russian transition to democracy has been sobering for many, as
a country that seems to possess at least some of the requisites for democracy –
for example, competitive (more or less) elections and a very high level of
literacy – appears as of this date (2002) at least to be drifting again toward

---

[1] The question was raised this way by Gordon Tullock in "Why So Much Stability?" *Public Choice*
37, 1981, pp. 189–202.

authoritarianism as alternative sources of information and decision making are systematically neutralized by the government. Another problematic case is contemporary Italy, where the discovery of widespread corruption in 1992 has given rise to a number of attempts at reform, none of which seems to have been entirely satisfactory; and although the new prime minister does have a majority, his ownership of a large chunk of the country's media, and his use of this media to advance his candidacy, are disturbing. These two cases (Russia and Italy) illustrate the dilemma that may arise for those voters who, to get the policies that they consider as most important, may have to gloss over a number of other, more dubious democratic credentials of the team they support.

Lest these cases seem exceptional, or our thoughts about them overdrawn, the reader is asked to note that in the United States there is enormous concern with issues such as negative campaigning and campaign finance, that there was a substantial attempt to impeach the last American president, and that the current one (George W. Bush) obtained his office by a decision of the Supreme Court in what was perhaps the most contested presidential election result in U.S. history. Indeed, the behavior of the judicial system during that contest has led some to believe that it is not as independent of the other branches of government as might be desired. It seemed that at each level of the judiciary, both state and federal, the decision could be predicted with 100 percent success on the basis of what everybody knew of the partisan affiliation of the judges on that level. Finally, around the world there seem to be fewer governments every day that face effective opposition and even fewer that are not severely tainted by corruption.

One reflection of all this is that measures of trust in politicians in many democracies appear to be at a historic low,[2] and many people express the view that they do not believe any statistic that is uttered by a politician. So while the idea of democracy has never been more popular and the (sometimes) alleged virtues of dictatorship have never appeared so unpromising, examples of true, strong democracies in action seem to be harder and harder to find as we enter the twenty-first century.

The Italian case is important in another connection, as it was the laboratory for the celebrated initial work by Robert Putnam on what makes for good and responsive government. In his 1993 book, *Making Democracy Work*, Putnam popularized the idea that social capital, particularly in certain forms ("horizontal" rather than "vertical") was the central ingredient necessary for democracy to be responsive to the wishes of the people.[3] Thus, to oversimplify a bit, he argued

---

[2] See, for example, Chapter 1 of Susan J. Pharr and Robert D. Putnam, *Disaffected Democracies,* New Jersey: Princeton University Press, 2000; and Robert Putnam, *Bowling Alone: The Collapse and Revival of American Community*, New York: Simon and Schuster, 2000.

[3] Social capital, variously defined, is one avenue of giving meaning to the concept of civil society. But it is hardly uncontroversial, and indeed the issue of what is meant by the concept has of late become an industry in itself (See, for example, Mark E. Warren, *Democracy and Trust*, Cambridge: Cambridge University Press, 1999).

that the north in Italy has high social capital and good government, whereas the south is low on both counts. Of course, Edward Banfield had earlier advanced the proposition (in his *The Moral Basis of a Backward Society*[4]) that lack of social capital posed problems for the development of democracy in parts of the south of Italy. And Putnam's magisterial new book, *Bowling Alone* (2000), is essentially a lament for the decline of social capital in America and the decline of good government along with it.

At the same time, one could look at the current state of political life in the world in much different ways. Thus, the importance of human rights in political discourse has undergone a sea change, and emphasis on their observance has become entrenched. The decline in ideological competition as the result of the demise of the Soviet system of government has often meant a more pragmatic approach to government in the West. The rise of the Internet has meant a decline in the capacity of politicians to mislead, trick, or bully their peoples. These things would all seem to bode positively for democratic government. However, with the advent of globalization, many decisions have been taken out of the democratic process and left to institutions such as central banks, international dispute settlement mechanisms, and other nonrepresentational organizations, causing many people to complain of a loss of sovereignty.

With these mostly dark thoughts in mind, we thought it would be important and interesting to bring together several scholars from North America and Europe and ask them to explore in a more rigorous and scholarly way what they thought were the ingredients that made democracy successful, that is, the *binds* and *bonds* of democratic politics, and to present their analyses of how these binds and bonds have functioned and how well or badly they currently function to sustain democracy around the world. By these phrases, we mean two things: First, we refer to all the constraints, restrictions, rules, and requirements that govern democratic political competition. These include the formal rules of the constitution, but also changes in them such as those that are the product of judicial interpretation, as well as the informal agreements among competing parties and other political actors. Second, and no less important, we refer to the glue that ties the members of the polity together, such as social capital or a common belief in the rule of law, and democratic rights, such as the right to free speech or the right to participate in a demonstration. Many institutions perform both these roles, that is, they both bind individuals in the sense of restricting their capacity to act, and they bond or link them more closely, or raise their awareness of being linked together, in a common polity. Both binds

---

[4] *The Moral Basis of a Backward Society*, by Edward C. Banfield with the assistance of Laura Fasano Banfield, Glencoe, IL: Free Press, 1958. Even before Banfield's work, there were the Italian economists of the eighteenth century, Doria and Genovese, as discussed in A. Pagden, "The destruction of trust and its economic consequences in the case of eighteenth century Naples," in Diego Gambetta (ed.), *Trust*, Oxford: Blackwell, 1988, pp. 126–141.

and bonds are, we believe, the foundations of democratic politics. We invited these scholars to participate in a seminar to discuss these matters.

As in previous Villa Colombella Seminars, it was expected that scholars would seek to develop positive models based on the assumption of rational decision making and rational behavior. Some of the issues we suggested were worthy of exploration included the following: Does social capital always underpin the rule of law in desirable ways? Can there be too much social capital? On constitutions, an important issue is that of the flexibility of constitutions in the presence of a changing social, political, or economic environment. Why do people accept constitutional reinterpretations and adaptations at one time that were rejected previously? The tradeoff between the requirements of constitutional maintenance versus that of flexibility is a subject that is continually being debated. A third issue is whether democratic politics has generated institutions and institutional devices to make commitments possible – or alternatively to make reneging on commitments costly – and thus ensure the determination of stable equilibrium outcomes. It has to do with the notion that democracy is founded on the principle of the sovereignty of the people. One implication of this principle is that one parliament representing the people at a particular historical moment cannot bind a future parliament. It might appear therefore that the ability to commit is not a feature of democratic politics. But in the absence of commitment virtually every equilibrium outcome is unstable. Perhaps this is one reason why most members of parliaments tend to get reelected most of the time under all voting rules. But in turn, this appears to shield them from voters' control under some systems.

As the reader will discover, we received provocative answers to a number of these questions. In addition, some authors took a rather different approach to them than what we had anticipated and asked new questions. The chapters are wide ranging, and consider such diverse aspects of democratic governance as negative advertising, the role of morals or virtue in political life, the role of social capital and civil society in sustaining democracy, secessionism and the constitutional and cultural prerequisites of democracy, and how representative democracies interact with the evolution of the market economy. Overall, however we are gratified at the unity which the book appears to display. To provide a brief overview, the chapters in the first part of the book, "Some Problems with Democratic Institutions and Trends in Their Evolution," describe and analyze in detail from a variety of points of view some of the problems and trends in democracy to which we have just been referring, from negative campaigning to the decline in public discourse to the increase in activities which are often said to constitute civil society. Perhaps one way to read the rest of the book is that, in it, the authors look at different possible solutions to these dilemmas. Thus, Part 2, "Morals in Politics," contains two chapters, both of which ask whether a more virtuous or altruistic citizenry can ameliorate weaknesses in the institutions of democracy themselves. The third part, "Social Capital," is devoted to issues surrounding the concept and workings of social capital, currently felt by many to be, in one form or another, a *sine qua non* for effective democracy. The fourth part, "The Role of Constitutions," addresses a number of aspects of these institutions: how the demand for constitutions as solutions to democratic dilemmas arises, and how constitutions actually function in this regard and in other ways.

The chapters can be summarized as follows.

In Chapter 2 Michael Munger considers the effects of negative campaigning or "attack" tactics on the electoral system. His conclusion is that ideological attacks "loosen the bonds" that tie democracies together. Perhaps more importantly he argues that once the bonds that tie a democracy together are loosened they tend to stay loose, and he is not sanguine that such measures as restrictions on campaign measures will necessarily improve matters. The reason is that restrictions on spending or contributions tend to benefit incumbents, reducing competition and insulating officials from the electoral forces that assure accountability.

Stergios Skaperdas's basic point in Chapter 3 is that the level of public discourse in the West has deteriorated in the post-WWII period. He suggests that this process has taken place very gradually and imperceptibly. That deterioration can be thought to be a by-product of material growth. Public discourse requires time – to read, think, and interact with others. It is also assisted by the presence of public space, the *agora*, the corner café, bar, or tavern. With economic growth, both the time spent with others and public space are shown to decline in the formal model he examines. Allowing for feedback from public discourse on economic growth does not qualitatively change these effects.

Roger Congleton points out in Chapter 4 that most modern analyses of democracy take it for granted that democratic government is feasible. However, this point of view neglects the fact that democracy has become a dominant constitutional arrangement only recently. Perhaps democracy is not always feasible. Democratic politics have to overcome several defects in majority rule if they are to succeed. His chapter analyzes cultural and economic prerequisites for avoiding three fundamental problems of majoritarian decision making – indecisiveness, redistributory pressures, and subversion of the process by the governing party – that would otherwise tend to hobble democratic government.

Frédérique Chaumont-Chancellier analyzes the impact of civil society on the contemporary social order in Chapter 5. Relying on a Hayekian analytic framework, she explores the part played by individual incentives in the preservation or decline of pre-existing social rules as well as in the generation of new ones. New rules are generated by a five-step process. The first step is the appearance of some recurrent interaction problem. In the Hayekian framework this generates pioneer action to address it, the emergence of one or more relational rules, competition among them, and ends in the institutionalization of a rule once a certain critical mass has been reached. She further proposes an explanation of the different appearances of civil actions – from incivilities to civil engagement directed to the provision of collective goods – in contemporary France. Finally, she argues that some aspects of civil actions can be understood as an exit from the political society and should not be attributed to the good health of democracy.

The second part of the book, "Morals in Politics," contains chapters by Don Wittman and Alan Hamlin. These two authors chose to write on morality or virtue as a foundation for democratic politics, and ask whether democracy works better when the population is more virtuous.

The first chapter (Chapter 6) on virtue or altruism is by Donald Wittman. He develops a positive theory of elections when some or all of the voters temper their selfish interests with some concern for the distribution of income. As is well known, when people are selfish, there is no permanent majority and intransitivity arises. Wittman considers the situation where voters have, in addition to their own selfish preferences, some concern for the average income and the distribution of income around the average. He argues that a certain degree of altruism is indeed the glue that binds people together to prevent such instability. In addition, majority rule encourages altruism because the transfers are imposed on a set of people rather than just on one person at a time.

In the second chapter on morals (Chapter 7), Alan Hamlin also analyzes the role of virtuous rather than self-interested motivations in the operation of democratic institutions. He investigates whether democratic institutions operate in a way that is resilient to alternative specifications of the characters and motivations of individuals. Hamlin follows Montesquieu in suggesting that different forms of government thrive on the basis of different human characteristics: a monarchy, for example, thrives on honor while a despotic government survives on the basis of fear. A democratic government requires virtue. Hamlin argues that virtue in turn is not a stock that is consumed by use. On the contrary, it is more useful to think of democratic institutions as mechanisms that can screen for the virtuous (elections), enhance virtue (as suggested by Condorcet's jury theorem), or even produce it. The chapter concludes with a simple modelling exercise that illustrates how the screening and enhancement of virtue might operate.

The third part of the book contains two chapters on social capital. In Chapter 8, Ronald Wintrobe takes as his starting point the recent revival and spectacular growth of interest in the subject of social capital, particularly inspired by the work of Putnam mentioned earlier. He focuses on the concept of solidarity, which may or may not be a synonym for social capital. He argues that while Putnam produces a vast array of evidence about trends in social capital, he does not supply an analysis of how social capital is produced or accumulated. Wintrobe suggests one model of this process. In this model, people acquire solidarity with a group by giving up their own views and adopting the views of the group. In effect, they give up autonomy for solidarity. To the extent that this process of trade takes place, the person who holds a belief which appears on the surface to be irrational is not behaving irrationally. The rationality consists not in the content of the belief, but in the reason for holding it, which is to obtain social cohesion or a feeling of "belonging-ness." The more extreme the views of the group, the greater sacrifice in autonomy a person will have to make in order to join, and the greater the amount of solidarity he will demand from the group in return. Hence extremist groups are typically characterized by high solidarity as well as extremist views.

Stefan Voigt's Chapter 9 is an attempt to analyze the bonds of democracy. In a wide-ranging chapter, which surveys a large literature on this subject including experimental games and contributions from sociology as well as economics and political science, he argues that only those societies that have at their disposition certain kinds of bonds will be able to sustain democracy. For example, an extended welfare state only seems sustainable if those who are net-payers feel some sort of solidarity for those who they are supporting. He suggests, however, that an extensive welfare state can lead to a loosening of personal bonds. He compares the bonds of democratic politics with those of non-democratic politics, and also asks whether democracy is a precondition for certain kinds of bonds to survive. Perhaps surprisingly, he concludes that the differential effects of democratic versus non-democratic regimes on the strength of bonds are rather weak. But then again, he argues, this is not the only relevant distinction, and different kinds of democratic institutions might well have an effect on the prevalent bonds found in a society.

The fourth and last part of the book, "The Role of Constitutions," contains three chapters on constitutional economics, by Gianluigi Galeotti, Albert Breton and Pierre Salmon, and Viktor Vanberg. Breton and Salmon's chapter concerns the economics of secession; Galeotti's chapter some shortcomings of all voting rules; and Vanberg's chapter the issue of whether under a democracy it is possible to bind future legislators.

Galeotti's Chapter 10 develops an early cue suggested by Anthony Downs on "the paradox of delegation." He identifies a basic tension between voters' information costs – requiring more delegation of decision authority – and the dissonance of principals' and agents' goals which would require less delegation. That tension is eased in a setting where representatives' uncertainty of citizens' votes is an efficient spur to make the principals' authority effective. Incumbent politicians, however, find that setting uncongenial and try their best to bind voters through the cultivation of political loyalties or by making themselves indispensable (as also happens with managerial entrenchment in the case of corporate control). Thus, Galeotti presents four different settings of the life of a representative democracy. The four depend on the combinations of incumbents' confidence of voters' support on the one hand and voters' reliance on the incumbents on the other. Empirical evidence shows that voters are often trapped by their own choices under both the plurality and the proportional rule, thus leading to waves of inconsistent expectations. The constitutional quandary is how to combine permanence and change of the electoral system. The problem is that no permanent voting rule seems able to keep the required level of asymmetric mistrust constant. With the elapsing of time incumbents are always able to find ways around any stable set of rules.

Victor Vanberg, in Chapter 11, discusses the issue of commitment in democratic politics from a constitutional economics perspective. More specifically, he examines the conjecture that the principle of popular sovereignty inherently limits the ability of democratic polities to commit. If this conjecture were true, democratic constituencies would be incapable of realizing the benefits that a capacity to enter into binding commitments might generate. Looking at a democratic polity as, in Rawls's words, a "cooperative venture for mutual advantage," Vanberg seeks to show that such a pessimistic conclusion need not be drawn from the principle of popular sovereignty. Interpreting commitments as social contracts among citizens, the commitment issue is analyzed in terms of two distinctions, that is, on the one hand, the contrast between *original* versus *ongoing* agreement in such social contracts, and, on the other hand, the distinction between "transaction agreements" and "constitutional agreements" as the two principal ways in which citizens can use the political process to realize mutual benefits. It is argued, in particular, that *ongoing* agreement is not only the relevant standard of legitimacy in constitutional agreements, but that it is also a workable foundation for constitutional commitments when certain requirements are met.

In Chapter 12, Albert Breton and Pierre Salmon argue that the effects of constitutional rules depend on the nature of political competition and on some meta-rules that contain procedures regulating the application and the modification of constitutional rules. They outline two models of competition, electoral competition and compound government competition, and describe the nature of the transactions between the parties involved in the two corresponding settings. In both, the transactions are over constitutional rules and ordinary goods and services, all of which are arguments in the utility functions of citizens. To make the discussion more concrete, the chapter focuses on the demand for political autonomy, a variable that, at the limit, becomes a demand for secession and independence. This allows the specification of some meta-rules applicable to secessionism. In this particular context, it appears that relatively small differences in the content of the meta-rules lead to large differences in equilibrium outcomes.

POSTSCRIPT: SOME TENTATIVE CONCLUSIONS AND SUGGESTIONS FOR FURTHER RESEARCH

Readers of this book will of course want to draw their own conclusions about the state of democracy and its foundations. Perhaps it would be useful to them if we, the editors, take this opportunity to offer our own reflections, based not only on our participation in the conference, but also on listening to the papers and comments of others there, reading the referee reports for the volume and rereading the final versions of the various chapters. In our view, four broad themes seem to emerge. The first of these is that the pessimism on these matters mentioned earlier seems to have been shared by a number of the participants at the seminar. In particular, most (but not all) of the authors appear to believe that, left to themselves, political markets do not function very well. The classic public choice problems of cycling or indecisiveness, the tendency for redistributory issues to dwarf the concern for resource allocation, and the ever-present possibility of subversion of the democratic process by the party in power are well identified by Congleton. To this list, two newer dilemmas are added by Skaperdas and Munger. Skaperdas argues that growing material wealth increases the value of time and reduces the capacity for public discourse. Public discourse requires time to read, think, and interact with others. Chapter 3 is a lament for the decline of the *agora*, the corner café, bar, or tavern, and of media that provide fodder for real debate. Lack of public discourse reduces the number of alternatives considered and allows small minorities to have an inordinate influence on public decisions. He speculates on the etymology of the word *idiot* and notes that it initially referred to a private person who had no time for public affairs. He discusses whether we could become, if we are not already, *idiots* in both senses of the term.

Munger also discusses the depreciation of the common culture and describes another force that has led to this phenomenon: the increasing tendency for negative campaigning in elections. In the simplest model of this process, negative campaigning is individually rational for the candidates in an election in that it appears to win support, but is easily matched by the other candidate. The resulting equilibrium is one where both candidates engage in it. Neither wins by the strategy but the common culture is depreciated. Munger shows how important this result can be. Because elections tend to be fought on simple ideological dimensions, the basis of political competition can be changed by a depreciation of the common culture, and the result can be a distortion of voters' choices and a degradation of the public sector. In turn, voters react by becoming, as he puts it, demoralized and demobilized.

The second theme is the possible replenishment of the foundations of politics through what is variously termed morals, culture, virtue, bonds, or social capital. In this vein, Wittman's mathematical model shows how the problem of intransitivity can be overcome when voters temper their selfish interests through altruism, or a concern for the distribution of income. Hamlin is in one sense less pessimistic in that he argues that democracy can be *flexible*. It may function tolerably well with the various motivational characters of the individual citizens. But he nevertheless argues that without some modicum of virtue, so that individuals feel themselves bound together in a common enterprise, the human aspect of democracy may be undermined. Congleton also tries to show how culture can solve the standard dilemmas of public choice, and Voigt suggests as well that a sense of solidarity among voters is necessary for many forms of public decision-making, for example, the maintenance of the welfare state, to survive.

A third theme which emerges in several papers is the specification of the mechanisms and processes by which the bonds or virtue or social capital are produced and maintained. That is, virtue, morals, bonds, or social capital are not merely exogenous forces in a society but are produced endogenously through the functioning of political, economic, or social systems. We have already mentioned Munger's model of the depreciation of common culture through negative campaigning and Skaperdas's model of how economic growth reduces the possibility of public discourse. To these must be added Chaumont-Chancellier's Hayekian model that implies that such events do not go unnoticed, but become the staple of political entrepreneurship to address these problems. She shows how such problems tend to get recognized, how relational rules tend to emerge, and how competition among these rules tends to produce new rules to solve recurrent problems. From this point of view, civic action appears as a sign of discontent with existing institutions, and quietism an indication that they are working well. Indeed, one way to read Chaumont-Chancellier's chapter is as a (despite differences in methodology) challenge to those who decry the apparent results of the workings of an open society to show why openness itself does not provide a solution to the problems it is said to create.

One possible line of counter-argument to Chaumont-Chancellier's thesis is provided by Voigt, who argues that it is possible that sustained democracy depends on preconditions that it is not always capable of reproducing or bringing about itself. For example, he suggests that participatory rights will be granted only as a consequence of changes in the bargaining power of various groups, and that horizontal bonds or trust might be a precondition for vertical bonds (trust in government) which in turn is a necessary condition for sustainable democracy.

Of course, pessimistic or gloomy views on the way democracy works have a long tradition. However, considering the matter over longer periods of time or over a larger sample of countries often changes the perspective. The phenomena or trends apparently accounted for or revealed by the theory appear then to be more local or temporary than the theory suggests. Some readers may apply such caution to the currently fashionable thesis of decreasing social capital a la Putnam and others or to some of the ideas mentioned here. Are the parts of the contemporary world which are poorer, and where the opportunity cost of time has less value, those in which political life and the level of political discourse are the most democratically healthy? And is the virulence of negative campaigning, though perhaps greater today than 10 or 20 years ago, really much greater today than it was in many democracies in the interwar period or earlier?

Research from a longer time perspective would undoubtedly help to clarify these issues.

Another point of view on these matters is provided by Wintrobe's paper. He does not take issue with the various stories and evidence of the decline of social capital in the United States. But he notes that what to Putnam, for example, was the golden age of social capital in the United States, the 1950s, was also an era of conformism and racism. It was an era in the United States in which blacks were systematically excluded from public life and Jews were excluded from many private and public organizations, and it is perhaps best symbolized by the book, *The Organization Man*, and the film, *Gentleman's Agreement*. Wintrobe's model of the process by which solidarity or social capital is created highlights this point by showing one of the costs of social capital, which is increased conformity to the dominant values of the organization or political culture. By this standard, the politics of the 1990s at least were open and vibrant and inclusive.

Clearly, the mechanisms by which the foundations of political markets are capable of being produced and the conditions that make this possible are important avenues for future research.

The fourth theme, which naturally emerges from this line of thought, is the role and functioning of constitutions. Can rules substitute for morals or civic virtue? All of the papers in this section of the book raise or address problems with the functioning of constitutional rules. At the general level, Viktor Vanberg addresses the important and perennial issue of whether popular sovereignty inherently limits the ability of democratic governments to make binding commitments. He argues that the only relevant standard of legitimacy is *ongoing* agreement, not some original agreement. Constitutional agreements are about joint commitments to submit to common rules of the game. Within this framework, the classic issues of opportunism and renegotiation can be dealt with. Thus the issue is not whether some party should not be allowed to exit if they no longer agree with the rules of the game: Obviously, this possibility should be allowed for. But this does not mean that they should be allowed to escape obligations that they have contracted for under agreed-on-rules.

Albert Breton and Pierre Salmon also deal with the issue of exit from the polity, but they focus on a different point. They stress that the rules that govern the implementation of constitutional rules (which they call meta-rules) are as important as the constitutional rules themselves. One example of a meta-rule is the so-called Clarity Act passed recently by the Canadian federal government. This meta-rule states that any question posed in a referendum on the secession from the federation of a province such as Quebec must be clear if the central government is to be obligated to negotiate secession with the province. This makes it difficult for secessionist forces to obfuscate the issue. Thus the government of Quebec would not be in a position to pose a question such as "Are you in favor of Quebec independence provided this independence will not require you to give up your Canadian passport nor hamper your ability to continue to receive services and transfer payments from the Canadian government?" and declare that a "yes" vote in such a referendum would constitute a mandate for secession.

While stability in constitutions is usually much admired, Gianluigi Galeotti challenges this conventional wisdom by showing that any stable constitutional regime has an inherent weakness: Under any stable rule, elected representatives are better able to take advantage of whatever weaknesses it has than voters and are able to find ways to bind voters to them. Thus they are able to use the rule to encourage voters' loyalty. But this in turn weakens representatives' discipline, by making the threat of dismissal less credible. Hence the dilemma at the heart of constitutional design is to combine stability and change in voting rules.

Whether the solution to the dilemmas of democracy lies in constitutional rule-making, or in the strengthening of moral codes or social capital, or whether indeed these dilemmas have been overdrawn in this book (after all, as has been said many times but perhaps bears repeating once more, democracy is always the worst system of government, except for the alternatives) is something we leave to the reader to decide. But we hope the reader will find, as we believe we have, a wealth of information about these binds or bonds – the foundations of democracy – and about the functioning of democratic systems, in the chapters that follow.

We thank Massimo Bordignon, Vani Borooah, Luisa Giuriato, Donato Masciandaro, Fabio Padovano, Janez Sustersic, and Pietro Vagliasindi for acting as discussants and Angela Fraschini as well as Margaret Levi for their participation in the seminar. We are grateful to the Lynde and Harry Bradley Foundation and to the Italian Ministry of Education (National Research Grant, 1999–2000) for their continuing financial support that has made this seminar possible. We thank in a special way Luisa Giuriato and Pietro Vagliasindi for their help in organizing the seminar.

REFERENCES

Downs, Anthony. *An Economic Theory of Democracy*. New York: Harper and Row, 1957.
Schumpeter, J. A. *Capitalism, Socialism, and Democracy*. 3rd ed. New York: Harper and Row, 1950.

PART ONE

SOME PROBLEMS WITH DEMOCRATIC INSTITUTIONS AND TRENDS IN THEIR EVOLUTION

2

Demobilized and Demoralized: Negative Ads and Loosening Bonds

Michael C. Munger

I don't like this backbiting – this putting someone down to build yourself up.

> Betty Norden, administrative assistant, Washington, North Carolina, quoted in Raleigh *News and Observer*, April 30, 1996.

NEGATIVE ADVERTISING AND THE QUALITY OF ELECTIONS

Ms. Norden raises two important theoretical questions. I have fleshed out the questions, and given what I believe to be the answers:

Q: Is it possible for political candidates to use negative advertising to "put someone down to build yourself up"? This is clearly the popular perception, but is it consistent with an equilibrium model that allows the best response to advertising messages?

A: *As is often the case, the answer is, "It depends." If you mean, "Are candidates usually able to win more votes if they 'go negative," the answer is* **YES**. *If you mean "Are all candidates able to increase their net vote percentages by negative ads, in equilibrium," the answer is clearly* **NO**.

Q: Is Ms. Norden's "dislike" of mudslinging simply a matter of taste, or is there something deeper at work?

A: *There is something much deeper at work. Negative ads are individually rational, in the sense that they "work" for the candidates. But the utility citizens derive from living in such a political system is sharply reduced.*

In this chapter, I review briefly some of the results on negative campaigning, and then consider the effects of attack tactics on the citizens and the electoral

The author thanks John Aldrich, Gianluigi Galeotti, Bernard Grofman, Melvin Hinich, William Keech, Joseph Oppenheimer, and Ronald Wintrobe for helpful comments and suggestions. All mistakes are author's own, however.

system. My conclusion, as the title suggests, is that ideological attacks loosen the bonds that tie democracies together. The final section, the one that should contain policy prescriptions that flow from this conclusion, is unfortunately not very optimistic. The bonds that tie democracies together, once loosened, may stay loose.

BACKGROUND AND PREVIOUS LITERATURE

The idea that negative advertising may harm consumers is an old one (see, e.g., Wheatley and Oshikawa, 1970). The notion that negative campaigning in elections may harm citizens is perhaps not quite so old, but it is well established (for results, and a much more complete review, see Ansolobehere, et al., 1994; Chappell, 1994; Garramone, 1984; Harrington and Hess, 1996; Hinich and Munger, 1994; Skaperdas and Grofman, 1995). The idea behind this work is simple: Negative advertising appears empirically to benefit the advertiser, by hurting the target of the attack. But because access to negative tactics is symmetric, there is no net benefit in equilibrium, except in the sense that going negative avoids the sure loss, as in any prisoner's dilemma setting.

It is worth considering the strategic situation as a 2×2 game, as pictured in Table 2.1. Assume that the election is otherwise a dead heat, with the likely outcome too close to call in advance. Each candidate has access to enough money to run a positive or a negative campaign. Obviously, there are two pareto optimal outcomes ([negative, negative] and [positive, positive]), but only one equilibrium ([negative, negative]). To put it another way, even though the candidates may be indifferent between the outcomes, since both result in ties, there is a dominant strategy for each player: Go negative. This result is robust to a variety of more realistic asymmetric specifications of the contest (Harrington, 1992; Skaperdas and Grofman, 1995). Harrington derives explicit results under which the "corner solution" ($p > 0, n = 0$) for the mix of positive and negative ads in a campaign should be observed. These results reveal that such conditions can rarely, if ever, be met in a noncooperative setting.

There is no reason, however, to believe that societies, or individual citizens, are indifferent between the two types of campaigns. As Ansolobehere, et al. (1994) argued, there is growing evidence of two types of effects observed empirically in voter groups exposed to attack tactics. One effect is *demobilization*, or decreased participation in voting and other expressive forms of activity. The

Table 2.1. Campaign Strategy

		Player 2: Run Negative Ads	Run Only Issue Ads
Player 1:	**Run Negative Ads**	50–50 tie	Player 1 wins in landslide
	Run Only Issue Ads	Player 2 wins in landslide	50–50 tie

other is increases in measures of cynicism, or the attribution of bad motives and likely bad behavior to candidates for electoral office. The latter effect may be the real problem, since it is an attitudinal change that is almost certainly behind the behavior change of demobilization. I will call this increased cynicism by a more descriptive name: *demoralization*. While the size of these effects (see, e.g., Wattenberg and Brians, 1999), the direction is increasingly clear: I will argue that negative advertising hurts voters and the electoral system.

Much of the focus in the literature has been on the demobilization effect, because it is amenable to treatment as a strategic consideration in the campaign. But the demoralization effect is more important in the long run, both because it is likely logically prior (i.e., demoralization causes demobilization) and because the effect on the welfare of citizens is much larger. To be able to describe the aggregate effects of negative campaigning in an ideological setting more fully, it is useful to spell out the conception of ideology that will be used here.

IDEOLOGY

Ideology may be defined as either (a) a set of ideas with implications for good policy, or (b) a widely shared belief system. Neither of these notions requires internal consistency among ideas or beliefs. Instead, an ideology provides a means to organize political thinking, and to let people understand each other. The key evidence that ideology is important is the now-established empirical regularity (Enelow and Hinich, 1984; 1989; Laver and Schofield, 1990; Poole and Rosenthal, 1984; 1991; 1993) that the space of political competition is of much lower dimensionality than the number of issues.

Issue positions cluster: If I know what you think on defense policy, abortion rights, and environmental policy, I can guess (with some error) what you think of school lunch subsidies. Further, this clustering phenomenon is not purely atomistic, so that ideological positions such as liberal and conservative have similar meanings to different people. If the understanding of clusters of issues is shared, the particular form of clustering is an ideology. If platforms are ideological, the strategies of candidates in the policy space are highly constrained.

There are at least three theoretical justifications for this claim: *communication*, *commitment*, and *budgets*. The justifications are not mutually exclusive, and share one essential element: They imply empirically demonstrable linkages across issues, so that the relevant space of political debate is of low dimensionality.

- *Communication.* To provide voters with a message they can understand and use to make choices, parties must simplify their message. Because only broad statements of principles can be used in advertising and position-taking, the latitude for more subtle distinctions and differences is highly circumscribed. Ideologies are a means of solving problems of uncertainty and lack of information.

- *Commitment.* To be able to persuade voters that they can trust the party to do as promised after the election, parties must give reasons and explanations rather than just take positions. But explanations require some sort of overarching system of justifications, and the advancement of values that can be applied to a variety of issues. Parties trade on reputations, but reputations are meaningful only if they provide coherent (that is, "separating") signals. If parties act on their ideologies when such actions do not appear self-interested, reputations gain value.
- *Budgets.* Increasing spending in one area forces decreases elsewhere in the budget, or else forces increased present or future taxes. Thus, any change from the status quo forces a linkage to other issues, if only in terms of taxes or opportunity cost.

Is it useful to model political competition as constrained by ideology? After all, Converse (1964) pointed out that voter preferences do not seem to be constrained by any shared ideology. I concede the point, as Converse made it, but would still argue that ideology is a useful concept. Ideologies are shared understandings of political alternatives, not internal constraints on individual belief schema.

Ideology is not the mark of sophistication and education, but of uncertainty and lack of ability to connect policies with benefits. . . . They do this because voters do not perceive all the differences, cannot remember all the past performances, and cannot relate all future policies to their own benefits. . . . But unavailability of data is not the only reason voters revert to default values. They do this when they are so satisfied with their past choices that they see no reason to collect any data. (Popkin, 1994; pp. 51–52)

Ideologies do not constrain voter preferences. Instead, ideological divisions constrain choices, because only a small number of alternatives are available. To put it another way, ideologies may not organize voter preferences, but a political system cannot function without the structure imposed by ideology. The key question, then, is this: How does negative advertising affect voter perceptions of the legitimacy of political systems? One answer is that mudslinging increases the uncertainty citizens feel about political messages, because they are no longer very sure about the meaning of those messages. In the limit, we may not even be able to talk to each other and be believed. We may not even be understood.

The reason that the ability to commit and communicate through ideologies is so important may not be obvious without some careful reflection. The problem is that there are two spaces, separate both conceptually and empirically (as far as I know, this was first argued by Peter Ordeshook (1976), but it has been an on-again, off-again research program ever since). The first space is the space people care about, where local and national public goods are supplied (or not supplied). That is, people care about the outputs of government: Is the garbage picked up, are children educated, is the home and other property safe from theft and violence, and is foreign aggression deterred or defeated. I will call this the *policy space*, as in earlier work (Hinich and Munger, 1994).

The second space is the actual arena of political conflict: ideology. Politicians rarely take specific policy positions, at least not on all issues. Instead, they give general statements of values and principles. But voters can draw inferences from these statements; these inferences form the mappings, in voters' minds, from the world of political rhetoric to the practical world of preferences. The mapping in voters' minds is not a logical inference, however. Rather, voters use their experience with the meaning and consistency of political messages to make inferences.

It is useful to see how this might work, using an example adapted from Chapter 9 in Hinich and Munger (1997). Imagine that there are two issues that voters care about, tanks (read: defense policy) and school lunches (read: social policy). In spatial theory terms, it is possible to represent the preferences of a voter in such a two-dimensional policy world using an ideal point and indifference curves based on an assumption about the relative importance of the two issues to the voter's perception of his welfare. This preference representation is depicted in Figure 2.1.

There are some important things to note about this figure, because I will use it to make some significant points about my argument. First, I have arbitrarily repositioned the origin in the space to represent the status quo budget or policy choice. Movements along any of the axes therefore represent changes in the status quo. For example, moving into the northeast quadrant is an increase in both tanks and school lunch spending; moving into the northwest quadrant is an increase in school spending, but a cut in tanks spending; and so on.

I have also positioned a representative voter's ideal point in the southwest quadrant. The indifference curves describing the preferences of that voter show that the voter places more importance on the vertical dimension (school lunches), as small vertical movements cross more indifference curves than an equal horizontal movement.[1]

Having represented the policy space, and arbitrarily placed voter's preferences in that space, I now turn to ideology, the space in which political conflict and debate actually takes place. As argued above, political conflict collapses to only a few dimensions, because of the complexities of communicating and committing in higher dimensional spaces. The ideological space, in the case of two parties, is of necessity a line. Two points in space can never support more than one independent dimension, so in a two-party system political conflict

---

[1] Technically, of course, any discrete movement crosses an infinite number of indifference curves, since they are dense everywhere. It is more correct to say that the ratio of the absolute value of the marginal utility of school lunch spending to the absolute value of the marginal utility of tanks spending always exceeds 1 when the marginal utilities are measured in terms of equal movements along the respective axes away from the voter's ideal point.

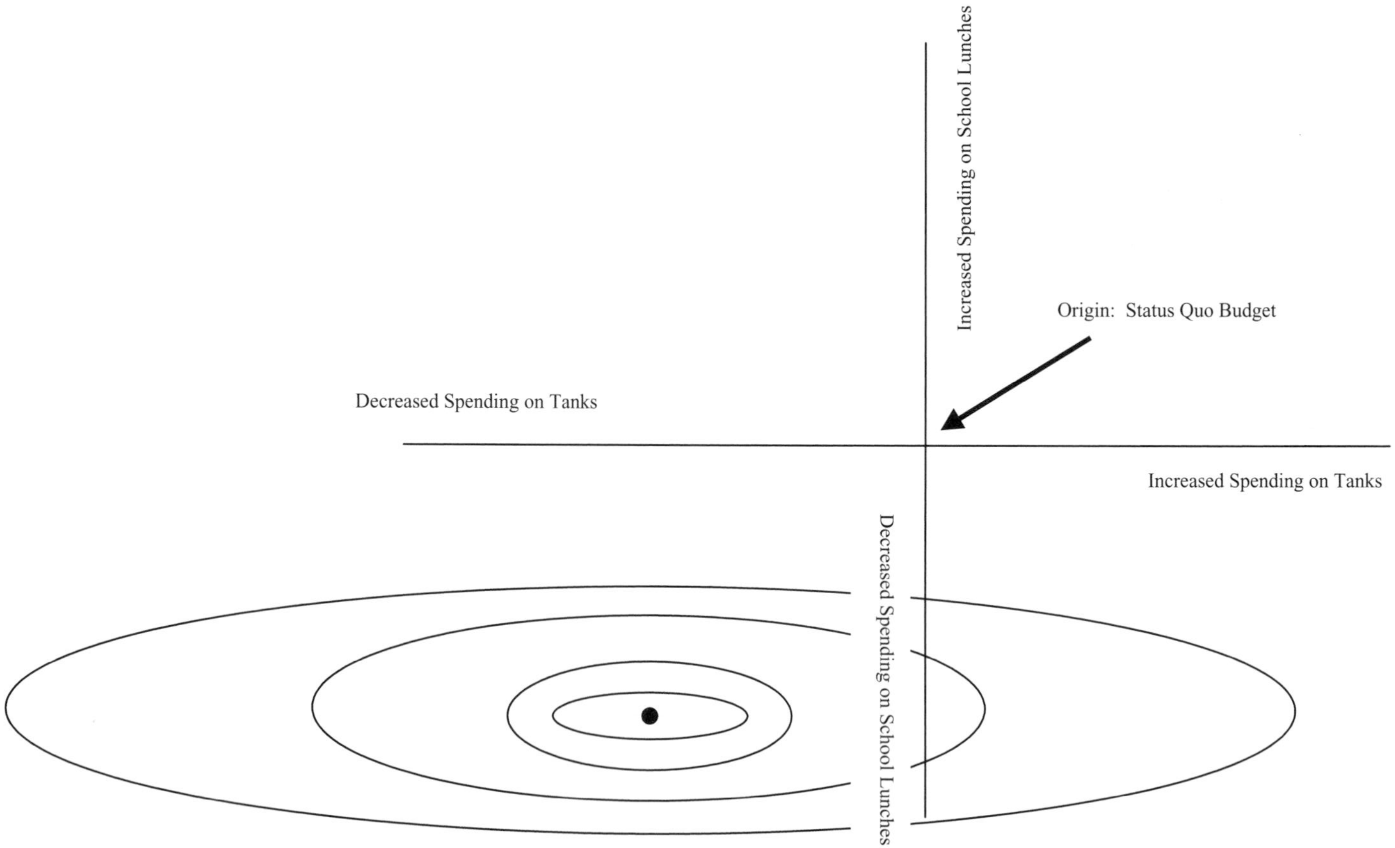

Figure 2.1. The basic policy space, with a voter's preference map

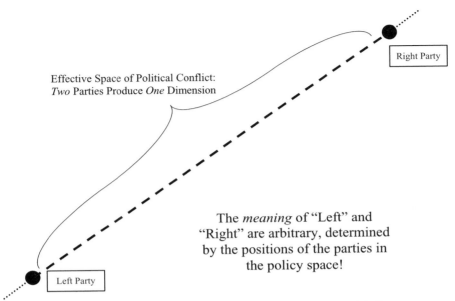

Effective Space of Political Conflict:
Two Parties Produce *One* Dimension

The *meaning* of "Left" and
"Right" are arbitrary, determined
by the positions of the parties in
the policy space!

Right Party

Left Party

Figure 2.2. The ideological policy space, with a Left Party and a Right Party

is one-dimensional.[2] The ideological space, with two parties (one leftist, one rightist) is depicted in Figure 2.2. The dimension is canted to remind the reader that the position of the ideological space in the larger policy space is the product of mappings in voters' minds, not a logically coherent set of principles of correspondence.

The next task is to superimpose the ideological space on the policy space, with an implied correspondence or mapping from ideology to policy. In Figure 2.3, I have used the same policies and voter preferences as in Figure 2.1, but have added an ideological dimension. In this political culture, the meaning of *Left* is: Cut military spending, and increase social spending. The meaning of *Right* is: Add military spending, offset by cuts in social spending. Both parties (apparently) support a balanced budget, with no increased spending over the current status quo (the origin in the figure). Consequently, the ideological space is a line, passing through the origin and sloping from northwest to southeast. It is a 45-degree line, because issues are linked by the budget constraint: Adding a dollar to one budget requires a one dollar cut in the other.

The interesting thing about this figure is that it implies that the voter votes as, and in fact considers himself to be, a rightist. Though neither of the two party positions is very close to the voter's ideal point, the fact that social spending has

[2] This suggests that the dimension of the political space is always $m - 1$, where $m =$ number of effective parties, as suggested by Hinich and Munger (1997).

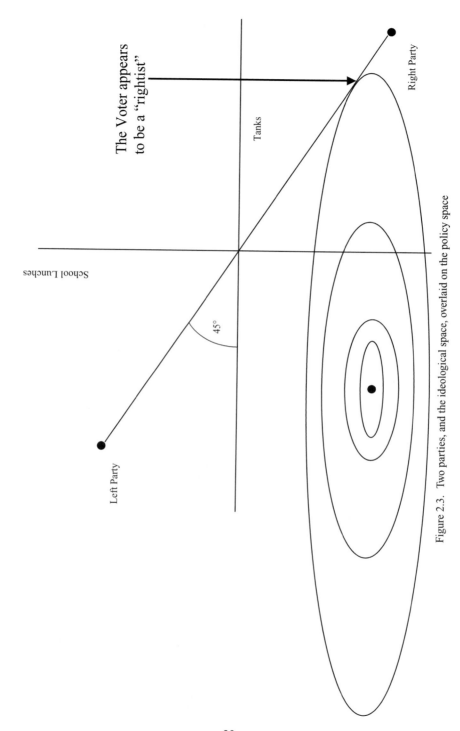

Figure 2.3. Two parties, and the ideological space, overlaid on the policy space

higher salience for the voter means that the best feasible policy (in terms of the highest indifference curve) is the Right Party. This is clear from the fact that the voter's induced ideal point (the tangency point of the indifference curve on the ideological dimension) is much closer to the platform of the Right Party. So, if a pollster were to ask the voter what his ideology is, the voter would confidently answer, "I am a rightist."

Now, however, let's do something interesting. Let's keep everything the same about the basic space (same policies, same voter ideal point, same origin). However, let us now suppose that the political culture is organized around a very different ideological principle. In this case, imagine that the political conflict in the society is centered on libertarianism versus facism/statism. In that case, *Left* means a reduction in the all the powers and activities of the state, with the expectation that those activities will be taken over by markets or private action. *Right* means an increase, compared to the status quo, in both social spending and military spending, so that there is more government activity in all aspects of citizen's lives. This would imply an ideological space leading upward from southwest to northeast, as depicted in Figure 2.4.

What has happened to our Rightist voter now? He has changed completely, and become an ardent (and much happier, compared to the situation in Figure 2.3!) Leftist. The highest indifference curve available, at the tangency with the ideological dimension, is much closer to the Left party. However, nothing at all has changed: The voter has exactly the same preferences as before. What has changed is the mental construct of ideology, or the mappings voters use to go from political speech to political choice.

The point of this extended example is that an important part of the social capital of the society is the understanding and reliance it places on the rhetorical mappings attached to ideological statements. If it is possible to devalue or discredit ideological statements, then the socially constructed infrastructure of politics collapses. These are the "ties that bind" in a democracy. In the next section, I will discuss a little more formally the implications of these binds, and how rational candidates may unintentionally weaken or even destroy the ability of citizens and political leaders to communicate and make commitments.

MODEL AND ASSUMPTIONS

At a formal level, the model advanced by Hinich and Munger (1994), and discussed very briefly in the beginning of the previous section, has two key assumptions:

- There are two spaces relevant to understanding political competition: an n-dimensional *policy* space Ω, and a p-dimensional *ideological* space Π, where $p \ll n$. Voters have ideal points $x_i \in \Omega$. Political competition between candidates alpha and beta, however, takes place in Π, because alpha and beta are constrained (by the twin problems of communication and

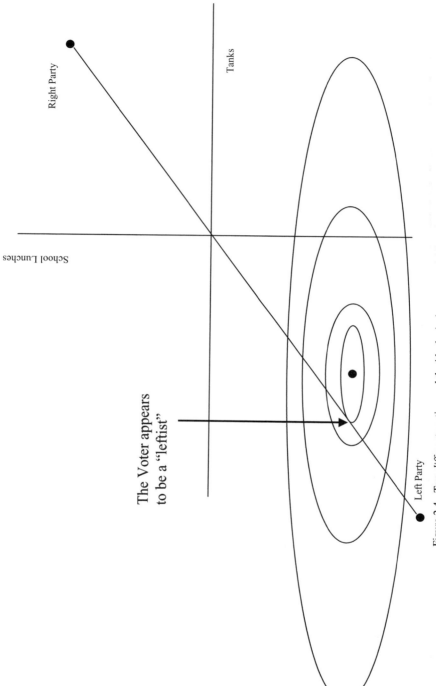

The Voter appears
to be a "leftist"

Figure 2.4. Two *different* parties, and the ideological space, overlaid on the policy space

commitment) the prevailing ideology cleavage of the society. The correspondence, or mapping, from the ideological to policy spaces can be expressed as a linear function of the various ideological dimensions. Though the model can handle multiple dimensions (see Hinich and Munger, 1994), assume $p = 1$ for simplicity.

- Voter preferences are strictly concave in the expected difference between a candidate's ideological position and their (induced) ideal point in the ideological space. That is, voters do not like uncertainty.

These two assumptions have an important implication, one that is obvious yet not often recognized explicitly. Each voter i, with ideal point x_i in the policy space Ω, chooses between two candidates (alpha and beta) based on their platforms $\{\omega_\alpha, \omega_\beta\}$ in Ω. For simplicity, I will use a well-know concave function, the quadratic, to represent utility. Let [] mean simple Euclidean Distance calculated from vector differences:

$$U(\omega_\alpha) = -[x_i - \omega_\alpha]^2 \qquad U(\omega_\beta) = -[x_i - \omega_\beta]^2 \qquad (1)$$

The imputed platforms ω_α and ω_β come from the voter's perception of the candidate's ideological position, and the mapping from ideology to policy. The imputed platform (for alpha, for example) is:

$$\omega_\alpha = \mathbf{b} + \mathbf{v}\pi_\alpha \qquad (2)$$

The $(n \times 1)$ $\mathbf{b}$ vector is the set of status quo policies. The $(n \times 1)$ $\mathbf{v}$ vector is the set of mappings from the ideological space to the policy space. The ideological position of each candidate is drawn from the set of feasible positions (that is, $\pi_j \in \Pi$, where in this case π_j is scalar).

The elements of $\mathbf{v}$ reflect the beliefs of voters that the prevailing ideology has implications for policies. For example, if v_k is large (positive or negative), the voter believes abstract ideological statements are highly meaningful for policy k. Conversely, if v_k is near zero in absolute value, the issue is not accounted for by the ideology of the prevailing party system. This does *not* mean voters don't care about the issue. Instead, if $v_k = 0$, issue k is outside the issues voters associate with the orthodox political debate they hear from parties and candidates.

We rewrite Equation 2 to reflect the fact that voter perceptions are uncertain (Hinich and Munger [1994] derive posterior parameters of the normal distribution derived using Bayes's Theorem). For voter i

$$\hat{\omega}_{\alpha i} = \mathbf{b} + \hat{\pi}_{\alpha i}\mathbf{v} \qquad (3)$$

(An analogous expression describes beta's position). Notice that the $\mathbf{v}$ terms, or mappings, are not subscripted here by voter. *Only the posterior distributions of candidate positions are voter-specific.* Further, I am not allowing uncertainty in the mapping ($\mathbf{v}$) terms, though this is another likely source of error.

Voters acquire information about alpha from campaign advertising. Alpha can use his resources to say "trust alpha"; beta can use his resources to say "don't trust alpha." The strategies for affecting perceptions of beta are symmetric. Although changing the mean of the posterior distribution is possible, let's assume that the campaign focuses on variance. Spending on reducing self variance I will call s; spending increasing opponent variance I will call o.

The ith voter's spatial utility function and net candidate differential NCD_i (arbitrarily defined as the value of alpha over beta) can now be defined:

$$NCD_i = u_i[\hat{\omega}_{\alpha i} - x_i] - u_i[\hat{\omega}_{\beta i} - x_i] \tag{4}$$

Substituting for $\hat{\omega}_\alpha$ and $\hat{\omega}_\beta$, using the Bayesian posterior distribution parameters for mean and variance assuming quadratic utility and taking expectations, we arrive at:

$$NCD_i = -(v\mu_\alpha - x_i)^2 + (v\mu_\beta - x_i)^2 + v^2[\sigma_{i\beta}^2(s_\beta, o_\alpha) - \sigma_{i\alpha}^2(s_\alpha, o_\beta)] \tag{5}$$

Two things are immediately obvious from inspecting this expression. First, if the two candidates take what look like identical ideological positions, the voter will choose the candidate with the lower variance. Second, the higher the variance of the "best" candidate, the lower the utility of the voter. Thus, even if both candidates pledge to pursue exactly the voter's ideal point if elected, the utility of the voter is reduced by negative advertising if the consequence of negative advertising is to increase the perceived variance of both candidates' positions.

Importantly (because this result differs from the classical spatial model), the larger the mapping terms v_k on the n issues, the lower the voter's utility. The logic underpinning this conclusion is straightforward. The larger the v_k, the more related the voter's perception of ideological position is to actual policy. Since small changes in ideology cause big changes in policy, variance in ideology produces magnified variance in expected policy. The greater the relation between ideology and policy, the greater the increase in variance.

IMPLICATIONS OF THE GAME BETWEEN CANDIDATES FOR THE VOTERS

Hinich and Munger (1994) outline a game between candidates in spending, where campaign funds are endogenously determined by self-interested interest group contributions. If neither candidate has an advantage in terms of policy (ideological locations π_α and π_β represent an equilibrium for the parties), the technology of changing variances by advertising (both parties can hire consultants of equal competence), or the private benefits to be offered in exchange for contributions, then strategies will be the same, because the game is formally symmetric.

The "result" is a foolish equilibrium: Each candidate exhausts his electoral resources (private benefits) for exactly zero net gain. Remember what the

Red Queen told Alice: "It takes all the running you can do, to keep in the same place. If you want to get somewhere else, you must run at least twice as fast as that!" The reason is that each candidate can respond to expenditures by the other with exactly matching, offsetting spending. Since strategies are defined over a scaled difference term $(v^2[\sigma^2_{i\beta}(s_\beta, o_\alpha) - \sigma^2_{i\alpha}(s_\alpha, o_\beta)])$, and strategies are symmetric, the net impact is zero and candidates cannot improve their expected pluralities. This is true *no matter how many private benefits*, up to and including the Gross National Product, the two candidates have to give out.

Hinich and Munger (1994) assume that the technologies of affecting self and opponent variance were identical. But as Alesina and Cukierman (1990), Page (1976), and Shepsle (1972) suggest, the symmetry condition is unlikely to hold. It is easier (more precisely, for our purposes, cheaper) to cloud the likely position of an opponent than to illuminate and focus on one's own position, implying a strategy of ambiguity. If it is comparatively cheaper to campaign negatively (i.e., attack one's opponent), then self-oriented campaigning will be observed (if at all) only if the available budget is large enough to equalize the marginal electoral gains. It is entirely possible that, for poorly financed campaigns with a candidate known to voters, this condition is never met, and all money is spent on negative campaigning.

The asymmetry in the technologies of using positive versus negative campaigning to affect elections becomes especially important in light of the discussion earlier regarding voter utility in high variance races. To recapitulate, (1) voters will choose the lower variance candidate if positions are similar or are equidistant from the center of the distribution of voters, but (2) the higher the variance of the perception of each candidate's actions, the worse off *all* voters are. In the limit, the very community of understanding on which any political system depends can be destroyed or changed by negative advertising.

If voters become more uncertain about *both* candidates' positions, this affects the level of utility, though it does not affect the choices they make, or the outcome of the election. Candidate j's position in the ideological space can be represented as a random variable with mean μ_j, and with an error ε_j whose mean is 0 and whose variance is fixed but allowed to differ by candidate.

$$\hat{\Omega}_j = \mu_j + \epsilon_j \tag{6}$$

$$E(\epsilon_j) = 0$$
$$\text{Var}(\epsilon_j) = E\left(\epsilon_j^2\right) = \sigma^2 \tag{7}$$

What this means, of course, is that the level of utility of the voter, when the winner (whoever it is) is selected, can be stated this way:

$$E(U_I) = -(\mu_j - x)^2 - \sigma_j^2 \tag{8}$$

where j can be either alpha or beta, depending on who wins the election.

As the variance term grows large, the utility of the voter declines. The particular quadratic model depicted here of course assumes a particular scale, but it is trivial to rescale the expression for utility, and the result will always be the same.

CONCLUSION

The results here do not paint an optimistic picture for the chances for reform of the campaign finance process. Restrictions on spending or contributions tend to benefit incumbents, reducing competition and insulating officials from the electoral forces that ensure accountability. The alternative is little better, however, since the absence of such restrictions implies an ever-expanding quantity of resources will be spent of elections. Worse, such a result implies no real consequent increase in competitiveness, because incumbents can still win by simply matching the challenger's spending.

It is important to point out that there is no illogic in agents' actions. In fact, the problem is that actions are individually rational, but harmful to the collective interest. Candidates who use negative campaigning are more likely to win, all else equal and across many races, than those who emphasize positive themes or (worst of all) "stick to the issues." The problem for society is created when *both* candidates act on the incentives to use negative campaigning. Neither candidate realizes any net electoral gain, though each does better than if he had stayed positive, but the campaign, itself, imposes enormous and uncompensated utility losses on voters. Voters are made worse off by the breakdown of trust and communication, or (more precisely) by the increase in variability of their own perceptions of the implications of a particular ideological position for policy outcomes.

Within a community, it is possible to achieve collective, apparently altruistic ends because what Schofield calls the "common knowledge basis of cooperation" is satisfied. As Schofield points out:

> The fundamental theoretical problem underlying the question of cooperation is the manner by which individuals attain knowledge of each others' preferences and likely behavior. Moreover, the problem is one of common knowledge, since each individual, i, is required not only to have information about others' preferences, but also to know that the others have knowledge of i's own preferences and strategies. (Schofield 1985, p. 218)

Community is a sufficient basis for cooperation, but is not necessary. Ideology provides an alternative means by which the common knowledge basis of cooperation can be achieved. Common knowledge of this sort is itself a collective good, however, and is subject to depreciation because of the incentives facing candidates who want to win, for negative campaigning serves the candidate but hurts the electorate. The ultimate effect is the erosion of the common knowledge basis for cooperation, as ideological messages lose their meaning, and campaigns lose their importance as a means for making effective and wise political choices.

REFERENCES

Alesina, Alberto, and Alex Cukierman. "The Politics of Ambiguity." *Quarterly Journal of Economics*, 105 (1990): 829–848.

Ansolobehere, Stephen, Shanto Iyengar, Adam Simon, and Nicholas Valentino. "Does Attack Advertising Demobilize the Electorate?" *American Political Science Review*, 88(1994): 829–838.

Chappell, Henry W. "Campaign Advertising and Political Ambiguity." *Public Choice*. 79(1994): 281–303.

Converse, Phillip. "The Nature of Belief Systems in Mass Publics." In *Ideology and Discontent*, ed. David Apter, New York: Free Press, 1964.

Enelow, James, and Melvin Hinich. *The Spatial Theory of Voting: An Introduction*. New York: Cambridge University Press, 1984.

Garramone, Gina M. "Voter Response to Negative Political Ads." *Journalism Quarterly*, 61(1984): 250–259.

Harrington, Joseph. "The Revelation of Information through the Political Process." *Economics and Politics*, 4(1992): 255–276.

Harrington, Joseph, and Gregory Hess. "A Spatial Theory of Positive and Negative Campaigning." *Games and Economic Behavior*, 17(1996): 209–229.

Hinich, Melvin, and Michael Munger. *Ideology and the Theory of Political Choice*, Ann Arbor: University of Michigan Press, 1994.

Hinich, Melvin, and Michael Munger. *Analytical Politics*. New York: Cambridge University Press, 1997.

Laver, Michael, and Norman Schofield. *Multiparty Government: The Politics of Coalition in Europe*. Oxford: Oxford University Press, 1990.

Ordeshook, Peter. "The Spatial Theory of Elections: A Review and Critique." In *Party Identification and Beyond*, eds. Ian Budge, Ivor Crewe, and Dennis Farlie, New York: Wiley, 1976, pp. 271–296.

Page, Benjamin. *Choices and Echoes in Presidential Elections*. Chicago: University of Chicago Press, 1976.

Poole, Keith, and Howard Rosenthal. "The Polarization of American Politics." *Journal of Politics*, 46 (1984): 1061–1079.

Popkin, Samuel. *The Reasoning Voter: Communication and Persuasion in Presidential Campaigns*. Chicago: University of Chicago Press, 1994.

Schofield, Norman. "Anarchy, Altruism, and Cooperation: A Review." *Social Choice and Welfare*, 2 (1985): 207–219.

Shepsle, Kenneth. "The Strategy of Ambiguity, Uncertainty, and Competition." *American Political Science Review*, 66 (1972): 551–568.

Skaperdas, Stergios, and Bernard Grofman. "Modeling Negative Compaigning." *American Political Science Review*, 89 (1995): 49–61.

Wattenberg, Martin P., and Craig Brians. "Negative Campaign Advertising: Demobilizer or Mobilizer?" *American Political Sceince Review*, 93(1999): 891–899.

Wheatley, John, and Sadaomi Oshikawa. "The Relationship Between Anxiety and Positive and Negative Advertising Appeals." *Journal of Marketing Research*, 7(1970): 85–89.

3

Turning "Citizens" into "Consumers": Economic Growth and the Level of Public Discourse

Stergios Skaperdas

> There is little hope that the Italians will achieve a state of prosperity and internal calm until they start to be more interested in the respective merits of cornflakes and cigarettes than in the relative abilities of their political leaders.
>
> American official, 1947 (quoted in Mazower, 1998, p. 308)

> Individualism, at first, only saps the virtues of public life; but, in the long-run, it attacks and destroys all others, and is at length absorbed in downright egotism.
>
> de Tocqueville, *Second Book*, chapter II (p. 620, [1835] 2000)

INTRODUCTION

Gathered around a big table, a company consisting mostly of young adults produces much noise and fury. They are arguing about some, in the big scheme of things, inconsequential legislation proposed in parliament. There is much talking past each other, the stentorian voice of the conversation's would-be monopolist, the repetition of cliches from the mass media, but also much wit and belly-laughs. After the company's break-up, discussions linger at home, in some cases threatening domestic tranquility. Bits of the topic are picked up at subsequent gatherings in which new controversies might emerge as the center of argument. Newspapers and magazines, aware of the underlying demand,

Presented at the Villa Colombella Group conference on "The Binds of Democratic Politics," held in Parma, Italy, September 7–9, 2000. I would like to thank the conference participants for valuable comments. For discussions or comments I would also like to thank Marina Arseniev, Frank Cancian, John DiNardo, Tasos Karanastasis, Gary Milante, Jim Robinson, Loula Skaperda, three anonymous referees, and numerous symposium co-participants over the years (who have become fewer over time). Although many of the individuals mentioned above have very different views from mine, all have influenced me in at least some small way and cannot be completely absolved from responsibility; I do however grant them legal absolution from having anything whatsoever to do with the views expressed in this chapter.

provide plenty of both serious and lightweight fodder for argument in such gatherings.

This is the spice of life for the folks trying to find respite from the drudgery of trying to make a living. As a by-product, the prime minister's propagandists and media consultants feel restrained in the sleek claims they can make about the white being black and the black being white because of the ridicule they are likely to receive in such gatherings as well as elsewhere; or, at least, they are more restrained than foreign spin doctors from whom they have learned the art. Debate with friends, relatives, and acquaintances therefore plays a dual role: as a simple consumption good which has the attributes of a collective good and as a contributor to public political discourse.

One prerequisite, of course, for such forums of public debate is that one does not live in a police state, there is some openness, although having all the characteristics of a full-fledged democracy is unnecessary. Another prerequisite is that some basic material needs are satisfied and people do not go to bed on an empty stomach – the level of material well being of Western Europe during the late 1940s would probably be a safe lower bound for which the hypotheses developed in this article would apply. Then, given some openness and the satisfaction of basic material necessities, it appears that, other things being equal, increases in material welfare are associated with a decline in public discourse and political participation.[1] A smaller percentage of the electorate votes; political debate becomes less contentious; time spent getting together and arguing with friends and relatives is reduced; newspapers and other media devote less space to politics; television news turns into infotainment; in some advanced cases, if any debate occurs at all, it is focused on the less contentious, horse-race aspects of political campaigns as norms develop against openly disagreeing with others on substantive issues and against advocating for a particular position; major decisions about governance, like the Maastricht treaty, are agreed upon with virtually no public debate or even reaction.[2] Along the way, gradually and imperceptibly, the primary designation of a human being changes from citizen into consumer.[3]

I will try to make sense of this trend by formally showing how material growth increases the time spent working in the market while it reduces the time spent in gatherings, in *symposia,* with others. Public discourse requires time

---

[1] For the United States, Chapter 2 of Putnam (2000) provides quantitative evidence on about a dozen measures of political participation, all pointing to declining levels over time. For Europe and elsewhere, the trends appear to be similar but no doubt with significant variation across countries. For example, political discourse in France and Denmark still appears to have a fiesty component that has disappeared elsewhere, although the trends might be similar there too.

[2] A major exception to this absence of wide debate on the Maastricht treaty has been France.

[3] In some cases the term "citizen" might not have enough time to establish itself. The transition into "consumer" might therefore take place directly from "subject," the most common designation of human beings before democracy's "citizens."

to read, think, and interact with others. It is also assisted by the presence of a public space, the *agora*, the corner café, bar, or tavern, as well as the presence of media that can provide fodder for debate. Public discourse could be considered akin, or perhaps even a subset, of "social capital" (Putnam, 1993, 2000) and similar types of collective goods. However, whereas the formal analysis that follows can apply to other types of collective goods that have time as an input, public discourse does not necessarily require the presence of the formal voluntary associations that have been primarily associated with social capital.[4]

One corollary of the analysis is that individual welfare could decline even though material well-being increases. This outcome could occur because welfare depends on a public good that requires the time of others, and whose provision can collapse at higher levels of material well-being. Such an outcome is consistent with the evidence reported by Easterlin (1998) and others, according to which reported measures of subjective well-being often do not increase, and sometimes decline, with economic growth. However, though this issue is important, since it is tangential to the focus of this chapter we do not analyze it in any detail.

Before we go on, let us very briefly outline another hypothesis that could also possibly provide insight into the relationship between economic growth and public discourse. Such a hypothesis would be based on Michels's (1962) "iron law of oligarchy" and its main argument would go as follows. At early stages of economic growth, political systems, like political parties in early stages of development, are not well-organized and consolidated, thereby allowing a broader range of opinions to be heard and more democracy. As the political system matures, though, the leadership learns how to manage opinion better and since the people, like the rank-and-file of political parties, do not have much time or expert knowledge, debate is increasingly stirred toward the direction that the leadership desires. Gradually, the people's old passions become spent and discourse abates. We will not pursue this idea further, but it is worth keeping it in mind as a hypothesis which is complementary to the one we pursue here, emphasizing the informational mechanism through which reductions in public discourse can occur.

The next section develops the basic model about the effects of economic growth on public discourse and derives the basic findings. The third section, "When Discourse Also Matters for Growth," allows for feedbacks from the level of public discourse back to economic growth and shows that the basic findings

---

[4] The absence of formal associations might be due precisely to the fact that people satisfy their need to associate and engage in discourse with others through informal gatherings. This view has been proposed, for example, by Cancian (1961, p. 15) in his critique of Banfield (1958).

are not altered. The final section of the chapter briefly ponders what the future might hold.

WHEN PUBLIC DISCOURSE IS JUST CONSUMPTION

We begin with a simple model in which public discourse, participation in symposia, is a public good that increases the welfare of each participant directly and does not have any external effects on growth. Each individual i has one unit of time that is allocated between *labor, l_i*, and participation in *symposia, s_i*:

$$1 = l_i + s_i \qquad (1)$$

Individual utility is a function of a material good that is obtained through labor and a spiritual or psychic good that is derived from participation in symposia. The quantity of the material good consumed equals wl_i, where w is the exogenously given wage rate and is the indicator of the level of economic growth that we use in this chapter. The good derived from participation in symposia is modelled for simplicity as a pure public good, so that for a group with N potential participants the quantity obtained by each participant is $S = b \sum_{i=1}^{N} s_i$.[5] b is a positive productivity or public space parameter that can be thought of as representing the infrastructure for symposia, the presence of public spaces and ease with which the potential participants to a symposium can get together. Whereas in each particular instance the participants consider this parameter exogenous, it could be influenced by growth and by the choices made in the past, and we shall discuss how such an endogeneity of the public space parameter affects participation in symposia later. Although the parameter N represents literally the number of participants, we shall occasionally interpret the parameter as an index of the level of publicness of the public good, with higher levels of its value representing higher levels of that characteristic. For concreteness, in order to obtain explicit solutions, we employ the CES utility function:[6]

$$U_i = \left[(wl_i)^{\rho} + \left(b \sum_{j=1}^{N} s_j \right)^{\rho} \right]^{1/\rho} \qquad \text{where} \quad 0 \leq \rho \leq 1 \qquad (2)$$

---

[5] All results would follow through, but at much greater analytical expense, if participation in symposia were modelled as a congestible public good.

[6] The elasticity of substitution is $\sigma = \frac{1}{1-\rho}$. Given the restrictions we assume in (2), we allow the elasticity of substitution to take values between 1 and ∞ and, thus, do no consider the cases with elasticities of substitution between 0 and 1. The reason for this choice is that elasticities of substitution in that range yield some perverse effects. For example, an increase in w reduces the share of total expenditures going to the material good that comes from work. Effectively, the assumption on the elasticity of substitution ensures that the two goods are normal.

Using (1) to eliminate s_i, the utility of individual i can be written as a function of the choices of labor time made by all participants:

$$U_i(l_i, l_{-i}) = \left[(wl_i)^\rho + \left(b \sum_{j=1}^{N} (1 - l_j) \right)^\rho \right]^{1/\rho}$$

where $l_{-i} = (l_1, \ldots, l_{i-1}, l_{i+1}, \ldots, l_N)$ (3)

We first examine the case in which choices are made by each individual noncooperatively. We then discuss how norms of cooperation, public pressure, and of public space could mediate the effect of economic growth on the level of public discourse.

Noncooperative Contributions

Here we suppose that each individual i chooses how much to work, and therefore how much to participate in symposia, noncooperatively. Accordingly, we are interested in finding combinations of choices that form a Nash equilibrium so that no individual has an incentive to change their choices. One such combination of choices is the one in which each individual spends all of his or her time working and does not participate in any symposia. Since in this starkly atomistic equilibrium there are no symposia regardless of the level of economic growth, there is not much to learn from it and we shall therefore not consider this equilibrium any further.

By differentiating (3) with respect to l_i and setting the derivative equal to zero, any interior equilibrium $(l_1^*, l_2^*, \ldots, l_N^*,)$ must satisfy the following equation for all $i = 1, \ldots, N$:

$$(wl_i^*)^{\rho-1} w - \left(b \sum_{j=1}^{N} (1 - l_j^*) \right)^{\rho-1} b = 0$$ (4)

We concentrate on the focal, symmetric equilibrium, whereby each individual works the same number of hours. Therefore, by solving (4) we obtain the following equilibrium levels of labor (l^*) and participation in symposia (s^*):

$$l^* = \frac{w^{\frac{\rho}{1-\rho}} N}{w^{\frac{\rho}{1-\rho}} N + b^{\frac{\rho}{1-\rho}}} \qquad s^* = 1 - l^* = \frac{b^{\frac{\rho}{1-\rho}}}{w^{\frac{\rho}{1-\rho}} N + b^{\frac{\rho}{1-\rho}}}$$ (5)

Time spent working rises with economic growth (that is, with an increase in w) whereas participation in symposia diminishes with economic growth. Naturally, as public space becomes more accommodating (when b is higher), less time is spent on work and more in symposia.[7]

---

[7] Although average working hours for individuals might have fallen in the West for some periods during the past 50 years, with the massive increase in female labor participation household working hours have increased during the same period. Thus, the effect of wages on working

By substituting the expressions in (5) back into the utility function in (3), we obtain the maximized level of utility, or the indirect utility function which can be considered a function of the growth and public space parameters w and b:

$$V(w, b) = U_i(l^*, l^*, \ldots, l^*) = \frac{N\left(w^{\frac{\rho}{1-\rho}} + b^{\frac{\rho}{1-\rho}}\right)^{\frac{1}{\rho}}}{w^{\frac{\rho}{1-\rho}} N + b^{\frac{\rho}{1-\rho}}} \tag{6}$$

Normally, we would expect economic growth to induce higher welfare, higher utility. However, growth reduces contributions to a public good – public discourse – and it is theoretically possible for the reductions to its provision being so precipitous so as to overcome the increase in utility that comes from material growth. For the particular utility function we use in this chapter, we can search for this possibility by differentiating $V(w, b)$ with respect to the growth parameter w:

$$\frac{\partial V(w, b)}{\partial w} = A \frac{Nw^{\frac{\rho}{1-\rho}}(1 - \rho) + b^{\frac{\rho}{1-\rho}}(1 - N\rho)}{w^{\frac{\rho}{1-\rho}} + b^{\frac{\rho}{1-\rho}}} \text{ where } A \text{ is a positive number.} \tag{7}$$

This derivative can be negative if the numerator is negative, which can occur if N or b are large enough. By inspecting (7), we can identify two possibilities for maximized utility as a function of the growth parameter w. First, there is the possibility that maximized utility is strictly increasing in growth. This would occur if public discourse had not had a strong enough "publicness," one could satisfy the need with a small number of symposium participants N, or the infrastructure, the public space as measured by the parameter b, were not large enough. The second possibility is that the relationship between growth and maximized utility is U-shaped, with utility first decreasing and then increasing after a certain level. This possibility would occur if the publicness of public discourse were high enough or public space were accommodating enough for symposia.

Optimal Contributions

The atomistic, noncooperative contributions we have just discussed should probably represent a lower bound on the amount of contributions to symposia that we would expect to find (if we were ever able to examine empirically our theoretical findings here, which would be a highly dicey endeavor anyway). In practice, communities and social groups invent many different ways of enforcing higher participation. In small groups, where everybody knows each other, the threat of ostracism and other pressures can easily induce contributions higher than the noncooperative ones. In larger groups and communities, there exist more sophisticated mechanisms, especially those that hard-wire

hours we find here is consistent with the postwar experience at the household level. I thank a referee for raising this issue.

choices in childhood. However, it would be difficult to deny that monitoring compliance in larger groups is not as easy as in smaller ones.

To have a sense of comparison, we now derive the choices of work and participation in symposia that would maximize the welfare of each individual. The optimal choices of work and participation in symposia can be shown to be the following:

$$
l^{\#} = \frac{w^{\frac{\rho}{1-\rho}}}{w^{\frac{\rho}{1-\rho}} + N^{\frac{\rho}{1-\rho}} b^{\frac{\rho}{1-\rho}}} \qquad s^{\#} = 1 - l^{\#} = \frac{N^{\frac{\rho}{1-\rho}} b^{\frac{\rho}{1-\rho}}}{w^{\frac{\rho}{1-\rho}} + N^{\frac{\rho}{1-\rho}} b^{\frac{\rho}{1-\rho}}} \qquad (8)
$$

Note that this optimal choice of labor is always lower than l^*. Moreover, it is decreasing in the publicness of the symposia, as represented by the parameter N, instead of being increasing as it is with l^* (because of the lower incentive to contribute to the pubic good as N increases). The maximized utility under these choices then equals:

$$
V^{\#} = \left[w^{\frac{\rho}{1-\rho}} + N^{\frac{\rho}{1-\rho}} b^{\frac{\rho}{1-\rho}} \right]^{\frac{1-\rho}{\rho}} \qquad (9)
$$

Obviously this level of utility is higher than the maximized utility under noncooperative contributions ($V(b, w)$) in (6). Moreover, it is always increasing in economic growth (that is, as w increases) since the substitution away from participation in symposia is much less dramatic here.

Public Space

Regardless of the mechanism that generates contributions to symposia – non-cooperative, public pressure inducing optimal behavior, or anything in between – we can expect these contributions to decrease with economic growth. This may have implications for the provision of symposia not just in the present but also in the future. As symposia become less common, taverns, cafes, and publications that facilitate them – in short, the associated public space – become less common as well; even the architecture of building and communities be- comes less accommodating to symposia and encourages privacy. In turn, that reduction in public space which we can identify in our model as a reduction in the parameter b, induces a reduction in participation in symposia that goes beyond that reduction that is solely due to growth.

Suppose then that b is a decreasing function of w, denoted by $b(w)$. The total effect of economic growth on equilibrium utility when contributions to symposia are chosen noncooperatively is as follows.

$$
\frac{dV(w, b(w))}{dw} = \frac{\partial V(w, b)}{\partial w} + B \frac{w^{\frac{\rho}{1-\rho}}(N - \rho) + b^{\frac{\rho}{1-\rho}}(1 - \rho)}{w^{\frac{\rho}{1-\rho}} + b^{\frac{\rho}{1-\rho}}} b'(w) \qquad (10)
$$

where B is a positive parameter.

The second term of this expression is always negative since $b'(w)$ is negative and everything else in the term is positive. Given that $\frac{\partial(w,b)}{\partial w}$ can be positive or negative and induce the two types of relationships between economic growth and maximized welfare discussed earlier, (10) shows that maximized utility can be increasing, have an inverted U-shaped with welfare maximized at particular level of w, or even be strictly decreasing everywhere. The same relationship between the level of growth and maximized welfare holds for $V^{\#}$ as well, although the range of parameters for which there is an inverted-U relationship holds for a narrower range of parameters.

We should note at this point that according to numerous measures of subjective well-being, the relationship between level of growth and subjective well-being is not monotonic. Easterlin (1998) interprets the evidence as showing an essentially flat relationship over time, whereas Lane (1998) considers the relationship to be negative for the US.[8] Easterlin (1998) and Frank (1997) attribute the non-increasing relationship between money and happiness to status-seeking, the tendency to judge our own welfare relative to that of our neighbors. Whereas status-seeking appears to be at least partly responsible, there is no reason that other factors might not come into play, like the reduction in the provision of public goods that have leisure as an input, which we have examined here.

Overall, when pubic discourse is just consumption and regardless of how the choice between participation in symposia and work is determined, participation in symposia decreases and work increases with economic growth. Because public discourse is a public good which decreases with economic growth, the effect of economic growth on welfare is ambiguous. When public space itself becomes negatively affected by economic growth, welfare can be strictly decreasing in economic growth, especially at higher levels of material well-being. Persons in such cases become richer, more private, and less happy. Public discourse, however, may affect well-being not just as consumption. We then turn next to the more intricate effects public discourse could have, especially its possibly reverse causality on economic growth, and see how our findings are affected.

WHEN DISCOURSE ALSO MATTERS FOR GROWTH

We could consider the exogeneity of economic growth that we have supposed thus far to be the outcome of technological change. While we will continue to consider this technological effect as exogenous, we will now consider effects that public discourse could have on institutional aspects of growth. Disentangling

---

[8] Oswald (1997) qualifies Easterlin's interpetation of the evidence, but also introduces additional evidence against the assumption that more money brings more happiness. This basic assumption of economics texts was also scrutinized by Scitovsky (1976), one of the first economists to do so in the postwar period.

It should also be mentioned that the evidence discussed is a time series. At any point in time, richer folks tend to report that they are happier.

such effects is not a simple affair. Our aim is to take account of the different effects that have been proposed, incorporate them into our model by assuming the least we can, and then determine the extent to which our previous findings continue to hold qualitatively.

The first quote at the beginning of this article is indicative of a view about the effect of political discourse on the economy that was common in the immediate postwar period. That view reflected the fear that the postwar prospects for democracy in Europe were no better than the interwar period, when democracy lost ground in most countries very quickly. During that time the perceived or real ineffectiveness of parliaments combined with economic malaise helped identify the term "democracy" with mob rule, just as Plato had done some time before that. Churchill thought that the parliamentary tradition was not for export out of the United Kingdom (Mazower, 1998, pp. 16–17) and George Kennan, a young American diplomat then, thought that "benevolent despotism . . . had greater possibilities for good" than democracy (quoted in Mazower, 1998, p. 27).

Public discourse can become all-consuming in some cases, with physical fights in parliaments as well as in the streets, possibly taking too much time, energy, and resources away from other endeavors and inducing political instability that saps economic growth. Such intensity of public discourse may also be considered an almost necessary outcome of the transition to more democratic forms of governance. Perhaps it is not an accident that parliamentary fights – from many interwar European capitals to Ankara, Moscow, and Taipei of a few years back – take place when the lid of political repression has come out recently and both the form of governance in the future is uncertain and rules and norms for compromise and cooperation are yet undeveloped. Regardless of the particulars though, it might be reasonable to hypothesize, as the American official in postwar Italy had done, a negative effect on economic growth when public discourse is too high.

Considering the opposite end of the spectrum, however, with Leibnitzian monads never getting together for a symposium, cannot be an optimal state either. The quote from de Tocqueville, the second one at the beginning of this article, hints at the problems of extreme individualism.

As with the external effects of education that endogenous growth theory considers central to modern economic growth (e.g., Aghion and Howitt, 1998), so we can suspect that public discourse at reasonable levels does not just have consumption externalities but growth externalities as well. Lack of public discourse reduces the alternatives considered and allows small minorities to have inordinate influence and make public policy decisions that could adversely impinge on economic growth. Reductions in public discourse erode governance and bad governance is typically not good for the economy. At low levels of public discourse, then, we can expect economic growth to increase when public discourse increases.

We incorporate these two effects of public discourse on economic growth by assuming that w is determined in the following fashion:

$$w = \phi\omega(S) \text{ where } \phi > 0; \omega'(S) \geq 0 \text{ if } S \leq S_o \tag{11}$$

and $\omega'(S) \leq 0$ if $S \geq S^o$ for some S_o and S^o such that $S_o \leq S^o$

The parameter ϕ represents the exogenous technological effect on economic growth; it plays the same role that w plays in the previous section, "When Public Discourse Is Just Consumption." The effect of public discourse, S, on economic growth goes through the function $\omega(\cdot)$; for low levels of public discourse (that is, those below S_o) growth is increasing in public discourse, whereas for high levels of public discourse (those above S^o) growth is decreasing in public discourse.[9]

By substituting for S in the utility function we employed earlier, we obtain the following payoff function for agent i:

$$U_i^g = \left[\left(\phi\omega \left(b \sum_{j=1}^{N} s_j \right) l_i \right)^\rho + \left(b \sum_{j=1}^{N} s_j \right)^\rho \right]^{1/\rho} \tag{12}$$

$$= \left[\left(\phi\omega \left(b \sum_{j=1}^{N} (1 - l_j) \right) l_i \right)^\rho + \left(b \sum_{j=1}^{N} (1 - l_j) \right)^\rho \right]^{1/\rho}$$

We now seek to determine the effect of exogenous technological change (that is, a change in ϕ) on the (noncooperative) equilibrium levels of labor and participation in symposia. Because the model of this section is more complex than the one of the previous section and we do not suppose a specific functional form for $\omega(\cdot)$, we cannot derive analytical solutions for these variables. We can derive comparative static results, however, which we do in the Appendix of this chapter.

When $\omega'(S) \leq 0$, at high enough levels of public discourse, we can show that growth-inducing technological change always increases the amount of time devoted to labor and reduces the amount of time spent on symposia (provided that $\omega(\cdot)$ is concave). This is to be expected, as too much public discourse in this case is supposed to have a negative feedback on growth, through its institutional component.

When $\omega'(S) > 0$, at low levels of public discourse, even though we cannot in general sign the effect of ϕ without additional restrictions, there appears to be a strong tendency not to have the effect on labor time reversed. For instance,

---

[9] Since we examine a static model the effect of public discourse on economic growth is assumed to be immediate. Of course, that effect in reality can take much time to work itself out. To allow for that long-term effect, we need to examine a dynamic model. That can be done, but we do not expect to find any effects that are qualitatively different from those we find here. If anything, because agents would tend to discount the effect of public discourse today on future growth, the underprovision of public discourse that we find would be accentuated in a dynamic framework.

when $\omega'(S)$ is constant, say some positive number γ, we show in the Appendix that, again, an increase in ϕ is accompanied by an increase in time devoted to labor and a reduction in the time spent on symposia.

Therefore, regardless of how public discourse affects the institutional aspects of growth, growth that emanates from technological change has the same qualitative effects: it reduces the time spent on, and the level of, public discourse. Following the argument at the end of the previous section, we can thus expect public space to be reduced as well, an effect that we have seen to induce an additional reduction in public discourse. The effect of technological growth on maximized welfare is ambiguous, as it was in the previous section, "When Public Discourse Is Just Consumption." Overall, taking account of the possible feedback of public discourse on economic growth through institutional channels does not appear to change any of the qualitative results we found when public discourse is a consumption good only. Nevertheless, the quantitative effects and how public discourse is viewed can be important, especially when a society is at low levels of public discourse and additional reductions can have dramatic long-run effects through the erosion of its institutions; the danger of having democracy in name only would then become real.

WHAT DOES THE FUTURE HOLD? SPORTS, WWW, OR IDIOCY?

Will public discourse continue to decline as material growth forges ahead? Or are we at the dawn of a new era, in which self-governance and public debate, abetted by technology, can reach forms that we cannot now imagine? We are not in a position to answer such questions, but we can at least close by briefly discussing two sets of forces at work and how they might influence the future.

If we were to consider public discourse as a collective good that only yields consumption, it could be argued that with increasing material prosperity new goods emerge that have quasi-collective good components but which can be supplied privately through the market. For the right price you can take a white-water rafting trip in an exotic river where you can expect to find new friends and possibly temporarily bond with them over the fire at night. But, perhaps a more realistic alternative for most people is simply to cheer for the home team along with thousands of others. The effective invention and explosive growth of spectator sports during the twentieth century must surely be related to the secular decline of community over the same period. Therefore, one route that society and polity can take is one in which sports and other similar goods provided through the market could serve as substitutes for public discourse and other collective goods traditionally provided through the time contributions of group members.

However, as we have seen, that condition could eventually undermine material prosperity itself through the erosion of institutions that support the economy. Furthermore, spectator sports or white-water rafting trips might prove inadequate substitutes for symposia for at least some people. Could, as with everything else, the Internet come to the rescue? This new medium allows unprecedented access to information and facilitates the formation of virtual communities; in other words, it could be considered to increase the public space that facilitates public discourse. And, by allowing almost instant and cheap interactive communication across the globe, it can help build the currently scarce *bridging* social capital. The Internet holds the promise of impact comparable to that the print media have had on thought and political practice over the past five centuries, but just as with print in its early stages, we cannot imagine the avenues that it could take in the future.

In closing, let us note an interesting linguistic tidbit. The etymology of *idiot* is that of private person, someone who does not participate in public affairs; gradually the word also acquired the connotation of someone who is incapable of participating in public affairs, and that was the meaning that passed through Latin into many modern European languages. Though the evolution of language as everything else involves many accidents, there is enough correlation between the two meanings to makes us pause. Erasing perhaps the temporary blip of Enlightenment thought, we could become, if we are not already, idiots in both senses, and of course we wouldn't know it. We would then come back, full circle, where we started – being "subjects," even if the name used to describe us were to be different.

APPENDIX

In this Appendix we derive the comparative static results reported in the chapter section titled, "When Discourse Also Matters for Growth."

As we did in the second chapter section, we consider the symmetric interior equilibrium in which each agent $i's$ payoff function is defined in (12). Letting l^* denote the equilibrium level of work, differentiating (12), and setting it equal to zero, we obtain the following expression:

$$[\phi\omega(N(1-l^*))l^*]^{\rho-1}\phi[\omega(N(1-l^*)) - l^*\omega'(N(1-l^*))] - [N(1-l^*)]$$

To find the effect of exogenous technological change (ϕ) on the equilibrium level of work (l^*), we totally differentiate this expression with respect to these two variables and obtain the following expression:

$$\frac{\partial l^*}{\partial \phi} = -\frac{Z}{\Lambda}$$

where $Z = \rho[\phi\omega(N(1-l^*))l^*]^{\rho-1}[\omega(N(1-l^*)) - l^*\omega'(N(1-l^*))]$

and $\Lambda = -[\phi\omega(N(1-l^*))l^*]\{(1-\rho)[\omega(N(1-l^*)) - l^*\omega'(N(1-l^*))]\phi$
$$\times [\omega(N(1-l^*)) - Nl^*\omega'(N(1-l^*))]$$
$$+ (N+1)\omega'(N(1-l^*)) - l^*\omega''(N(1-l^*))\}$$
$$- (1-\rho)N[N(1-l^*)]^{\rho-2}$$

When $\omega'(S) \leq 0$, Z is always positive. It is also somewhat more tedious to show that, under the same assumption, all the terms of Λ, except one, contribute to a negative sign of Λ. The term that can contribute to ambiguity is the one involving the second derivative ω''. To eliminate the ambiguity, however, we just need to assume concavity of $\omega(\cdot)$, so that ω'' is negative, which is a natural assumption (and also guarantees uniqueness of l^*, which we need to assume anyway).

Therefore, when $\omega'(S) \leq 0$ the effect technological growth on work ($\frac{\partial l^*}{\partial \phi}$) is positive. That is, growth-inducing technical change increases the time devoted to work and decreases the time devoted to pubic discourse.

When $\omega'(S) > 0$, the derivative in question cannot be signed in general. However, inspection of the expressions indicates that the effect is qualitatively similar, but quantitatively less important, than the effect when $\omega'(S) \leq 0$. In particular, when $\omega'(S) = \gamma > 0$ for some constant γ, the payoff function of player i over that range becomes:

$$b \sum_{j=1}^{N} (1 - l_j)[(\phi \gamma l_i)^\rho + 1]^{1/\rho}$$

In the interior, symmetric equilibrium, we can show that

$$\frac{\partial l^*}{\partial \phi} = \frac{\rho l^{*3-\rho}(N(1 - l^*)/l^* - 1]}{\phi[(1 - \rho)N + 2\rho l^*]}$$

Because at an interior equilibrium we can show that $N(1 - l^*)/l^* - 1$ is always positive, this derivative is positive as well.

REFERENCES

Aghion, Philippe and Howitt, Peter, *Endogenous Growth Theory*, 1998, Cambridge, MA: MIT Press.

Banfield, Edward C., *The Moral Basis of a Backward Society*, 1958, Glencoe, IL: The Free Press.

Cancian, Frank, "The Southern Italian Peasant," *Anthropological Quarterly*, January 1961, 34(1), 1–18.

De Tocqueville, Alexis, *Democracy in America*, translated by Henry Reeve, 2000, [1835], New York: Bantam Classic.

Easterlin, Richard, *Growth Triumphant. The 21st Century in Historical Perspective*, 1998, University of Michigan Press.

Frank, Robert, H., "The Frame of Reference as a Public Good," *Economic Journal*, November 1997, 107, 1832–1847.

Lane, Robert, "The Joyless Market Economy," in Avner Ben-Ner and Louis Putterman, (eds.), *Economics, Values, and Organization*, 1998, New York: Cambridge University Press.

Mazower, Mark, *Dark Continent. Europe's Twentieth Century*, 1998, New York: Random House.

Michels, Robert, *Political Parties; A Sociological Study of the Oligarchical Tendencies of Modern Democracy*, translated by Eden and Cedar Paul, 1962, New York: Free Press.

Oswald, Andrew J., "Happiness and Economic Performance," *Economic Journal*, November 1997, 107, 1815–1831.

Putnam, Robert D. (with Robert Leonardi and Rafaella Y. Nanetti), *Making Democracy Work. Civic Traditions in Modern Italy*, 1993, Princeton, NJ: Princeton University Press.

Putnam, Robert D., *Bowling Alone*, 2000, New York: Simon & Schuster.

Scitovsky, Tibor, *The Joyless Economy*, 1976, New York: Oxford University Press.

4

Economic and Cultural Prerequisites for Democracy

Roger D. Congleton

Just as the regimen of the healthy is not suited to the sick, one must not try to govern a corrupt people by the same Laws as those that suit a good people. *Nothing proves these maxims better than the long life of the Republic of Venice, which still retains a simulacrum of existence, solely because its laws are suited only to wicked men.*

Rousseau (1997/1755, p. 135).

INTRODUCTION: IMPLICIT ASSUMPTIONS IN DEMOCRATIC ANALYSIS

Modern scholars may disagree about the merits of alternative forms of democracy, but generally agree that democracy is self-sustaining in the sense that once in place it continues uninterrupted. Donald Wittman's (1995) book, *The Myth of Democratic Failure*, makes this presumption explicit with its title, but essentially all rational-choice-based analyses of democracy use this assumption as an uncontroversial point of departure. That is to say, modern analysis of democracy generally presumes that democratic governance is always a feasible method of making policy decisions. The question addressed in this chapter is whether this presumption is defensible. Are there implicit assumptions about the cultural or economic environment that are implicitly being made when the feasibility of democracy is taken for granted?

To get some sense of the problem that I am interested in here, recall the optimistic forecasts that were widely made by economists in the early 1990s as the Iron Curtain disappeared overnight. Economists evidently believed their models, which seemed to imply that a market only requires unimpeded trade to achieve competitive results. Under the Coase (1960) theorem, any form of privatization would be as good as any other, and, so, the specifics of privatization could be neglected. As long as control of the individual resources of a particular society is clear and tradable, the specific distribution of control would not affect the process of economic development. Given the relatively large apparent stocks of human and nonhuman capital available in Eastern Europe, it was widely believed that within 5 to 10 years the former communist economies would be entirely transformed, and for the most part would have income and markets comparable to Western ones. Fixed physical capital assets play a role in short-run neoclassical analysis, but not in the long run.

However, economic models had widely neglected the role of cultural and legal institutions for markets. As it turned out, the stock of human and physical capital was not simply homogenous K that could readily be (re)optimized for whatever institutional environment production takes place in, nor were all distributions of ownership rights equally effective at generating value-increasing transactions. It was not always, or perhaps even often, possible to take human capital accumulated for the purposes of succeeding in a nonmarket (political-bureaucratic) mode of production and use it to succeed in a cost-minimizing market-oriented mode of production. The particulars of property rights also seem to have affected prospects for growth. Getting the law right was a major concern of all reformers, but legal reform was also a potential source of rents that rent seekers used to advance their own narrow interests. The neglected cultural and political assumptions underlying most neoclassical analysis of long-standing market-based societies turned out to be critical in explaining market success, (North 1990). In the end, few Soviet-East European enterprises fully made the transition from command-and-control to market-based economies.

Similar optimism seems to be present in the assessments of the many new democratic governments launched in Eastern Europe and elsewhere during the 1990s. The question addressed in this paper is whether the same sort of neglected assumptions underlie the widespread optimism about the viability and appeal of democratic constitutional reform. Are analytical models of democracy abstracting from important cultural, legal, and constitutional preconditions that make it possible for majority rule to function as a mechanism for governance? The answer suggested here is yes. Economic and cultural conditions do contribute to the success of democratic governance in both the short and long run.

Before proceeding with the analysis, it bears noting that I do not mean this chapter to be a direct attack on all the fine work that has been done in public choice or rational politics traditions. Substantial value added is produced by abstraction – that is to say, by focusing attention on a subset of larger phenomena that can be analyzed holding other things constant. I will certainly employ that methodology in the following analysis. The neglected cultural and economic prerequisites for democracy often can be safely neglected for short-term analyses, and especially for analyses of long-standing and well-functioning democracies and market systems. However, no presumption can be made that every society will have an easy time establishing a well-functioning majoritarian government. Within Europe, it is clear that many countries, for example, France and Germany, struggled for decades to develop democratic regimes that

worked tolerably well, and that success was not entirely a matter of constitutional design. Democratic governance has only very recently been the rule
rather than the exception in large scale political organization.

Historical experience, thus, suggests that democracies are far more frail
than most modern analytical analyses presume. This chapter demonstrates how
fortuitous economic and cultural conditions can make them less so.

To advance citizen interests, the governments constituted have to select rules,
tax methods, and regulations that will be enforced. A government that prospers may be said to have made good choices on such matters. A society that
prospers may be said to have a good government. However, if public choice
theorists are correct about the properties of simple majority rule, theory implies that all these tasks can be problematic for majoritarian governments. (1)
The majority cycling problems suggests that democratic governments may not
be able to make decisions. (2) The majoritarian demand for redistribution may
cause democracies to adopt overly generous transfer schemes that impoverish
democratic societies in the long run. Moreover, (3) elected government officials may use their powers to subvert the electoral process by which they are
selected.

The fact that these implications of majority rule are not obvious features of
long-standing democracies may lead some to conclude that public choice theories of democracy and democratic failure should be rejected. Perhaps models
of rational choice do not properly explain political life because it is a domain where narrow self-interest is never the dominant concern. Alternatively,
perhaps self-interest has lead individuals within government to construct institutional arrangements that solve many of the problems that theorists have
discovered.

This chapter explores a third possibility. Perhaps the problems identified by
public choice theorists are significant ones that do, in fact, undermine the viability of democratic governance. Institutional solutions do exist for most of these
problems, although effective reforms may be difficult to put in place. Many
democratic polities have failed over the years, and the problems identified by
public choice theorists often appear evident in those that fail. Democracies may
need a bit of luck to succeed. The analysis of this chapter shows how fortuitous
culture and economic circumstances can make the problems of majority decision making easier to overcome, and thereby allow democracy to become an
appealing and effective form of governance.[1]

---

[1] Ostrom (1998) provides a very complete overview of the role of norms in making collective
action both feasible and productive.

The tradeoff between good rules (constitutions) and good men (culture) has long been recognized. Consider, for example, Rousseau (1997/1755, p. 135): "Just as the regimen of the
healthy is not suited to the sick, one must not try to govern a corrupt people by the same Laws
as those that suit a good people. *Nothing proves these maxims better than the long life of the
Republic of Venice, which still retains a simulacrum of existence, solely because its laws are suited*

AVOIDING MAJORITY INDETERMINACY

Indecisiveness and Majority Rule

The first problem that has to be overcome by a democratic government is indecisiveness. A very large literature suggests that majority rule will not be able to consistently rank policy alternatives, nor make policy decisions that are stable through time. In unconstrained collective choice settings, every policy can be beaten by another, Arrow (1963). Theory, thus, suggests that unconstrained democracy will be unable to make policy decisions.

To illustrate this fundamental problem, consider a medieval city whose citizens have agreed to build a defensive wall around their city. Suppose that all relevant parties within the city (voters) have agreed on the design of the wall and its placement, and now confront the problem of paying for it.[2] Suppose, further that there are three equally sized groups of persons entitled to participate in the majoritarian decision making process used by the community: shepherds, masons, and merchants.

A broad range of methods for financing the wall can be proposed by those participating in the decision. The first proposal for financing the wall might require all citizens to make equal contributions toward building the wall. Such an apportionment may be plausibly justified from the public-good nature of the wall. The benefits of the wall are more or less uniformly distributed within the city. The distribution of the tax burden can be written as $(T_{shepherd}, T_{mason}, T_{merchant})$, which in this case is (4, 4, 4). A second proposal for funding the wall's construction might be based on comparative advantage. Perhaps, the wall should be provided by those best able to provide the needed services, which in this case would be those already skilled at wall construction. Some might argue that clearly the middle class masons should be public spirited and construct the wall for the city (2, 8, 2).

Another proposal might be developed based on differences in the ability of the townspeople to pay for the public services. Proponents of that view might reason that the community should take account of physical or wealth differences among citizens. After all, some persons can more readily shoulder the burden than others (1, 5, 6). A fourth proposal might attempt to account for the fact that poor persons could benefit from learning the craft of masonry, and, moreover, have more free time available for undertaking the required work. The

---

only to wicked men." Similarly, de Tocqueville (1972/1835, p. 319) notes that "the maintenance of democratic institutions in the United States is attributable to the circumstances, the laws, and the customs of that country" while emphasizing that the latter two causes are more important than the former.

[2] It bears noting that in this circumstance essentially any financial method sufficient to assure the wall's construction would be Pareto efficient. (That is, the result satisfies the familiar Samualsonian (1954) conditions for production of a pure public good.)

shepherds have the most to gain, or the least to lose by undertaking most of the work. Indeed, it could be claimed that the others groups were already busy carrying the burden of expanding the town's cathedral (6, 4, 2).

Since all four tax systems are sufficient to finance the public good of interest here, any will serve, but nonetheless, a decision has to be made. Consider that choice under majority rule. As rational voters, it is natural to assume that the members of each group will favor the tax regime that minimizes their tax burden. However, if votes are based only on anticipated tax burdens and the range of tax instruments is unconstrained, there may not be a stable majoritarian equilibrium. There is, for example, a majoritarian cycle among the first three proposals. In each case, two of the three groups benefit from lower taxes as the distribution of tax schedule used to fund the wall changes. Consequently, the second proposal can defeat the first, the third the second, and the first the third. As long as the previously defeated proposals can be reintroduced, majority rule will never reach a final decision, and the wall remains unfinanced and unbuilt. Our democratic city seems likely to disappear as the next roving military force conquers it, or expansionary neighbor annexes it, while the town deliberates.[3]

Arrow (1963) points out that this problem is surprisingly general and extends to other collective decision making rules as well as to majority rule. The theory of cycling problems has been analyzed by modern public choice and social choice theorists for half a century, although most attention has been directed at the extent to which cycling limits majority rule's appeal as a social welfare function, and the extent to which Arrow's assumptions regarding ideal methods of ranking social alternatives might be changed to escape from cycling. Few have noted that the cycling problem implies that *majoritarian democracy may not be a feasible method of governance* (Congleton and Tollison 1999). However, any policy issue that affects the distribution of income or wealth tends to exhibit the cyclic majority problem. In such policy areas, unconstrained majority rule can not make conclusive policy decisions in such policy areas, and clearly, governments can not govern unless they can make and enforce policy choices.

Institutionally Induced Stability

The fact that the possibility of majoritarian cycling has only recently been puzzled out by political theorists suggests that such problems have not often

---

[3] Of course, not every series of tax alternatives generate cycles. For example, the fourth option is weakly dominant among the four proposals listed. None of the alternatives makes a majority strictly better off than the proposal four. Thus, in this case, majority rule might be able to choose a method of finance if only these four alternatives can be considered.

However, it is clear that other proposals may dominate the fourth alternative as well. For example, the masons may be asked to do essentially all of the work since this is the fastest method of establishing the defensive wall (2, 8, 2).

been observed. There are at least three possible explanations for this. First, majoritarian cycles may be so critical for democracy that decision failures of this sort lead democracies to be rapidly replaced by other forms of government. If true, this explanation would explain the dearth of democratic regimes in recorded history. An obvious solution to majority indecision would be to let a prominent leader make the policy decisions for community of interest. Perhaps only a few democratic regimes have managed to avoid the cycling problem.

Second, majoritarian procedures might be modified or constrained in a manner that allows decisions to be reached. An ongoing cycling problem would be obvious to the participants of any democratic forum, and, once recognized, most participants would agree to adopt procedures that avoid cycles. Shepsle and Weingast (1981) and Bernholz (1986) have shown that restrictions on the order and range of alternatives can assure stable majoritarian outcomes in a broad range of issue spaces. Majoritarian decisiveness can be assured in our medieval town if a procedural rule is adopted that limits financing options to whole numbers, and rules out reconsideration of defeated proposals. Such procedural and domain constraints would assure an eventual decision, although the tax structure selected would be affected by the order in which proposals are considered.[4] Alternatively, majoritarian decisiveness can also be assured if an agenda setter is selected, although the outcomes may not look very democratic.

However, institutional solutions may be difficult to work out because the same cycling problems that are present in the funding of public good projects also tend to be associated with majority decisions over procedural rules and constraints for avoiding the cycling problem. There are many possible institutional designs. While a city or nation's constitutional committee ponders the best constitutional arrangements, the polity might well be at risk. It seems likely that the institutional arrangements that help solve cycling problems have been adopted for other reasons.

Culturally Induced Stability

A third possibility is that voter preferences or policy agendas may be such that the conditions for cyclic majorities rarely occur. Widely held norms may generate broad agreement about the proper way to fund public works or to organize the agenda of town meetings. For example, Buchanan and Congleton (1998) and Congleton (1997) demonstrate that the use of a generality norm – the norm that all citizens be treated equally by government – tends to increase the efficiency of governance, in part by avoiding cycling problems. In the wall

---

[4] In addition to constraints on the order or range of issues that may be voted on, groups could rely upon other voting rules that are less cycle prone. However for our purposes a majoritarian focus seems most appropriate.

illustration, agreement to equally divide the burden of the collective enterprise implies a single unique distribution of tax burden (4, 4, 4), and the wall gets built. Similar results also hold for the other normative theories in the example as well. If only one of them is widely supported, three of the tax schemes would be widely regarded to be unacceptable because they yield burdens that are improper or unfair. Insofar as the wall is a true public good, there is no conflict in this case between the use of widely accepted norms as a guide for policy development and narrow self-interest.

In the case where norms do not lead directly to particular policy outcomes, norms may limit the domain of policy alternatives in a manner that helps assure stability. For example, a consensus that taxes should be based on ability to pay tends to limit tax systems to a relatively small subset of those which can fund the desired public goods, although it does not imply a unique distribution of tax burdens.[5] Cycles may also be curtailed by procedural norms. For example, it may be widely regarded as improper or unsportsmanlike to reintroduce tax schemes that have already been defeated. Ideally, stability enhancing norms reduce the range of potentially acceptable policies to ones with a single peaked distribution of voter preferences, and limit acceptable procedures to ones that curtail cycling in cases where cycling would otherwise occur.

The same reason also implies that the existence of widely shared norms can also enhance prospects for constitutional building. Within a democracy, all formal constitutional constraints have to be voted on at some point, and to the extent that majoritarian procedures are used to make constitutional law, constitution deliberations are also prone to majoritarian cycling problems. In contrast, norm-based agenda and procedural restrictions are exogenous to political deliberations. That is to say, widely held norms are not matters voted on, but rather part of the existing culture in which policy alternatives are proposed and evaluated. Consequently, culture can serve as a super-constitutional foundation for decisive majoritarian decision making for the constitutional as well as for day-to-day democratic politics.

It bears noting that in order for norms to bind, normative theories have to be widely internalized by many individuals or broadly supported within the community of interest. That is to say, norms themselves have to influence day-to-day decision making as well as political deliberations, although such norms do not have to constrain everyone in the community. In the wall example, the normative arguments used by proponents of particular assignments of the cost of the wall might have been self-serving in the sense that each proponent appealed to the normative theory that minimizes their tax burden.[6]

---

[5] Usher (1981) demonstrates that tax systems that preserve the pretax rank order of income tend to be more stable under majority rule than those which do not.

[6] See Congleton (1991) for an illustration of how self-serving efforts at persuasion can be modeled in an environment where normative theories (ideology) are widely used by voters.

However, clearly, there is no reason to employ norm-based rhetoric unless normative arguments are convincing in a manner not directly tied to personal wealth or income. The widespread use of normative rhetoric by policy proponents suggests that some widely held norms do not always encourage wealth maximizing behavior. Otherwise, norm-based arguments would be no more effective than arguments based on wealth. *If only wealth or income matters when selecting norms, then only arguments based on wealth can be persuasive.*[7]

AVOIDING THE REDISTRIBUTIVE POVERTY TRAP

Once institutions or culture allow policy decisions to be made, the next problem confronted by a democratic polity is making the right policy decisions, namely those which advance the shared interests of community members. There is no guarantee that such policies will be forthcoming from majority rule decision making. After all, the pivotal member of the majority coalition is not normally the smartest, best informed, or most experienced person in his community. The median voter's policy analysis will naturally reflect his or her limitations, although the Condorcet's jury theorem suggests that the democratic policy choices tend to be better informed than the median's capabilities immediately suggest. However, if relatively few policy mistakes are made, the median voter's policy interests may not be those which lead to prosperous societies.

---

[7] Normative theories may still emerge as a consequence of self-interest. For example, Buchanan (1994, Ch. 3) argues that norms may emerge as rhetorical devices that get other persons to adopt the behavior that advances the interest of those using the rhetoric. In the present analysis, the shepherds would promote norms that support ability to pay policies. The merchants would promote norms that justify proportional or regressive taxation – as a work or self-improvement ethic does in the illustrating example. For this method of rhetoric to work, it is clear that those whose behavior is affected by mere rhetoric are likely to have internalized a particular normative theory.

Vanberg and Congleton (1992) provide a self-interest based explanation for the emergence and widespread use of norms in the long run. In a setting where players can choose their partners in joint enterprises, sorting into more or less homogeneous normative communities is possible. The least helpful (uncooperative) partners would be avoided and the most productive (cooperative) partners would be sought out. In such settings, those who apply normative theories that enhance joint production can avoid many Prisoner's Dilemma type problems and increase their own personal wealth and income.

Here the application of personal norms systematically improves the personal welfare of those using the norms through time, although not necessarily at every instant in time. In the end, the normative theories that come to be most broadly used are those that have best served those using them in a variety of circumstances. (Of course, neither explanation rules out the other.) For this method to work, those whose behavior is changed by mere rhetoric have to be inculcated with a particular norm.

Either case implies that "paying the preacher" may be a method by which those who can benefit from particular kinds of norm-driven behavior can realize those benefits.

One policy area in which median voter interests can easily lead to disaster is redistribution.[8]

The Meltzer-Richard Model and the Majoritarian Poverty Trap

A very influential paper by Meltzer and Richard (1981) characterizes incentives for a decisive democracy to redistribute income. The Meltzer and Richard (MR) model assures decisiveness by restricting the domain of permissible tax and transfer mechanisms. All tax revenues are generated by a proportional tax on income, and the tax revenue generated is entirely used to fund a demogrant program. Each voter pays the same flat-tax rate on his or her income, and each receives the same lump sum transfer payment. The restricted domain of fiscal policy together with the assumption that voters behave as income or wealth maximizers imply that the policy choice is effectively one-dimensional, and consequently, majority rule tends to yield the redistributive program preferred by the median voter.

MR demonstrates that the policy preferences of a wealth-maximizing median voter depend upon the magnitude of his or her income level relative to the average income in the community of interest. If the median voter has above average income, he or she will prefer no redistribution. In that case, the median voter always pays more in tax than is received from the demogrant program. If the median voter has below average income, he or she may prefer substantial redistribution. In that case, the demogrant exceeds the tax paid by the median voter. In the case emphasized in MR's work, the tax rates will be set so that marginal increases in the demogrant equal the marginal reduction in personal income generated by the tax's deadweight loss. Conditions for such an equilibrium are depicted in Figure 4.1. (People are presumed to work and save less as the tax rate is increased.) For median voters with nearly average income levels, optimal redistribution will be fairly moderate. This is the case stressed in MR's work, and in most of the subsequent research built upon the MR foundation.

There is, however, another possibility associated with settings in which the median income is below average income. In cases where the median voter's

---

[8] There have been cases where those fears were realized. Aristotle (330BC/1969) was among the earliest political theorists to note instances of this problem. For example, he recounts (p. 200) an instance in Megara where "the popular politicians in order to have money for doling out to the people, banished many of the notable citizens; this went on until the number of those thus exiled became so large that they returned, won a battle against the people and set up the oligarchy. The same thing happened also at Cyme . . . "

Montesquieu (1748/1966, p. 110) noted similar problems for democracies. "Democracy has, therefore, two excesses to avoid – the spirit of inequality, which leads to aristocracy or monarchy, and the spirit of excess equality, which leads to despotic power as the latter is completed by conquest." Similar concerns were often voiced in policy debates in the nineteenth century European democracies when expansions of suffrage (voting rights) were being contemplated. See for example: Verney (1957, p. 68) or Conacher (1971, p. 24–33).

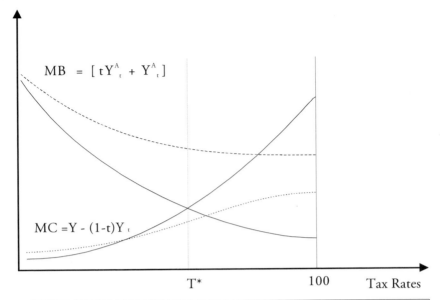

Consider the following model based on the Melzer and Richard assumptions:

Let $U = u(C)$ where $C = (1-t)y(t, i) + G$ and $G = tY^A$

Thus $U = u((1-t)y(t, i) + tY^A)$ (C is private consumption, Y is income, t is the proportional tax rate, and Y^A is average income.)

Consequently t^* is such that :

$U_C [(1-t)Y_t - Y + tY^A_t + Y^A_t] = 0$ where subscripts denote partial derivatives

or $(1-t)Y_t - Y + tY^A_t + Y^A_t = 0$ when $U_C > 0$

Grouping terms allows this first order condition to be written as:

$(1-t)Y_t - Y = - [tY^A_t + tY^A_t]$ The left-hand side is the individual's marginal loss of personal income as tax rates increase (MC) and the right-hand side is the individual's marginal increase in transfer receipts as the tax rate increases (MB).

This equality *may not be satisfied* within the feasible range of t, as illustrated with the dotted lines above.

Figure 4.1. The transfer poverty trap

income is well below average, the median voter's preferred level of redistribution may be very large. In the limit, the tax rate could be set at 100 percent and all of the polity's wealth would be redistributed via the demogrant program. In this case the majoritarian state would be all embracing, and financial incentives to work and save beyond that required for personal subsistence would disappear. Any person who earned above average income would have their above average income taxed away. The geometry of this case is characterized in Figure 4.1 by the dashed lines.

The high tax rates associated with such confiscatory regimes generally imply very low future demogrants relative to current ones, but may, none the less, yield a time path of demogrants that has a higher present discounted value than one generated by more moderate taxes. That is to say, the present value of increased future demogrants generated by the greater work and saving efforts associated with lower tax rates can be smaller than that associated with immediate and complete redistribution of existing wealth.

The maximal redistributive democracy would be permanently poor, and democratic institutions might rationally be rejected as a suboptimal form of government by those who find themselves in such societies or observe them.

Economic Escape from the Majoritarian Poverty Trap: A Broad Middle Class

The MR model, besides indirectly pointing to a potential failing of majority deci-sion making in societies with substantial income inequality, provides a possible solution for that problem. An implication of their analysis is that democracy will avoid the poverty trap whenever economic development reaches a stage where there is a large middle class, for example, where median income is suf-ficiently close to average income that radical redistribution is not undertaken. In such cases, material welfare will not be directly undermined by majoritarian policy decisions because the gains to the median voter from such policies are more than offset by the combination of their own tax costs and reductions in the aggregate tax base.

From this perspective, democracy may have been more viable in the United States than in Europe in 1800 because the United States had an advantageous distribution of income. Although there were many wealthy men in America, as evidenced by the founding fathers, the open frontier allowed the bulk of Americans to have sufficient holdings of fertile land to maintain a comfortable middle class existence as independent farmers or shopkeepers. There were no famines in America. Democracy may have worked in 19th-century America because economic conditions were sufficient to avoid the majoritarian poverty trap by providing the right median voter. This economic-based majoritarian logic also provides a possible defense of the wealth requirements for suffrage that were used throughout democratic Europe during the 19th century. Such requirements generated a median voter whose income exceeded the average of an electorate composed of all adult citizens. Perhaps Europe had to await sufficient industrialization to produce a median voter who would be less disposed to redistribution before universal suffrage could be adopted. There can be economic prerequisites for democracy.

Constitutional and Cultural Escapes from the Majoritarian Poverty Trap

In addition to favorable economic conditions, there are also constitutional and cultural solutions to the redistributive poverty trap. For example, a polity's constitutional law may require the government to compensate owners for any resources taken over for public purposes. Since, a good deal of wealth consists of tangible assets, such a constraint implicitly removes a good deal of the potential tax base from the tax roles.[9] Income tax rates, budget size, and state borrowing can also be constrained procedurally or limited constitutionally.[10] Alternatively, as noted above, the electorate could be limited to those with the least propensities for redistribution.

The problem with such constitutional restrictions is that it is difficult to motivate their adoption via broad majoritarian procedures. That is to say, a majority of the adult electorate would normally oppose such limitations in the circumstances of interest here, because those restrictions would reduce the present discounted value of transfers received by the median voter. The troublesome policies of interest here are actually in the interest of a majority of current voters.[11]

Fortunately, broadly held norms can also reduce the desired scope and the undesired effects of redistribution.[12] Any internal norm that raises the marginal

---

[9] Some assets require no such protection. For example, human capital is very difficult to take or tax, as is leisure.

[10] See Buchanan and Brennan (1999) for an analysis of constitutional rules and tax regimes that would limit state revenues to levels far below national income.

[11] It is possible that constitutional restrictions on redistribution would be favored by a majority if there is considerable uncertainty about each voter's own place in the future distribution of income (or perhaps that of their children). If constitutional issues generate a sufficient "veil of uncertainty" it is possible that long term implications for the average person would be decisive. In that case, each voter's expected future income would approach that of the average voter, and voters would favor rules that increase long run average income over alternative policies.

[12] Other norms such as the work ethic may also reduce the dead weight loss of redistribution by changing the leisure-labor tradeoff or by increasing the propensity for individuals to engage in entrepreneurship. For example, a society with a strong work ethic will be less likely to be impoverished by a given tax and transfer scheme because the labor supply curve is less elastic and the deadweight loss of taxation is smaller within such societies. For those with a strong work ethic, gainful employment is partly an end in itself, and both net transfer payers and net transfer receivers who have internalized a work ethic will continue to engage in productive activity even as tax and transfer rates become relatively high. Conversely, a leisure or income oriented culture

cost of redistribution tends to reduce the level of redistribution that will be favored by the median voter.[13] Figure 4.2 illustrates the effect of such a norm on the MR demogrant program. In the case illustrated, the median voter has internalized a norm that calls for some idealized program of social insurance/demogrant program, perhaps subsistence demogrants. Such a norm implies that taxes below that required to fund the ideal would be more desirable than those based on narrow self-interest alone and taxes above that ideal would be less desirable. The result illustrated avoids the poverty trap. Taxes and redistribution are higher than justified by the norms because economic interests in redistribution remain, but are not impoverishing.

Of course, norms do not have to be directly concerned with optimal redistribution to solve the redistributive problem. Any norm that inhibits taking from current owners whether for public or private purposes tends to reduce redistribution in a manner that makes the redistributive poverty trap less likely. For example, the modern Western characterization of ownership is often regarded as a legitimate and important personal right. Taking property from legitimate owners violates that norm regardless of the purpose advanced. Rules regarding what Richard Epstein (1985) calls *takings* are not always part of written constitutional documents, but are generally part of the public law in successful polities.

Ideology and political philosophy may also constrain economic self-interest. For example, if a minimal level of prosperity is a prerequisite for the democracy in question to be viable, those interested in democratic governance would accept constitutional rules that imply lower tax rates and accept smaller demogrants rather than risk its demise. In this manner, a widespread preference for democratic over other forms of government may be sufficient to defend a government against policies that would be in the interest of particular voters, but undermine support for democracy.[14] Utilitarian norms and various forms of altruism also have this property over a significant range of transfers insofar as the interests of future citizens are taken account of. Libertarian and liberal norms also discourage large scale redistribution insofar as they oppose the development of a more

---

tends to be more sensitive to marginal tax rates and more interested in receiving transfers, and thus more susceptible to the redistributive poverty trap.

[13] Mathematically, violations of such norms reduce the utility of the transgressor in a manner which increases with the size of the transgression, as with $U = u(|G - G^*|, G, C)$ with G^* being the norm of interest, and $U_{|G-G^*|} < 0$. Many internalized norms appear to have this property, and clearly can constrain policy development by raising the subjective marginal cost of deviating from G^*.

[14] Gordon (1999) notes that a strong preference for democracy is often associated with democratic governance. For example, he notes that such a preference was present in Athens (p. 66) and in the Roman Republic. Such a preference was strong enough that democracy reestablished itself in Athens shortly after the Sparta conquest, and also was partly responsible for intense efforts by many leading Romans to preserve the republic. In part, Cicero (Grant, 1993, p. 11) was executed for his efforts to encourage reestablishment of the republic.

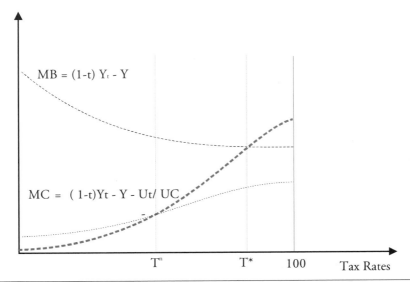

Consider now an extention of the the Melzer and Richard assumptions that includes tax norm t^n:

Let $U = u(C, |t-t^n|)$ where $C = (1-t)y(t, i) + G$ and $G = tY^A$

Thus $U = u((1-t)y(t, i) + tY^A, t^n - t)$

(C is private consumption, Y is income, t is the proportional tax rate, and Y^A is average income.) Consequently t^* is such that:

$U_C [(1-t)Y_t - Y + tY^A_t + Y^A_t] - U_t = 0$ where subscripts denote partial derivatives

or $(1-t)Y_t - Y + tY^A_t + Y^A_t = U_t/U_C$ (Note that the right hand side formerly was zero.)

Grouping terms allows this first order condition to be written as:

$(1-t)Y_t - Y - U_t/U_C = - [tY^A_t + tY^A_t]$

The left-hand side is the individual's marginal loss of personal income and of utility from violating tax norms as tax rates increase (MC) and the right-hand side is the individual's marginal increase in transfer receipts as the tax rate increases (MB).

This equality *may now be satisfied* within the feasible range of t, as illustrated above.

Figure 4.2. The normative escape from the transfer poverty trap

intrusive state. (It bears noting that such theories were widely in use during the 19th century when democracy began to be more widely used to decide national policies throughout Europe.)

Of course, it is also clear that broadly held norms can also reduce prospects for democratic success. A community with strong egalitarian norms will re-distribute more than required to advance the material interests of the median voter. Similarly, a community that encourages envy and jealousy would also be inclined to redistribute more than an electorate motivated by narrow self-interest. Philosophical and ideological views that undermine the legitimacy of the current pattern of ownership, similarly tend to reduce inhibitions about such redistributive policies. By making redistributive policies more desirable or less costly, such theories and norms clearly make the majoritarian poverty trap more likely to arise for a given distribution of income.

CAN WINNER TAKE ALL ELECTIONS BE AVOIDED?

Suppose that a democratic polity has successfully overcome the problem of decisiveness and also successfully avoided the poverty trap through some com-bination of institutional and cultural devices. At this point, the resulting demo-cratic society may be regarded as successful in that policy decisions are routinely made, and the policies adopted, if not perfect, at least avoid disaster. The econ-omy thrives and citizens lead pleasant lives. We now turn to problems that can arise when democracy is sufficiently successful that those in power have an interest in holding on to power.

Once the political process is decisive and policies have generated a mod-erately prosperous and pleasant society, holding political power becomes a valuable asset. A stable majority coalition with control over policy making will naturally wish to retain that control in order to put in place policies which it fa-vors and protect those already in place, whether constrained by a generality rule or not. The power, prestige, and wealth associated with holding governmental of-fice give elective representatives a clear interest in remaining in power *ad infini-tum*. That is to say, neither the majority coalition nor its elected representatives have a direct interest in subjecting themselves to the next round of electoral com-petition if there is any chance that they might lose control over policy making.

This problem clearly differs from the previous ones. Cycling can undermine support for democratic institutions insofar as policy decisions are in a constant state of flux, government services are poor or nonexistent, and laws are only temporary measures that are weakly enforced. The redistributive poverty trap implies that a policy choice is made, but that tax rates may be at such high levels that economic development is discouraged. Excessive redistribution may also clearly undermine support for democracy insofar as it leads to widespread poverty. Both these problems imply that democracy may not work very well or lead to attractive societies. Yet these problems only indirectly threaten the majoritarian decision making process itself by reducing public support for democracy and making a polity less resistant to conquest. The possibility of majoritarian takeovers explored in this section implies that democracies may not be sustainable, even if they are decisive and prosperous, because majoritarian governments may adopt policies that undermine the ongoing electoral process that makes a polity democratic.[15]

Avoiding Majoritarian Takeovers – Binding Electoral Winners

In the previous cases, the majority was presumed to get what it desired by voting for policies or parties that advanced its interests, whether broadly or narrowly construed. Such policies may fail to be implemented or adopted if there are political agency problems. The agency problems of interest for the purposes of this section of the chapter are not the relatively minor ones explored by the literature on political shirking and bureaucratic discretion, but rather is the constitutional problem of assuring that the next election takes place, and that the election is both competitive and fair.

Once a representative government is elected to office, the powers of the state become concentrated in the hands of a relatively small number of persons until the next election. If holding elective office is desirable for whatever reason, it is clear that elected representatives will use their policy making power to increase their own prospects for retaining office. This desire to remain in office is, of course, an essential feature of a well-functioning representative democracy, and is one of the reasons why a properly constrained representative government may be expected to advance the interests of a majority of the electorate through time. Providing good service is one method by which members of the current government may increase their chances for reelection. However, without constitutional or other constraints, a party's desire for continuation in office can also be advanced by indefinitely postponing the next election, or by passing laws that restrict or eliminate the ability of opposition parties to organize and solicit votes. In the absence of other constraints, changing the electoral rules and the circumstances of electoral competition to advance the incumbent government's own interests must often appear to be an easier road to reelection than adopting policies that please the next election's median voter.[16]

---

[15] It also bears noting that solutions to the first two problems tend to increase incentives for majoritarian takeovers. Without solving the first problem, no coalition could control the course of public policy. Without avoiding the second, there would be few resources potentially available for a dominant coalition to enjoy. It is only after those problems are solved that political power becomes a valuable asset.

[16] There have been many examples of such behavior by elected government. For example, very few of the African democracies established at the end of the colonial period in the 1950s and 1960s had a second competitive election. See, for example, Tordoff (1984).

The most significant example of takeover in the last century was that by the Nazi political party in Germany. The National Socialist Party had become the largest party in the Reichstag

In this sense, representative democracies are potentially more frail than direct democracies because a relatively small subset of the citizenry comes to have control over the procedures and constraints of governance and may not wish to give up that control. Such anti-majoritarian behavior by incumbents is difficult to rule out constitutionally, because it is unlikely that a written constitution will be rigorously enforced by the same persons that it is designed to constrain, particularly in cases where the government has a monopoly on force. In order to avoid majoritarian takeovers, those elected to rule must have, or be given, a broader interest in both prosperity and majoritarian procedures than can be assured by their efforts to win a single election.

How to Guarantee Constitutional Guarantees?

A constitution can attempt to address the problem of elective takeover by dividing policy-making power between a number of branches of government with the power sufficiently decentralized that no single branch has decisive policy-making ability or legitimacy. Gordon (1999) argues that the long lasting republics of Athens, Rome, Venice, the Netherlands, and the United States all use this organizational device with great success.[17] In such cases, a single election does not create an entirely new government because the other branches are chosen in a manner that is more or less independent of a particular electoral outcome. For example, terms of office may differ and be staggered, or different electoral procedures may be used to select members of different branches of government.[18] Moreover, one of the weaker branches of government can be assigned special responsibility to monitor the constitutionality of the rest of the government.

by 1932 with 230 representatives. In 1933, Hitler was asked to form a coalition government. By 1934, his party had "prohibited those parties that did not dissolve themselves" so that the National Socialists became the only legal political party. A last election was held which under the circumstances naturally solidified Nazi control. No further elections were held until after the regime was deposed by a world war, although the Reichstag continued to meet. See for example, Strayer and Gatzke (1979, p. 757).

In the previous century a similar democratic take over was engineered by Louis-Napoleon in 1852. Prince Louis-Napoleon was elected president under the new constitution of the 2nd republic by a huge popular margin along (with universal suffrage) with a more or less royalist popular assembly. In the following year, Louis-Napoleon declared the empire, and used the army to dissolve the elected assembly, Palmer and Colton (1965, p. 477).

[17] Similar arguments regarding the success of divided government within a broader array of government forms (including nondemocratic ones) were made by Montesquieu (1748/1966, bk. 9). Gordon credits Montesquieu with the first systematic analysis of the balance of power. Breton (1996) suggests that modern public choice scholars take too little account of competitive pressures within governmental organizations.

[18] In classical Athens this independence was often literal in the statistical sense, insofar as many important positions were chosen by lot, that is, randomly. See Gordon (1999, p. 70) or Levy (1989).

Critics of divided governments often complain that divided governments are not fully democratic in that policy decisions are not immediately determined by the current electoral majority. However, in cases where the elections and electoral pressures effectively determine the membership of all branches of government over the course of several elections, such governments are majoritarian in the long run. That is to say, a durable majority can eventually determine all government agents and essentially all of its policies. There is not necessarily tension between democratic rule and divided government.

Cultural Support for Electoral Competition

Culture can also play a role in assuring that majoritarian procedures remain in place. Again, democratic ideology may play a role. There may be a widespread regard for democratic arrangements that make it impossible for legislators to pass laws that significantly restrict electoral competition or postpone elections. Such supporting political cultures were present in all of the cases explored by Gordon (1999) who notes many cases in which a republic's electoral procedures were defended by its citizens at great personal risk.[19]

However, democratic ideology is not a prerequisite for the viability of democratic polities. Even without a direct preference for particular forms of governance, other norms may make anti-majoritarian electoral procedures difficult to put in place. For example, norms of fair play and equal opportunity make laws favoring one candidate or party over another unacceptable, or at least less likely to be successful. A strong norm of promise keeping tends to inhibit elected officials from violating oaths of office and promises made to their electoral supporters. Norms favoring open and unrestricted debate tend to reduce the scope for one-sided policy pronouncements by dominant parties and encourage organized opposition.

Widely held norms can make the *mere consideration* of laws that undermine electoral competition a very risky strategy at the level of both individual legislators and political parties.[20] Not only would violating such norms be

---

[19] There have, of course, also been several popular rebellions launched with the aim of establishing more democratic forms of governance including the American and French revolutions in the 18th century, and those in South America in the 19th. Moreover, it could be said that half of the military history of the 20th century was substantially motivated by, in the words of President Wilson, efforts "to make the world safe for democracy."

[20] Even fairly well-functioning democracies have not managed to completely avoid such problems. For example, many democratic governments have adopted rules which tend to protect incumbents and incumbent political parties to a limited extent, in spite of constitutional and cultural predispositions that broadly favor open elections. Miller (1999, Ch. 5) analyzes several examples of such policies, some involving campaign limits within the United States.

Moreover, even a generally dutiful or faithful government may fear that the next government may not abide by democratic electoral norms, and choose to avoid the risk of permanent exclusion by undermining the competitiveness of the next election.

directly costly insofar as those norms are internalized by individual legislatures, but any legislator who violated or planned to violate such widely held
norms would risk losing the next election.[21] By ruling out a wide range of
anti-majoritarian policies, such norms clearly reduce prospects for takeovers
by unfaithful agents of the median voter or majority coalition.

Reducing Electoral Opposition to the Next Election

Unfortunately, unfaithful office holders are not the only electoral threat to democratic procedures. A substantial block of voters is also always made worse off
by the prospect of the next election, namely those supporting the current government. Consequently, self-interested electoral support for policies that bias
elections in favor of the incumbent government always tend to exist, and even a
suitably constrained government that is always a faithful agent of the electorate
may adopt policies that limit competition in future elections. No self-interested
member of a stable coalition that finds itself in power has a direct interest in
being replaced in the next election. These self-interested antidemocratic electoral pressures can be reinforced or resisted by constitutional arrangements and
cultural norms.

A polity's existing political institutions, cultural norms, and prosperity all
play a role in generating a consensus favoring majoritarian politics. For example,
constitutional measures can reduce the advantages associated with control of
government and reduce the risk of future losses from election turnovers. Equal
protection laws, a takings clause, and generality norms for new laws and public
programs limit the ability of the current majority to transfer the minority's wealth
to the majority. Such constitutional provisions reduce the current majority's
interest in holding on to power.

Others reduce the ability of the current majority to hold onto power once in
office. Constitutional provisions that support open policy debate, a free press,
free assembly, openness in the deliberation of governments, together with a
general interest in politics as a source of entertainment, tend to assure a wide
range of forums for policy debate. To the extent that voters disagree about ideal
policies, such policy debates tend to promote the existence of strong opposition
parties and competitive elections. Election campaigns themselves may remind
voters of the long term advantages of unbiased electoral arrangements, even
among those favoring the current majority party.

---

[21] In Madison's words: "The aim of every political constitution is, or ought to be, first to obtain for
rulers men who possess most wisdom to discern, and most virtue to pursue, the common good
of society; and in the next place to take the most effectual precautions for keeping them virtuous
whilst they continue to hold their public trust." *Federalist Paper 57*.
   Madison evidently believed that the virtue of office holders is partly exogenous – an aspect
of culture or personality – and partly endogenous – generated by the institutional environment
in which elected rule makers find themselves.

Still other norms shape the perceived self-interest of the political community. Cultural norms may directly support democracy by enshrining majoritarian procedures. The normative mainstream might be sufficiently democratic so that antidemocratic majorities never arise, and adherence to constitutional procedures is taken for granted. (In the United States, the importance of following the constitution is widely taught in schools, and widely accepted.) Broad cultural support for constitutional procedures and restrictions clearly reduces the likelihood that a majority favoring the end of democratic governance will emerge.

The electorate does not, of course, have to have a taste for electoral competition and majoritarian voting procedures in order to prefer democracy to dictatorship, but the overall value of majoritarian rule does have to be clear enough that a majority of voters prefer it to other alternatives. In order for democracy to remain viable, a majority of the electorate has to regard majority decisionmaking to be sufficiently attractive that no majority will attempt to end democratic rule through legislation. The existence of widely accepted democratic norms provides candidates with a clear incentive to espouse policies that are consistent with those normative theories and to establish a reputation that makes such rhetoric and commitments credible.

On the other hand, not all widely held normative theories encourage democratic procedures. It bears noting that majoritarian problems can arise from both anti and pro majoritarian cultural trends. Elitists and paternalists may favor laws that discourage open debate, which limit political news coverage, and punish unconventional political views. Alternatively, majoritarians may lobby for constitutions that grant every temporary majority complete control over government policy, including the constitution. If the former policy advocates are successful, constitutions may be amended to limit electoral competition. By undermining constitutional support for majoritarian procedures, such reforms clearly increase the importance of cultural support and self restraint – especially within political elites – for the continuation of democratic polities.[22] If the latter are successful, impediments to the popular will may be eliminated and a system of governance put in place that unshackles every transient majority.

The risk anti-majoritarians will take control of majoritarian governments clearly increases with antidemocratic ideological tides and with democratic failures.[23] (The first two sections of the chapter suggest that democratic

---

[22] Denmark and Sweden replaced their bicameral institutions with unicameral ones in 1952 and 1970 respectively.

　　The United Kingdom has effectively had a unicameral system of governance for much of the last century. The House of Commons has had the power to overrule the House of Lords since 1911, while the royal veto has not been exercised since 1707. See, for example, Hollis (1973, p. 11).

[23] There is also at least one modern example of a government being elected on a platform that promised the elimination of democracy. The resulting civil war in Algeria has created a difficult conundrum for proponents of popular sovereignty.

governance can generate such results.) In the absence of a solid track record, history suggests that a majority will opt for a form of government that abandons democratic procedures.

CONCLUSION: HOW DIFFICULT IS DEMOCRATIC GOVERNANCE?

The public choice literature suggests that majority rule is not a very robust form of collective decision making. It is prone to cycles. It may yield very high tax rates. Moreover, incumbents may use the power of the state to secure permanent advantages from even short periods of office. Indeed, a majority may not even favor holding the next election. If these problems are as difficult to solve as the literature seems to suggest, they provide a plausible explanation for the dearth of democratic regimes through most of recorded history.

Many of those problems, once recognized, can be addressed by well-conceived constitutions that advance the long-run interests of narrowly self-interested individuals as has been emphasized by analysts working within the constitutional political economy tradition. Constitutions may usefully address such matters as election law, freedom in political debate, access to information, and freedom to run for office and organized politically interested groups. Additional support for democratic procedures can be provided by specifying an appropriate division of power and by specifying formal constraints that attempt to broadly align the interests of elected rulers with those of the constitution and the electorate. Moreover, a good constitution affects both economic conditions and political culture. Culture is not entirely exogenous. By making some patterns of behavior more attractive than others, and by promoting prosperity, constitutions indirectly affect the evolution of norms.

However, the extent to which a very good constitution can assure good governance in the absence of a supporting culture is an empirical question. Many of the constitutions that failed in Africa during the 1960s or which have proven problematic in South America for much of the last century are based on constitutional models that have worked very well elsewhere. The analysis of this paper suggests that a polity that lacks favorable social circumstances will need far better institutions to achieve effective democratic governance than one that has fortuitous cultural and economic endowments. However, the same problems of nondecisiveness, impoverishing transfers, and interest in permanent political power that may undermine the effectiveness of ordinary day-to-day majoritarian decision making can also undermine majoritarian efforts at constitutional design and reform. For example, a polity whose citizens have only financial interests in majoritarian procedures may find itself unable to adopt suitable constitutional means to achieve an attractive and sustainable democracy. Without a supporting culture, it may be very difficult to devise a constitution that ensures a well-functioning democracy. It is, thus, possible that only a relatively small subset of cultures readily support and sustain well-functioning democracies.[24]

The significance of culture in the performance of democratic governance does not mean that constitutional design is irrelevant, nor that culture is decisive. Rather it implies that the constitutional design problem facing a given polity is partly determined by the broadly held values and the economic circumstances of that polity. Culturally transmitted norms can help a society get effective constitutional rules in place, and once adopted, reinforce them by providing unwritten rules that circumscribe policy making and reduce the effects of unavoidable policy errors. However, widely held norms can also make the constitutional design problem much more difficult.[25] Overall, the analysis of this paper suggests that successful democracies have cultural and legal foundations that go well beyond the use of majority rule to select policies and leaders. It seems likely that successful democracies have developed a combination of political and legal institutions that is grounded and enhanced by widely shared norms within the community of interest that jointly serve as a springboard for escaping the fundamental binds of majoritarian decision making.

REFERENCES

Abrams, B. A., and Lewis, K. A. (1995) "Cultural and Institutional Determinants of Economic Growth: A Cross Section Analysis," *Public Choice* 83: 273–289.

Aristotle (1962) *The Politics*. Baltimore: Penguin Books.

Arrow, K. J. (1963) *Social Choice and Individual Values*, 2nd Ed. New Haven, CT: Yale University Press.

Bernholz, P. (1986) "A General Constitutional Possibility Theorem," *Public Choice* 51: 249–265.

Brennan, G., and Hamlin, A. (2000) *Democratic Devices and Desires*. New York: Cambridge University Press.

Breton, A. (1996) *Competitive Governments: An Economic Theory of Politics and Public Finance*. Cambridge: Cambridge University Press.

---

[24] It also bears noting the norms of persons outside a particular polity can play a role in establishing and supporting effective majoritarian government. For example, Western governments have recently been conditioning foreign aid on democratic reform. International transfers and access to markets that are conditioned on democratic procedures clearly create a broader domestic constituency for democratic institutions insofar as such conditional policies increase the net benefits associated with democracy in the countries subject to conditional grants. In this manner, the norms of a single nation or group of wealthy nations may cause majoritarian governmental forms to become more widely adopted than would have been anticipated on the basis of local political conditions. If the aid or access are sufficiently valuable such international norms may generate forms of governance that lack broad normative support within the polities of interest.

[25] This is one implication of Bernholz (1986) who demonstrates that there exists a constitution that can ensure stable outcomes for any given population of voters. Brennan and Hamlin (2000) also discuss how constitutional design might profitably take account of ethics and ethical persons within the community of interest.

Buchanan, J. M., and Brennan, G. (1980) *The Power to Tax*. New York: Cambridge University Press.

Buchanan, J. M., and Congleton, R. D. (1998) *Politics by Principle Not Interest*. New York: Cambridge University Press.

Buchanan, J. M. (1994) *Ethics and Economic Progress*. Norman, OK: University of Oklahoma.

Coase, R. H. (1960) "The Problem Of Social Cost," *Journal of Law and Economics* 3:1–44.

Conacher, J. B., ed. (1971) *The Emergence of British Parliamentary Democracy in the Nineteenth Century*. New York: Wiley.

Congleton, R. D. (1991) "Ideological Conviction and Persuasion in the Rent-Seeking Society," *Journal of Public Economics* 44: 65–86.

Congleton, R. D. (1997) "Political Efficiency and Equal Protection of the Law," *Kyklos* 50: 485–505.

Congleton, R. D., and Tollison, R. D. (1999) "The Stability Inducing Propensity of Unstable Coalitions: Some Constitutional Implications of the Downward Spiral of Majoritarian Rent Seeking," *European Journal of Political Economy* 15:193–206.

Epstein, R. A. (1985) *Takings: Private Property and the Power of Eminent Domain*. Cambridge, MA: Harvard University Press.

Feld, Lars P., and Savioz, Marcel R. (1997) "Direct Democracy Matters for Economic Performance: An Empirical Investigation," *Kyklos* 50: 507–538.

Fukuyama, F. (1992) *The End of History and the Last Man*. New York: Bard.

Gordon, S. (1999) *Controlling the State: Constitutionalism from Ancient Athens to Today*. Cambridge, MA: Harvard University Press.

Grant, M. (1993) *Cicero: On Government*. New York: Penguin Books.

Hollis, C. (1973). *Parliament and Its Sovereignty*. London: Hollis and Carter.

Levy, D. M. (1989) "The Statistical Basis of the Athenian-American Constitutional Theory," *Journal of Legal Studies* 18: 79–103.

Madison, James. *Federalist Paper no. 57*, p. 383.

Miller, J. C. (1999). *Monopoly Politics*. Stanford, CA: Hoover Press.

Meltzer, A. H. and Richard, S. F. (1981) "A Rational Theory of the Size of Government," *Journal of Political Economy* 89: 914–927.

Montesquien, C. L. (1748/1966) *The Spirit of the Laws* (translated by T. Nugent). New York: Hafner.

Mueller, D. C. (1989) *Public Choice II*. New York: Cambridge University Press.

North, D. C. (1990) *Institutions, Institutional Change and Economic Performance*. New York: Cambridge University Press.

Ostrom, E. (1998) "A Behavioral Approach to the Rational Choice Theory of Collective Action," *American Political Science Review* 92: 1–22.

Palmer, R. R., and Colton, I. (1965) *A History of the Modern World*. New York: Alfred Knopf.

Plott, C. R. (1967) "A Notion of Equilibrium and its Possibility under Majority Rule," *American Economic Review* 57: 787–806.

Rousean, J. J. (1997) *The Social Contract and Other Later Political Writing*. New York: Cambridge University Press.

Rubinstein, A. (1980) "Stability of Decision Systems under Majority Rule," *Journal of Economic Theory* 23: 150–159.

Samuelson, P. A. (1954) "The Pure Theory of Public Expenditures," *Review of Economics and Statistics* 36: 387–389.

Schap, D. (1986) "Executive Veto and Informational Strategy: A Structure-Induced Equilibrium Analysis," *American Journal of Political Science* 30: 755–770.

Shepsle, K. A. (1979) "Institutional Arrangements and Equilibrium in Multidimensional Voting Models," *American Journal of Political Science* 23: 27–59.

Shepsle, K. A., and Weingast, B. R. (1981) "Structure Induced Equilibrium and Legislative Choice," *Public Choice* 37: 503–519.

Strayer, J. R., and Gatzke, H. W. (1979) *The Mainstream of Civilization*. New York: Harcourt, Brace, Jovanovich.

de Tocqueville, A. (1972/1835) *Democracy in America*. New York: Knopf.

Tordoff, W. (1984) *Government and Politics in Africa*. Bloomington, IN: Indiana University Press.

Tullock, G. (1974) *The Social Dilemma*. Blacksburg: Center for Study of Public Choice.

Usher, D. (1981) *The Economic Prerequisite to Democracy*. Oxford: Blackwell.

Vanberg, V., and Congleton, R. D. (1992) "Rationality, Morality, and Exit," *American Political Science Review* 86: 418–431.

Verney, D.V. (1957) *Parliamentary Reform in Sweden, 1866–1921*. Oxford: Clarendon Press.

Wittman, D. (1995) *The Myth of Democratic Failure*. Chicago: University of Chicago Press.

5

Civil Society and the Contemporary Social Order

Frédérique Chaumont-Chancelier

> In a totalitarian State or in a field already made into State monopoly,
> those dissatisfied with the institutions that they find can seek a
> remedy only by seeking to change the Government of the country.
> In a free society and a free field they have a different remedy;
> discontented individuals with new ideas can make a new institution
> to meet their needs. The field is open to experiment and success
> or failure; secession is the midwife of invention.[1]

INTRODUCTION: REDISCOVERING CIVIL SOCIETY

One of the most fascinating social facts in France is probably the formidable
explosion of civil actions. This civil activism has various appearances and goals;
however, it seems that people not only increasingly engage in humanitarian
causes, they also try to solve institutional problems that fall into the public
domain such as pollution, violence, illiteracy, and social exclusion. On the
other side, the citizens' desertion from the political arena and the growth of
incivilities in schools or suburbs suggest that the French society does not display
only such a beautiful side. The point of departure of this chapter is the idea that
all those social facts could be linked to each other with the help of an appropriate
explanatory framework.

The recognition of the modern growth of civil activism directed to the provision of collective goods has lead to various reactions. Most of them are unsatis-
factory since they exclusively rely on preferences such as impulses of solidarity.
The question is sometimes formulated as follows: Why do people prefer doing
voluntary services instead of being political activists?

I thank Pierre Salmon, the participants at the 9th Villa Colombella Seminar, 2000, and three
anonymous referees for useful comments and suggestions. I also thank Elisabeth Krecke and
Alexandre Padilla for their help in the translation. The usual disclaimer applies.
[1] L. Beveridge, quoted in D. Green, 1993, p. 45.

E. Ostrom (Ostrom, 1998) proposes "a behavioural approach to rational choice theory of collective action." If my point of departure is similar, that is, the assertion that there exist civil societies which are "neither markets nor states" and that civil societies provide collective goods, I will nevertheless deal with the issue differently. My conjecture is that we can understand the modern growth of civil society as a rebirth of spontaneity. There are two reasons why a renewed analytical interest in civil society should lead to a renewed interest in the spontaneous order perspective.

First, the tradition of spontaneous order (Hamowy, 1987), whose most famous representative is Hayek, explains that there have always existed human societies without states. People without any political plans have spontaneously generated and followed some common rules. Stated differently, societies were always civil before being political. This is the reason why the modern definitions of civil societies such as non-profit associations or non-governmental associations cannot satisfy an evolutionist. Such a residual way to cope with the essence, the goals, and the modalities of civil actions is probably inherited from the rationalist perspective. If we admit that a society is a group of people following some common rules, and if we admit that civil societies existed prior to any political organization and can be independent of any collective action, we have some good reasons to rely on a Hayekian framework. Of course, this perspective also needs to explain this kind of modern civil activism which is organized in non-profit or non-governmental associations.

Second, most of the criticisms addressed to the spontaneous order perspective are related to the scope attributed to the free-rider problem by the rationalist approach. According to Vanberg, the spontaneous tradition underestimates the fact that the generation of cooperative social institutions raises a collective-good problem subject to free-riding (Vanberg, 1986, Vanberg, 1994). However, some modalities of civil actions strengthen empirical evidence that people in their daily life cope with free-riding problems more often than predicted by the rationalist approach. They could help to stop the contemporary decline of spontaneity in the social order: spontaneity versus design theoretical debate.

I start with a specification of a spontaneous order analytical framework that has been deconstructed by the rationalist approach. Then, I try to identify the impacts of civil actions on our social order. The third section is dedicated to those civil actions that are directed to institutional dynamics. In the following section, I propose an interpretation of the multiple appearances of civil actions. Relying on the interplay between political and civil societies, I argue that the explosion of civil engagement can be seen as an exit from the political society. Then, I examine some implications derived from such an interpretation of all the modalities and goals of civil society.

THE ANALYTICAL FRAMEWORK: AN HAYEKIAN APPROACH

I argued elsewhere (Chaumont-Chancelier, 1999b) that most of the criticisms addressed to the spontaneous order perspective are external. This tradition stands in the middle of a continuum, somewhere between evolutionary game theory and the design approach. Design theories model rational agents creating their institutions from a state of nature (Buchanan, 1975). Social institutions are seen as chosen constraints generated by a social contract. Evolutionary game theory models individuals who are completely exempt of any institutional needs, who are interacting repeatedly, and it assumes that, through these interactions, emerges a regularity in the social behavior that it identifies as the birth of a specific social institution (Schotter, 1981; Sugden, 1986). However, a presentation of the Hayekian concepts shall show the specificity of his spontaneous approach.[2]

Complex social order: A "spontaneous order" approach, as its name indicates, is not concerned with the formation of any particular rule. It tries to explain the existence of the social order, of this complex web of rules and institutions leading to a recurrent social pattern of cooperation and coordination. This order is complex since it can be seen as a network of interrelated institutions,[3] as an interweaving of many kinds of rules, some of them designed as spontaneous, explicit or tacit, enforced deliberately or spontaneously, and so on. But this "whole is more than the mere sum of its parts" (Hayek, 1967, p. 70).

If social complexity is the main object of study, it is also an anti-reductionist method relying on the importance of emergent effects on institutional dynamics. For instance, interactions in real time can give rise to something totally new, which was not initially comprehended in the human plans. If individuals are able to feel some kinds of institutional needs and act in order to satisfy them, the result of their actions and interactions can be completely different from their purposes. Interactions, relations, and evolution give rise to emergent effects.

Evolution and complexity: The ideas of evolution and spontaneous order are intertwined, that is to say, evolutionary processes are the main providers of complex institutional systems. Most institutions have evolved: They did not appear in their finalized shapes, they have undergone change. A small, simple rule – or relational rule – originally generated in order to manage a particular interaction problem evolves over time. When stabilized, it becomes an "institutional rule," covering a different problem. For instance, the state might have appeared in its embryonic form well before becoming the monopoly of coercion. Moreover, during their evolution, institutions intertwined with each other.

---

[2] No distinction will be made here between "invisible hand" explanations and explanations grounded on selection mechanisms.

[3] See also Vanberg, 1993 in U. Maki, p. 189.

Individual ignorance: The individual is ignorant. This means that individual makes mistakes and learns by a process of trial and error – which is also an evolutionary process.[4] But, at the same time, the hypothesis of ignorance implies the human ability to discover (O'Driscoll & Rizzo, 1985).

Order and change: The recurrent coordination between individual plans is the manifestation of the existence of a social order, but the notion of order does not imply any sort of conservatism.[5] Maintaining the social order does not necessitate the preservation of all of the social rules that bring it about. In fact, the social order can be seen as evolving between "coherence and flexibility" (Langlois, 1986b). Flexibility emanates from the decline of some rules and the gradual birth of new ones.[6] This evolution without disorder necessitates the compatibility between new rules and the others and the coherence between formal rules – legislation – and tacit rules – invisible institutions. For instance, formal rules like constitutions have to be compatible with the invisible institutions of the country which imports them (North, 1990).

Social institutions are seen as a set of intertwined stabilized rules. The various definitions found in the New Institutional Economics (Langlois, 1986a), with some modifications, can be integrated into that perspective. Social institutions reveal their very existence by the appearance of regularity in social behavior (Schotter, 1981). They can be felt by citizens as specific constraints (North, 1990). Their function, at their beginning, is to solve specific problems posed by interaction (Vanberg, 1994) and as soon as they are stabilized, they provide information on other people's normal behavior in given situations (O'Driscoll & Rizzo, 1985).

The Great Society: First, Hayek adopted a particular view on what is a human society. He considered that the very existence of a society is characterized by the fact that a majority of individuals follow some common rules (Hayek, 1967, p. 67). So, to have a society, we do not need to have a state (Benson 1990) nor prior political contracts between individuals. And, to have a society, we don't need to have a territory. This suggests the very contemporary idea of virtual societies, disconnected from territorial or political spaces. A society could be composed by people who live in different countries, while a given political territory could display no society, or several societies.

Second, Hayek described the structure of the Great Society as a tissue of micro societies or suborders ruled by more or less tight relationships between

---

[4] For a more complete discussion on evolutionary processes, see the volume edited by Witt (1993); see also Vromen, 1995.
[5] In Hayek's words: ". . . *the order can be preserved throughout a process of change*," Hayek, 1975, p. 184.
[6] And, also, a new combination of old rules.

their members:

> The spontaneous order which we call a society also need not have such sharp boundaries as an organization will usually possess. There will often be a nucleus, or several nuclei, of more extensive order. Such particular societies within the Great Society may arise as the result of spatial proximity, or of some other special circumstances which produce closer relations among their members. And different spatial societies of this sort will often overlap and every individual may, in addition of being a member of the Great Society, be a member of numerous other spontaneous suborders or partial societies of this sort, as well as of various organizations existing within the comprehensive Great Society. (Hayek, 1973, p. 47)

Let us call these suborders or partial societies relational networks.[7] Even in the Great Society, every individual is engaged in repeated relational interactions: family relationships, business contacts, associative relationships, neighborhood relationships, Internet relationships, and so on. If relational networks are most of the time peripheral to organizations and communities, they are different from both of them. They do not need to be based either on a common origin – ethnic for instance – or on a common goal. They are formed by repeated and related interactions, by concrete relationships. Of course, different individuals' relational networks, although unique, overlap with each other.

The main difference between opened and closed societies is probably not the fact of anonymity, but rather the fact of choice in partnership. The Great Society provides a particular advantage to all of us: the possibility to choose, at low cost, our partners. What the market society offers – and what the tribe could not – is the possibility to exit from particular interactions with opportunistic partners without losing the advantages of social cooperation (Congleton & Vanberg, 1992).

The second consequence is that most of our actions are located within particular contexts. So people are more affected by the system of rules (call it the relational order) followed in those contexts than by the system of rules followed at the macroscopic level.

The third consequence concerns the individual's proximity with specific kinds of problems. This proximity can be territorial or virtual, that is to say, relational networks are based either on territorial proximity like neighborhood, or on virtual proximity like chat lines. This proximity can be economic or ethic: For instance, if you are a farmer, you are interested in farmer interactive problems. If you are an artist with a lot of friends suffering from AIDS, you are mostly interested in the resolution of this disease.

INSTITUTIONAL DYNAMICS ENGINEERED BY CIVIL SOCIETY

In spite of the modern invasion of legislation, individual initiatives still play a major part in the maintenance or decline of pre-existing rules as in the generation

---

[7] A concept very similar to "personal network." See Granovetter, 2000.

of new rules. A spontaneous order approach is not only retrospective, it can also provide some routes about the way this dynamic has operated in the past, as well as the way it is operating now.

Relational Networks and the Spontaneous Maintenance of "Cooperation Rules"

The New Institutional Economics (NIE) concedes to the spontaneous approach the capacity to retrospectively explain the beginning and development of co-ordination rules. These rules benefit from cumulative effects: The more they are adopted, the more it is advantageous for an individual to follow them, the more they are followed, and so on. So, it is about those rules, called co-operation rules, that the polemics is engaged. Such rules as Hayek's "rules of just conduct" (Hayek, 1973), necessary to the operation of the market or-der, belong to that category. The various papers from the NIE provide a good reason why those rules cannot be maintained by private or spontaneous pro-cesses: the non-compatibility between *constitutional interests* and *action in-terests* (Vanberg, 1994, p. 22). This is the reason why a rational individual could perfectly well prefer to live in a group where there are some coopera-tion rules – constitutional interest – while having no advantage in conforming to them – action interest. Everything happens as if he wishes to consume the collective good – namely, the order – without contributing to its production. The means by which it is possible to reconcile these two types of interests is the addition of the costs for deviating and/or the gains for complying (Vanberg, 1986).

Amongst those additional costs is sanction. To assure these cooperation rules the label of spontaneous rules, the sanctions should themselves be spontaneous. And to be spontaneous, they should be rewarding or rational. It is possible to distinguish three different processes of spontaneous sanction: self-sanction, reciprocity (Axelrod, 1984), and relational sanction. The first type is psycho-logical: It consists of guilt and shame feelings, which are costs inflicted by an individual on himself when he is deviating from the rules and moral values he thinks to be fundamental. This self-sanction is probably underestimated by eco-nomic theory. Nevertheless, it is clear that this argument alone cannot explain the maintenance of cooperation rules.

Today, it is admitted that reciprocity pays as long as the partners in inter-action are meeting repeatedly[8] (Vanberg, 1986, pp. 95–96). This occurrence is generally correlated with the size of the social group of reference. In the Great Society, reciprocity would be neither individually advantageous nor realistic. In other words, it is not rational to sanction a partner in interactions if we are not to meet him again.

---

[8] There are some additional conditions.

To some degree, the hypothesis of relational networks can justify that of reciprocity and thus of spontaneous maintenance of cooperation rules.[9] However, Buchanan and Vanberg (Vanberg, 1994, p. 68–71) underline that the scope for this mechanism also depends on the nature of the cooperative rule. Reciprocity does not fit all types of rules. The authors perceive a new distinction within the category of cooperation rules: a difference between trust-rules and solidarity-rules. *"Trust-rules are rules such as 'keeping promises,' 'telling the truth,' or 'respecting others' property.' Solidarity-rules are rules such as 'not littering in public places,' 'respecting waiting lines,' 'not driving recklessly'"* (Vanberg, 1994, pp. 68–69). This second category raises a free-riding problem: Negative effects of the deviation are not targeted on one person in particular but on the group at large; they are public and external. Consequently, there are not any – or enough – selective incentives to sanction deviators. Only some centralised and organized sanction could explain the maintenance of solidarity-rules.

But is the free-riding problem so decisive? In the same way that each of us interacts for the most part of his daily interactions with a certain number of acquaintances, it seems that we act within particular contexts: our area, our work place, our sport club, and so on. Our actions are located. The system of rules followed in these contexts constitutes a kind of capital of a community type in opposition to individual or societal capital. It is still left to explain who, among the agents concerned by the problem of a communal type, is likely to provide an act of relational sanction. If we succeed in identifying the necessary selective incentives to sanction, this will suggest that the public good problem is less serious.

One hypothesis is that these agents would be those for whom the destruction of the situation of relational order would be the most detrimental. It would be the case if their economic activity necessitates this situation of order. For example, a shopkeeper does have an interest in keeping his area free of violence and making sure that the streets do not become rubbish dumps. He will be motivated to play the "cops" role. Another category of agents susceptible to offer a relational sanction is constituted by people who may be called the "elder" people. Their selective incentive comes from the fact that their mobility toward other relational networks would imply reducing their private relational capital to nothing. This private capital has been accumulated by their anterior compliance with the rules, as we will see later, when studying the additive advantages of rule-following.

One of the main reasons to follow rules is ignorance. In Hayek (1967; 1973) as well as in Simon (1978, p. 9), we find the idea that the mental resources of humans are limited relatively to the complexity of the environment – be it natural or social – in which decisions are made.[10] If this is the case, it is advantageous for individuals to use their scarce mental resources of alertness,

---

[9] See also Granovetter, 2000.
[10] See also R. Heiner, 1983.

calculation, and so on, in order to realize their priorities. For the rest, they lean on rules. In this way, individuals categorize situations and avoid looking at their singularity, as it is necessary for case-by-case maximization (Vanberg, 1993, pp. 175–178).

Another advantage of rule-following is that it constitutes "a mark of recognition of membership of the group" (Hayek, 1967, p. 78). To interact in the framework of specific relational networks, it is obvious that the individual has to conform to a package of rules. Everything happens as if the individual was buying an entrance ticket and a right to evolve within the relational space, while sacrificing the immediate benefits of case-by-case maximization, which is implied by deviation. The risk of being excluded from the relational network, which is possible without being excluded from the organization or the territory,[11] and from the advantages which the network procures, is acting as a counterweight to action interest. A relational network provides advantages such as specific information conveyed by chats, friendships, and solidarity.

Finally, conformity to the relational network's rules allows the individual to accumulate a relational capital. This capital is composed of the sum of the differences between what deviation would have benefited and what compliance will cost the individual, concerning each interaction – or action – framed by the rules. The more the deviation is rewarding in the short term, the larger the relational capital given to the one who conforms. Take note that it is the "other" who concedes this capital to the one who complies, and that the "other" is not solely the partner in interaction, but also the one who observes the action or the interaction. This relational capital has three characteristics. The first is that it takes a long time to be constituted: It is not enough to follow one or several rules from time to time. Entrants always have a nil capital. This explains why the relational capital of the "elders" is generally higher than that of the teenagers.[12] The second is that it is extremely elastic to free-riding: It could come back down to zero at any noticed deviation from a main rule.[13] Last, it is embedded in the relational network: If individuals leave a network, they do not take along their relational capital; they will have to start again from scratch – which constitutes a difference from reputation.

I am not trying to imply that the individual is a rule-follower but, rather, that there are good reasons not to deviate or free-ride too often and to sanction deviants. Obviously, all depends on the type of prejudice caused by conformity and the risk individuals run: To protect their lives, individuals are generally going to transgress the "thou shall not kill" rule.

---

[11] For example, the fact of non-belonging to a union or not being on strike could exclude employees from the advantages of specific relational spaces, but they will not be excluded from the company and will keep their jobs.

[12] Older people would therefore not be conformists by taste or by disposition but by calculation.

[13] With the exception of cases where the deviant has a specific status, leaders, for instance.

Up to now, I have situated myself in the NIE problematic. But it is difficult to approach the dynamic of institutions in a reductionist way, seeking to explain the rules of a market order as if they appeared one by one. What happens if a cooperation rule is embedded in a coordination rule? For instance, the rule of exchange[14] is tied in with that of respect other's private property – a cooperation rule. Furthermore, to interact among specific relational networks, it will be difficult to exclusively follow the rules that are immediately and individually advantageous: This is another modality of rules interweaving.

I have also supposed so far that rules and institutions only procure indirect advantages. But it is not excluded that actions themselves, and not only their consequences, could be part of individuals' ultimate needs (Hausman, 1994, p. 63; Chaumont-Chancelier, 1999a). As social institutions prescribe or prohibit some kinds of interactions, they could interfere in a more direct way with individuals' life plans. What happens if people prefer exchange to stealing or living from charity?

The Emergence of Relational Rules

Technological discoveries, such as the Internet or genetic research, create problematic interactive situations that are sometimes considered a "juridical void." With progress, some new institutional problems appear. The common attitude consists in waiting for the legislator to solve them. But civil society also solves these problems, often in a prompter way.

The standard economic approach is the following: Due to the fact that social institutions are collective goods, one cannot expect them to emerge and develop spontaneously in adequate quantity and quality. Nevertheless, in the best of cases, an institution is a collective good once its evolution is ended. To better understand this process, it is useful to proceed to a division of the dynamics of an institution into sequences.

1. *Appearance of recurrent interaction problems.* These problems concern individuals interacting in a particular context:[15] problems of maritime commerce, of farmers, of the inhabitants of a village, and so on. In the beginning, it is a local problem. But nothing allows us to affirm that all the citizens perceive the situation as such: Perceiving a problem and perceiving its recurrence are like an intellectual discovery. At a certain time, some alert individuals discover a recurrent problem in the interaction. A growing latent discontentment will arise, not expressed because of the lack of an alternative.

2. *Pioneer action.* Pioneers discover or imagine a solution, a conjectural rule. For them, the range of possibilities is open-ended. Each time the

[14] Mostly considered as a coordination-rule in Smith's and Menger's works.
[15] See also Ostrom, 1998.

interaction situation is played without a rule, they incur a subjective opportunity cost: the advantage it would bring to everybody to act according to the conjectural rule of the pioneers. The perception of a problem added to the discovery of an alternative are constituting two of the three conditions to action; the third one being self-confidence (Mises, 1985, p. 16).

3. *Emergence of a relational rule.* Depending on the type of rule, the pioneer will show the example or convince a few relatives, at least one, to try the conjectural rule. Between the social contract and the random meeting in non-cooperative games, there is still scope for communication taking the form of arguments between individuals in relational networks.[16] The other individuals of the relational network, who, like the pioneer, perceived the problem but who, unlike the pioneer, had not found any alternative, are likely to become the pioneer's first recruits; who we should call the intermediaries.

At this stage, since ignorance prevails, the intermediaries cannot choose the rule with regard to its consequences. The pioneer's personality will act as a substitute for the knowledge of the rule's effects. The more ignorance prevails, the more the pioneer's personality matters in the process of adhesion to the rule. First, this *entrepreneur in institutions* needs to benefit from a kind of credibility capital. A necessary but not sufficient condition to be seen as a credible person is that the pioneer has accumulated a very high relational capital. In order to be credible enough to initiate novelty, a deep previous adherence to main social rules is required (Hayek, 1979, epilogue, p. 79); indeed any proposition of a conjectural rule emanating from either a marginal or unconditional defector[17] would seem suspicious.

If previous institutional conformity is a necessary condition, it is not enough to prevail. The pioneer also needs to produce signals of competence. Successful boosters of new rules probably are individuals who have proved their worth in other areas. In the past, they were in the war elites or the nobility; today, sports or cultural leaders are potential candidates.

Authority could sometimes complete – but not substitute for – credibility in making shorter the process of compliance to the rule. For instance, the part played in the past by strategic actors (Knight, 1992) should not be underestimated; nowadays, previous hierarchical positions in specific organizations could also help. However, I refer more specifically to natural authority; that is to say, the capacity to convince through charismatic abilities. A comparative advantage in discourse could be

---

[16] See also Ostrom, 1998.
[17] Or a case-by-case maximizer.

particularly decisive in the case of choices between several entrepreneurs offering different conjectural rules covering the same category of inter-active problems within the *same* relational network; that is to say, when a first kind of a competitive situation emerges.

4. *Competition between experienced relational rules.* The previous dis-cussion also suggests that several relational rules coping with the same category of problems in different ways may be initiated at the same time in several spaces. It gives rise to another kind of competition: a com-petition between experienced rules. Individuals who, by disposition or functions,[18] cross over many relational spaces, may play a major role in the effectiveness of this kind of competition. They could reveal to others, first, the non-universality of their rule and, second, the relative performances of experienced solutions. The best performing rule could spread by this entrepreneurial comparative process (Garello, 1999).

5. *Institutionalization of the rule.* If the rule complies with hopes, it will spread to other relational networks, eventually even to the social level. That is to say, individuals who do not know each other will act according to the rule as soon as the situation will be recognized. It is at this precise time that the rule might need a supplement of enforcement in order to protect the majority of individuals from a deviating minority – composed of beginners or forgetful or marginal people. The judge's role, according to Hayek (Hayek, 1973, pp. 92–94) or Benson (Benson, 2000, p. 17), is to write down the rule, to put it into words so as to avoid any conflict of interpretation.

If everything is all right, the institutionalized rule has now two charac-teristics. First, it has proved its capacity to solve the recurrent interaction problem, and not to bring up another problem or any feeling of injustice. The rule works. To work, it has been experienced in time and has proba-bly been transformed in articulation with previous rules. Second, it has spread in space: At a given point in time *t* and in a given society, we can expect a large majority of individuals to behave according to the rule. The information provided by the rule is reliable. At the outset we have a self-confident pioneer, some acquaintances who trust the pioneer and finally, individuals who trust the information contained in the institution. The institutional dynamics can then be seen as a dynamic of trust carried forward.

Even in this ideal scheme of institutionalized development, new prob-lems occur. The shift from tacit informal rules to explicit formal rules can generate some discontent. When Common Law judges write down rules, they cannot avoid introducing some change. Sometimes the rule will transform into a more rigid one, or a more encompassing one, or

---

[18] Merchants could have been decisive in this process.

one that is less compatible with the other existing tacit rules (Hayek, 1973). Language, itself an institution, is not a faithful translator of acts and opinions. Besides, nowadays, most of the new rules do not arise from that spontaneous development but from legislation. As I shall show, some institutional dissatisfaction might emerge.

Degeneration of Informal and Formal Rules

Institutional discontent might have two causes. First, the rule does not fill the function for which it has been generated: It is a maladjusted tool. Maybe the function for which it has been created has become obsolete. Second, the institutional rule appears to be not neutral enough from an ethical point of view; it creates feelings of indignation or injustice.

The process of degeneration of the rule will operate in the following way. The individuals whose interests are most at stake because they are embedded more often in the interactions controlled by the rule, will deviate from it, called a *behavioral exit*. At the same time, the majority of citizens are dissatisfied with the rule. Even if they do not feel like deviating from the rule themselves, they will nevertheless stop sanctioning transgressors with the same intensity or frequency.

The other reason for the weakening of the relational sanction is linked not to the rule itself but to the deviator's status. The relational sanction is considerably lessened when those who are deviating are either the youngest individuals, who are beginners with respect to the rules and benefit from a form of indulgence, or those who, by their previous position in the group, have acquired a high relational capital. Moreover, people do not infer the same information from the similar observed deviation depending from whom it comes. If deviators are worthy members of the group, not only will they not be targets of relational sanctions, but they are likely to be imitated. Whatever the spontaneous institutional change initiated – new rules or rules degeneration – a successful entrepreneur in institutions needs to be part of the group. Institutional spontaneous change should be upheld by previous institutional conformity. Once a specific critical mass of deviations has been reached (Boyer & Orlean, 1994), it becomes less costly for the other individuals to transgress the rule.

Obviously the process of degeneration is different in the case of formal rules, emanating from legislation and enforced by penal sanction. However, it remains very active. Not only will relational sanction decrease, but the formal sanction will follow the same evolution. It will happen that laws are maintained on paper, but not enforced by real formal or informal sanctions. This process is particularly adapted to the study of decline in prohibitions. An edifying example is the treatment of prostitution and procuring activities in France, where accosting is the object of a penal sanction. French prostitutes pay income taxes, and recently the Conseil d'Etat has given a decision enacting that procurers should be subjected to V.A.T. on their illicit activity! Moreover, legal actions taken against procurers have diminished by 50 percent over the past 10 years and the budget allocated to these pursuits has not increased since 1960. It is possible to interpret this as a recognition of the incapacity of the legal system to stop this kind of activity.

It should be noted that citizens, in their majority, do not have a real personal interest in the abolition of this type of rule: Most of them are not offering, or asking for, prostitution services. But they might consider that the law is inefficient with respect to its objective of decreasing the exchanges of prostitution services, and that prohibitions generate criminality. This is also true regarding the prohibition of drug dealing, or moonlight work. It is not necessary to be directly concerned by the prohibition to feel an institutional dissatisfaction that reflects theories about the non-performing characteristics of prohibition. Those more concerned by the prohibition will deviate; the others will decrease their sanction.

Nevertheless, it is true that it is not always possible to deviate unilaterally from formal rules: The change of formal rules cannot take the form of deviating from the rule. When this process of behavioral exit is costly or impossible, citizens will sometimes give *voice*. To analyse the decline or the change of the rule, it will be necessary then to study the reciprocal effects between civil society and political society. Moreover, it is time for our spontaneous approach to take more firmly into account the existence of the political society.

THE INTERPLAY BETWEEN THE CIVIL AND THE POLITICAL SOCIETY

According to Hirschman (1970), the processes of *voice* and *exit* are the alternative means by which citizens express their discontent toward firms or governing bodies and, in doing this, they act as essential correcting processes. Generally, *exit* operates in a competition situation, while *voice* acts in a monopoly situation. An Austrian perspective suggests that it is not so much the real situation of supply which is essential when we transpose these processes into the domain of social rules, but instead, the opinion which the agents have of the situation of institutional supply.

Institutional Dissatisfaction: Voice or Exit?

Let us suppose that citizens dissatisfied with an institutional situation[19] are divided into two factions: those who think that the political society – or the political market – is the unique institutional solution-maker (the M group), and those who think that there is an alternative, civil society (the C group). For the

---

[19] Their dissatisfaction may concern an existing social institution as well as an institutional void. In the second case, dissatisfaction will be less intense, as they will be free to act case by case.

first group, institutional discontent can be expressed by the "voice" option, while the second group uses the "exit" option.

Voice has different modes of expression or channels: The sanction vote is one form of voice, but citizens may not want to wait for an electoral consultation. Furthermore, during elections, most of the time they are brought to give their opinion about a complex bundle of collective goods, measures, and institutions (Gwartney & Wagner, 1988, p. 10). At the other extreme, there is the political engagement that means that this institutional dissatisfaction is such that the citizen is willing to change from a demander to a political supplier, thus engaging himself in the opposition. More often than not, voice is expressed discontinuously through channels like demonstrations.

Among the M people, we can distinguish those who trust political society in its competence as in its motivations (the MT) and those who do not trust it at all (the $\overline{MT}$[20]). Only the MT people, for whom the cost/advantage calculus works in the right order are willing to engage in the voice action. Let us call this group of citizens MTI.

What are the elements entering into this individual calculus about demonstrating? On a costs level, there are opportunity costs. The more economically active individuals are – including the domestic economy – the higher the opportunity cost of self expression. Consequently, *ceteris paribus*, the less individually wealth productive we are, the sooner we will show our institutional dissatisfaction: The jobless and students take to the streets faster than do-it-yourself persons, family mothers, or small-company bosses.

The expected advantage is constituted by the gain weighted by the probability of obtaining it. The probability of winning the case depends on the matching between the citizens' request and the political color of the government: *ceteris paribus*, demonstrations emanate from citizens close to the political ideas of the government. The probability also depends on the past attitude of the government with respect to the citizens' demands: Did it give in? Finally, it depends on the means of pressure available to the citizens. The more the citizen belongs to a profession[21] with a high propensity to generate social trouble, that is, to impose external costs on to the other citizens, the easier it will be to make the government give in: It is better to be a truck driver than a florist.

The gain may be economic or ethical, objective or subjective. It is obvious that the suppression of a prohibition can perfectly well be evaluated in monetary terms for some individuals. But sometimes, the expression of moral indignation and feelings of injustice can also be considered as an advantage (North, 1981, p. 54).

The type of rule generating institutional dissatisfaction conditions the degree to which its change or its disappearance is a collective good subject to

---

[20] The $\overline{MT}$ are maybe aware of incentive problems within the political decision process.

[21] I disregard here the role of unions. See Olson, 1966.

free-riding. The more specific the rule, that is, the narrower the particular category of agents it concerns, the more it interferes in an identifiable way with their personal interests (for example, the prohibition regarding the hunters). The more general the rule, the more diluted its effects, offers a more serious free-riding problem leading to a lack of reaction. Consequently, there will be more demonstrations expressing institutional dissatisfaction with specific rules than with general rules.

At the bottom line, only a minute part of the citizens feeling institutional dissatisfaction is likely to express itself to the political society.[22] In my example, as the (M + C) citizens are discontented, the government will only be informed about the MTI people's dissatisfaction. Thus, the *error* signal addressed to the political arena is not reliable. Even if the executives are very attentive to the *voice* emanating from civil society, they only receive a deforming prism of citizens' dissatisfactions. An apparent civil benevolence toward the party in power may hide deep institutional dissatisfaction notably if the main dissatisfaction is brought upon not the party, but the institution generating legislation, that is, the state.

This can explain the variety of dimensions of civil action (or inaction) and, to some degree, some new aspects of the French social reality.

Marginality and Incivilities

Consider citizens who think that the French state is the only provider of institutional solutions, but that the state is not competent; or that the state is competent but that it is too costly to express their preferences to politicians. These people will not vote and will not feel engaged by the rules and duties emanating from politics. For example, some suburbs' so-called difficult youth, people working illegally and cumulating this source of income with the unemployment benefits, and people living out on the streets, exit from the political society when not following most of its formal rules.[23]

Consider the C people, who think that the French state is not the only provider of order goods. Some will do nothing (CN), others will practice different forms of exit. Some of them will emigrate, which is a territorial exit (CE). Some of them will choose a social exit becoming a marginal citizen (CS), or an active exit by engaging themselves in civil action (CCE). The first two categories of exit, being radical and costly, open the way to civil engagement.

These tendencies can be observed in France. There is a rise of incivilities at school and in the suburbs. Some very enterprising individuals are settling

---

[22] All my claims are complementary to Aranson's work on public ignorance (Aranson, 1989; 1990) and Kuran's work on public opinion (Kuran, 1993).

[23] Sometimes, feelings of frustration can transform incivilities into true violence which is sometimes understood as a "voice."

abroad. Meanwhile, we also observe the formidable explosion of civil engagement, whether in the form of punctual collective action (as the thousands of
people volunteering to clean up the polluted beaches after the Ericka's oilspill),
or in associative community life. Civil engagement is to the political society
what the domestic economy is to the market. Moving from the role of demanding
goods, the citizen is now becoming a supplier.

The Rationality of Civil Engagement

The potential candidates for civil engagement in democratic countries are individuals feeling strong institutional dissatisfaction. They will not express themselves through political society, be it on the supply or the demand side, because
they have no trust in the intentions or abilities of the political society. They
estimate that there exists an alternative: civil society. It is because the CCE
citizens evaluate the political society as unable to perform its task, or sometimes overdoing it, that they decide to substitute themselves for it in solving
some institutional or collective problems. Civil engagement in the form of the
creation of associations that deal with problems normally in the hands of the
public sector is interpreted here as a signal of a discontent toward the political
market. For instance, the fact that in France, associations have developed to face
problems such social exclusion, violence in suburbs, illiteracy, the protection of
the environment, rare diseases, and so on, reflects an institutional dissatisfaction
with the public sector and the institutional solutions the government is offering.
When associative life takes control of some institutional problems answerable
to the state or already managed by the public sector, civil activism embodies a
competitive solution, which would not be rational if the agents were satisfied
with or confident in the abilities of political society.

   If we have explained who the potential candidates of civil activism are,
we still have to identify the selective incentive generating this engagement.
The previous discussion on the conditions for action directed to institutional
voids or change applies as well. First, with the discovery of an alternative, a
subjective and conjectural opportunity cost emerges. Second, civil actors think
their own actions could have an effect on the situation: There is a process
of appropriation of the problem, that is to say, a process of responsibility for
the resolution of the problem. Then, there are some exchanges between civil
entrepreneurs and their recruits: Entrepreneurs offer to exchange conjectural
solutions for support for their projects. There are some exchanges, too, between
those who give and those who need voluntary services. Voluntary work is a form
of exchange. For instance, retired people giving their time and competences to
help illiterate teenage pupils, explain how happy they are to feel socially useful,
to be still active. To be recognized as useful, to receive gratitude, all these
feelings – which are perhaps fundamental human tools to human flourishing –
are rarely integrated by economists although they are evident to psychologists
and noticeable by introspection.

It is fascinating to observe the way civil society behaves. Unlike political society, it does not deal with the social problem as a whole. The problem to be treated is seen as a local one: an illiteracy problem in that particular high school, not the problem of illiteracy in France. Civil society carves the general problem, violence for instance, into many little quantitative and qualitative problems: violence in *my* area, *that* kind of violence against senior citizens. And it trys many little solutions, directly feasible on a small scale. The alternative is never a large scale solution, global, and almost impossible to reverse.

Most certainly, the *public* characteristic of the problem to be solved maintains the existence of free-riding, but in a less serious way than in the case of a *social* problem. Reciprocally, the proximity – it can be an ethical or intellectual proximity – with the problem and its context, the knowledge of time and place the civil actor possesses, all this brings about an experimental solution which may be more or less well adapted. In case it is not adapted, it will not be applied for a long time. In case it reveals itself as efficient, it will spread. It is as if civil society was segmenting the social problem into many little problems for which numerous experimental solutions will compete with each other. We might assume that through this mechanism of segmentation, civil society, if it was left free to do so, would end up solving the problem in its entirety.

ADVERSE SELECTION IN THE CHOICE BETWEEN POLITICAL SOCIETY AND CIVIL SOCIETY

One of the main justifications of the state or political society is that it offers order goods, including social institutions, which are of a public character. The private sector could not produce a sufficient quantity of those order goods. The private sector, constituted by civil society and the market, would be able, under some conditions, to provide services corresponding to particular interests, whereas only the state would be able to provide order goods. Now, the foregoing discussion suggests that there is actually an evolution taking place concerning the repartition of institutional supply between political society and civil society. On one side, governments increasingly legislate, creating specific rules to serve particular problems and interests. For instance, in France, the Toubon law on broadcasting foreign language songs or the PACS, which allows homosexual couples to be recognized as fiscal couples, the pit-bull law, the norms of hygiene for outdoor markets, and so on. At the same time, governments are confronted with problems of order goods like violence, pollution, social exclusion, and so on. Conversely, the French civil society takes over more and more general goods considered as public, and hence pertaining to the state's prerogatives.

Public choice theory has explained how the rules of the game within the political market may lead to perverse effects. Political society rewards some suppliers and some demanders. Electoral logic leads those in power to attribute some privileges in legal form to some active minorities, which is detrimental to the silent majority (Gwartney & Wagner, 1988, p. 19). Political society serves specific kinds of demands just as it rewards specific politician profiles. Thus, it is logical for entrepreneurs possessing the required disposition, like eloquence or the ability to make alliances, to engage themselves in the political market.

Let us now assume that some individuals exist who, having no confidence whatsoever in the political society, think they have a solution to some institutional problems. They will not engage in politics. Even if they did, they would not be selected. Therefore it makes more sense for them to engage in civil action. Their recruits will emanate from some of the C citizens. The distribution of agents and hence, of abilities between civil society and political society, illustrates a form of adverse selection. The entrepreneur in institutions, likely to provide experimental solutions to generic problems that address the priorities of the citizens' majority, will go less and less towards the political market.

CIVIL SOCIETY AND DEMOCRACY

The democratic[24] ideal suggests the idea that political products – notably institutions – should correspond to most citizens' preferences. Which kind of information about institutional preferences can be inferred by the observation of civil society?

First, civil activism trying to solve institutional problems that are in the public domain should be seen by politics as an error signal. More often than not, the governing bodies, all parties included, are congratulating themselves for this civil activism or for the punctual collective actions. They attribute these actions either to the good health of democracy, or to the solidarity impetus, which is not false since democracy lowers the costs of civil engagement. But these actions are probably more reflections of institutional discontent. This means that the explosion of the associative life and experimental solutions is not to be put to the credit of democracy's good work. This is, of course, a counter-intuitive idea, since the liberty to associate was seen as a main request from those fighting for democracy – French revolutionaries, for instance – and sometimes, as one of the main characteristics of a well-working democracy itself.

Second, politicians could infer some precious information about citizen's institutional priorities. In the case of existing social institutions, behaviors of spontaneous conformity could give a first indication on institutional preferences. Yet the problem is the conflict between personal and constitutional interest, implying that deviations do not necessarily signify that individuals do not prefer to live in a society in which the rule is implemented. Perhaps the observation of different kinds of spontaneous sanctions constitutes a better indicator. For example, the Americans invest in more and more elaborate and costly protection

---

[24] For a description of democracy, see Breton et al., 1997.

and defense systems (Benson, 1998). This is their way of having their property rights respected. From this, it is possible to say that Americans (or French) are very attached to the institution of private property. I am not sure, however, whether civil society would invest many resources to enforce legislative rules mentioned earlier, such as the Toubon law, the outdoor market norms of hygiene, or even pit-bull castration. To evaluate institutional priorities, do we have to imagine what civil society would do in the absence of an organized and centralized system of enforcement? We might observe what happens in cases where this system is failing locally. Of course, the information we draw out of this observation has to be taken cautiously, since civil society sometimes acts against minorities, that is, is not necessarily democratic.

Finally, how do we assess institutional preferences with respect to the emerging interactive problems? The true question is not to know whether citizens prefer a particular legislated rule to another one, but rather whether they prefer a conjectural rule to the absence of rules. As soon as we adopt the vision of relational networks, it suggests looking toward private and spontaneous initiatives. The absence of initiatives could be interpreted in two ways. The common way consists in saying that free-riding behaviors are at work, and that Parliament should legislate. But it could also mean that citizens prefer an institutional void, and the local disorder it produces, to the risk of global institutional errors.

CONCLUSION: THE STRENGTH OF THE INVISIBLE HAND

Even in democratic countries where growing legislative interventions are so pervasive, invisible-hand processes have found their ways. Spontaneous institutional dynamics is given a new embodiment in the form of civil actions that contribute to the maintenance of some cooperation rules as well as the generation of minor new rules and the decline of some formal rules. Sometimes, its role leads to a social situation in which the set of formal rules is very different from the set of rules effectively followed and enforced by citizens – that is to say, *real* social order. In those decentralized processes of change, the part played by entrepreneurs in institutions is decisive. But even if frequent and important, institutional entrepreneurship is most of the time anonymous. A part of our social order, that is to say, an important part of social patterns of cooperation and coordination, comes from the persistence of decentralized spontaneous processes mostly imperceptible to the eye (or invisible).

Some other modalities of French civil actions – from incivilities to humanitarian commitment – are more present and easier to observe. But if they can be understood as several kinds of *exit* from the political society, it suggests the apparition of multiple societies, some of which are unwilling to express themselves to the political bodies – new kinds of underground societies. If my vision of such a French social schizophrenia is realistic, something of a democratic ideal could be lost.

REFERENCES

Aranson, P. 1989–1990. "Rational Ignorance in Politics, Economics and Law," *Journal des Economistes et des Etudes Humaines*, Vol. 1, No. 1, pp. 25–42.

Axelrod, R. 1984. *The Evolution of Cooperation.* New York: Basic Books.

Benson, B. 1990. *The Enterprise of Law: Justice without the State.* San Francisco: Pacific Research Institute.

Benson, B. 1998. *To Serve and Protect: Privatization and Community in Criminal Justice.* New York: New York University Press.

Benson, B. 2000. "Jurisdictional Choice in International Trade: Implications for lex Cybernatoria," *Journal des Economistes et des Etudes Humaines*, Vol. X, No. 1, pp. 3–31.

Boyer, R., Orlean A. 1994. "Persistance et Changement des Conventions. Deux Modèles Simples et quelques Illustrations," in Orlean, A. (ed.), *Analyse économique des conventions*, Paris: Presses Universitaires de France, Chapter 9, pp. 219–241.

Breton, A., Galeotti, G., Salonon, P., and Wintrobe, R. (eds.). 1997. *Understanding Democracy: Economic and Political Perspectives*, Cambridge: Cambridge University Press.

Buchanan, J. 1975. *The Limits of Liberty.* Chicago: University of Chicago Press.

Buchanan, J. 1982. "Cultural Evolution and Institutional Reform," in Buchanan, J. 1987. *Liberty, Market and State*, Brighton, Wheastheaf Books, pp. 75–86.

Buchanan, J. 1988. "The Constitution of Economic Policy," in *Public Choice and Constitutional Economics*, Vol. 6, Political Economy and Public Policy. London: Jai Press.

Chaumont-Chancelier, F. 1999a. *Action humaine et évolution culturelle. Vers un entrepreneur en institutions*, thèse de doctorat de l'Université d'Aix-Marseille III.

Chaumont-Chancelier, F. 1999b. "Hayek's Complexity," *Journal des Economistes et des Etudes Humaines*, Vol. 9, No. 4, pp. 543–564.

Congleton, R., and Vanberg V. 1992. "Rationality, Morality and Exit," *American Political Science Review*, Vol. 86, No. 2, pp. 418–431.

Friedman, J. 1998. "Introduction: Public Ignorance and Democratic theory," *Critical Review, Public Ignorance*, Vol. 12, No. 4 pp. 397–411.

Garello, J. 1999. "Hayek's Unconventionalism," *Journal des Economistes et des Etudes Humaines*, Vol. 9, N0. 4, pp. 513–527.

Granovetter, M. 2000. *Le Marché Autrement*, Paris: Desclée-de-Brouwer.

Green, D. 1993. *Reinventing Civil Society.* London: The IEA Health and Welfare Unit, Choice in Welfare No. 17.

Gwartney J.D., and Wagner, R.E. 1988. "Public Choice and the Conduct of Representative Government," in *Public Choice and Constitutional Economics*, Vol. 6, Political Economy and Public Policy. London: Jai Press.

Hamowy, R. 1987. "The Scottish Enlightenment and the Theory of Spontaneous Order," *Journal of History of Philosophy*, Monograph Series, eds. R. Podkin and R. Watson, Southern Illinois University Press: Carbondale and Edwardsville.

Hayek, F. 1967. "Notes on the Evolution of Systems of Rules of Conduct," in Hayek, F. (ed.), *Studies in Philosophy, Politics and Economics*. London: Routledge and Kegan, pp. 66–81.

Hayek, F. 1973. *Law, Legislation and Liberty*, Vol. I. *Rules and Order*. London: Routledge and Kegan.

Hayek, F. 1975. "Competition as a Discovery Procedure," in Hayek, F., (ed.), *New Studies in Philosophy, Politics, Economics and the History of Ideas*. Chicago: University of Chicago Press, pp. 179–190.

Hayek, F. 1976. "Law, Legislation and Liberty," Vol. II: *The Mirage of Social Justice*. London and Henley: Routledge and Kegan.

Hayek, F. 1979. "Law, Legislation and Liberty," Vol. III. *The Political Order of a Free People*. London and Henley: Routledge and Kegan.

Heiner, R. 1983. "The Origin of Predictable Behaviour," *American Economic Review*, Vol. 73, No. 4, pp. 561–589.

Hirschman, A.O. 1970. *Exit, Voice and Loyalty*. Cambridge, MA: Harvard University Press.

Knight, J. 1992/1994. *Institutions and Social Conflict*. Cambridge: Cambridge University Press.

Knudsen, C. 1993b. "Modelling Rationality, Institutions and Processes in Economic Theory," in Mäki U., Gustafson, B., and Knudsen, C. (eds.), *Rationality, Institutions and Economic Methodology*, London and New York: Routledge, pp. 265–299.

Kuran, T. 1993. "Mitigating the Tyranny of Public Opinion," *Constitutional Political Economy*, Vol. 4, No. 1, pp. 41–78.

Langlois, R. (ed). 1986a. *Economics as a Process: Essays in the New Institutional Economics*. New York: Cambridge University Press.

Langlois, R. 1986b. "Coherence and Flexibility: Social Institutions in a World of Radical Uncertainty," in Kirzner, I. (ed), *Subjectivism, Intelligibility, and Economic Understanding: Essays in Honor of the Eightieth Birthday of Ludwig Lachmann*. New York: New York University Press, pp. 171–191.

Mäki, U., Gustafsson, B., and Knudsen, C. (eds). 1993. *Rationality, Institutions and Economic Methodology,* London and New York: Routledge.

Mises, L. 1949/1985. *L'Action Humaine*, Paris: Libre Echange, Presses Universitaires de France.

Mueller, D. 1997. "Constitutional Democracy: An Interpretation," in Breton A., Galeotti, G., Salmon, P., and Wintrobe, R. (eds.), *Understanding Democracy: Economic and Political Perspectives*, Cambridge: Cambridge University Press, pp. 64–87.

North, D. 1981. *Structure and Change in Economic History*. New York: Norton.

North, D. 1990. *Institutions, Institutional Change and Economic Performance*. Cambridge: Cambridge University Press.

O'Driscoll, G., and Rizzo, M. 1985. *The Economics of Time and Ignorance*. London and New York: Routledge.

Olson, M. 1966/1978. *La Logique de l'action Collective*. Paris: Presses Universitaires de France.

Ostrom, E. 1998. "A Behavioral Approach to the Rational Choice Theory of Collective Action," *American Political Science Review*, Vol. 92, No. 1, March.

Schotter, A. 1981. *The Economic Theory of Social Institutions*. Cambridge: Cambridge University Press.

Simon, H. 1978. "Rationality as Process and a Product of Thought," *American Economic Review*, Papers and proceedings, pp. 1–16.

Sugden, R. 1986. *The Evolution of Rights, Cooperation and Welfare*. Oxford: Basic Blackwell.

Vanberg, V. 1986. "Spontaneous Market Order and Social Rules: A Critical Examination of F.A. Hayek's Theory of Cultural Evolution," *Economics and Philosophy*, Vol 2, pp. 75–100.

Vanberg, V. 1993. "Rational Choice, Rule-following and Institutions: An Evolutionary Perspective," in Mäki, U., Gustafsson, B., and Knudsen, C. (eds.), *Rationality, Institutions and Economic Methodology,* London and New York: Routledge, pp. 171–200.

Vanberg, V. 1994. *Rules and Choice in Economics*. London and New York: Routledge.

Vromen, J. 1995. *Economic Evolution. An Enquiry into the Foundations of New Institutional Economics*, London and New York: Routledge.

Witt, U. (ed). 1993. *Evolutionary Economics*. Cambridge: Cambridge University Press.

PART TWO

MORALS IN POLITICS

6

When Does Altruism Overcome the Intransitivity of Income Redistribution?

Donald Wittman

Self-interest may work well in the economic sphere, but it wrecks havoc in the political sector. The ability of a majority to redistribute wealth from the minority to itself is ever present in a pure democratic system. When people are selfish there is no permanent majority and intransitivity arises. With each election, a totally different distribution of wealth is possible. Can a modest degree of altruism prevents such centrifugal forces? Here we answer in the affirmative by showing that a certain level of altruism creates the conditions for stability and equality.

More than 40 years ago, Ward (1961) demonstrated that majority rule is intransitive when selfish voters vote on income distribution. The following simple example will illustrate:

Table 6.1. Majority Rule Income Distribution

	A	B	C
X	33.33	33.33	33.33
Y	50	40	0
Z	0	45	10

A majority prefers allocation Y to allocation X (A prefers 50 over 33.33, and B prefers 40 over 33.33). In turn, a majority of voters (this time B and C) prefer Z to Y. But a majority of voters (A and C) prefer X to Z.

What degree of altruism is necessary to overcome this divisiveness of wealth distribution?

To answer this question, we first consider a reasonable altruism function that yields Pareto optimal results. We then show the conditions for this utility function to lead to a majority-rule equilibrium.

I would like to thank the participants at the Villa Colombella conference in Parma for inspiration and helpful suggestions.

THE THEORETICAL MODEL

We assume that voters have the following utility function:

$$U^i(X) = U^i(x_1, x_2, \ldots, x_N) = x_i + B\Sigma x_j/N - BC\Sigma(|x_j - \bar{x}|)/N.$$

x_i is i's utility from income, $x_i \geq 0$. This is the self-interest component. $B > 0$ is the voter's altruism weight. The larger B is, the less the voter weights his/her own income. $\Sigma x_j/N$ is average income. Thus, $B \Sigma x_j/N$ is the utility that the voter gets from high average income. $\Sigma(|x_j - \bar{x}|)/N$ is the average absolute deviation in income. The voter suffers a utility loss from an unequal distribution of income. $C > 0$ is the weight a person places on the distribution of income relative to average income.

There are, of course, a great many possible altruism functions. The advantage of this function is that it is readily understood and, because of its linearity, easy to calculate. One possible disadvantage of the formulation is that it may go against notions of fair distribution. For example, the formula says that person i would be indifferent between case A where j's income was 2 units below the average income and k's income was the average income, and case B where both j and k's income were 1 unit below average. This can be easily remedied by adding a small cost to extreme variation in incomes. Alternatively, one can argue that with linear utility of income, the loss due to unequal distribution should be linear, as well. In any event, one could choose other functions with other more complicated restrictions and obtain parallel propositions to those presented here.

PROPOSITION 1: *If $C \leq .5$, the altruism measure is positively associated with Pareto improvements. That is, an increase in any voter's income, holding other voters' income constant, will result in a greater welfare measure.*

PROOF: For any given total income, the greatest welfare loss occurs when all the income is allocated to one person. Therefore, we only need to concentrate on this extreme case for the proof. Suppose that all the income goes to j and that the remaining $N - 1$ voters receive 0. Then the total income is x_j and average income is x_j/N. The altruism component for i is then:

$$B x_j/N - BC (N - 1) |0 - x_j/N| /N - BC |x_j - x_j/N| /N$$
$$= (B/N) [1 - C(N - 1)/N - C(N - 1)/N]x_j = (B/N) [1 - 2C(N - 1)/N]x_j$$

Therefore, if $C \leq .5$, an increase in x_j results in an increase in the altruism measure. That is, a Pareto improvement results in a higher welfare measure, as well.

$$\text{QED}$$

Next, we show that a voting equilibrium exists.

PROPOSITION 2: *If $BC > N/(N+1)$, then a voting equilibrium exists with all voters having the same income.*

PROOF: Let $X = x_1, x_2, \ldots x_N$ be a distribution of income among the N voters. Let $X^* = x_1^*, x_2^*, \ldots x_N^*$ be an equal division of the maximal total wealth Y. That is, $x_i^* = x_j^* = Y/N$.

When the distribution of income is identical for all voters, we denote the utility of a voter by $U(X^*) = U^E$, where e stands for equitable and efficient. We do not use a superscript i in this case because all the voters have identical utility functions and identical incomes.

Let $X_{-i} = x_1, x_2, \ldots x_{i-1}, x_{i+1}, x_N$. That is, X_{-i} is the distribution of income to the j voters not including voter i.

We will concentrate on the case where $\Sigma x_j = Y$. If we can show that X^* is a Condorcet winner against all X such that $\Sigma x_j = Y$, then X^* is a Condorcet winner against all X such that $\Sigma x_j \leq Y$.

For a given total income, a necessary condition for the distribution X to be preferred by a majority to X^* is that the median income voter under X must have higher income than under X^*. This is because X^* beats all other X on distributional grounds; therefore, the median voter will only prefer X over X^* if he or she receives a higher income under X than under X^*.

Furthermore, for a given x_i, every voter i will prefer that X_{-i} is distributed as evenly as possible. This means that there are only $(N+1)/2$ voters in the winning coalition and that the median voter (the one who has the least to gain) prefers that none of the other voters in the winning coalition get more than the median voter. That is, the distribution that has the best chance of beating X^* is the one in which $(N+1)/2$ voters in the winning coalition (W) each get $x_W > Y/N$, and the $(N-1)/2$ voters in the losing coalition (L) each get $x_L = [Y - x_W(N+1)/2]/[(N-1)/2]$.[1]

Plugging this into our formula $U^i = x_i + B\ Y/N - BC\ \Sigma|x_j - \bar{x}|/N$, we get:

$$U^W = x_W + B\ Y/N - BC\ |x_W - Y/N|\ (N+1)/2N$$
$$-BC\ |Y/N - [Y - x_W(N+1)/2]/[(N-1)/2]|\ (N-1)/2N.$$

Since $BC\ \Sigma|x_i - \bar{x}|/N$ is based on deviations from the mean, we know that the sum of positive deviations from the mean (the last expression on the first line) is equal to the sum of negative deviations from the mean (the second line). Therefore, we ignore the second line and just multiply the last expression of the first line by two and get:

$$U^W = x_W + B\ Y/N - BC\ [x_W - Y/N]\ (N+1)/N.$$

X^* is a Condorcet winner if U^W is less than $U^E = U(X^*) = Y/N + B\ Y/N$.

$$U^E - U^W = Y/N - x_W + BC\ [x_W - Y/N]\ (N+1)/N$$
$$= (Y/N)[1 - BC\ (N+1)/N] - x_W\ [1 - BC\ (N+1)/N]$$

---

[1] Because the welfare function is based on absolute deviations, the $(N-1)/2N$ losers need not share the loss equally. This possibility does not change the analysis.

$x_W > Y/N$. Therefore, if $BC \geq N/(N+1)$, X^* is a Condorcet winner.

QED

PROPOSITION 3: *If $BC < N/(N+1)$, then majority voting is intransitive.*

PROOF: By the last equality in the preceding theorem, X^* will lose to another distribution. So suppose that we have an $X \neq X^*$. Let x_m be the median income.

If $x_m \leq Y/N$, then X^* will be preferred by a majority of voters to X.[2] The voters whose incomes were originally strictly less than Y/N will be better off on both selfish and altruistic grounds if everyone is at Y/N. Those who were originally at Y/N are indifferent on selfish grounds but are strictly better off because their altruism component leads them to prefer a universal income of Y/N. Since $x_m \leq Y/N$, there are a majority of voters who fit these two categories. So a majority of voters will vote for Y/N.

Next, suppose that $x_m > Y/N$. Let n be the voter with the highest income (if there is a tie for the highest income, arbitrarily choose one of these voters as voter n). Take $x_n - Y/N$ from x_n and distribute this amount to those voters whose incomes are initially below Y/N in such a way that none of these voters have more than Y/N after the redistribution. This is possible since the amount of income below Y/N equals the amount of income above Y/N. This method increases the utility of all voters except, possibly, voter n because the altruism component is increased for everyone and only one voter, n, is hurt on the selfish component. Indeed one or more voters may benefit on the selfish dimension as well. Therefore, $N-1$ voters will vote for this redistribution.

Therefore, every unequal allocation loses to some other allocation, and the equal allocation loses to some unequal allocation. Thus, we have intransitivity.

QED

Thus, we see that some altruism is necessary for majority rule voting on income distribution to be stable.

So far, we have analyzed the case where all of the voters are equally altruistic. It is insightful to ask what happens if there is a subset, *S*, of purely selfish voters. Clearly, if this subset is a majority, then intransitivity will again arise because this majority will vote to give itself more than the average income. But there is always another distribution that will take away the excess "pie" from the *K* member of this majority who received the most pie and redistribute this amount to the other members of the majority and the *K* people who originally received less than the average. A majority of voters will prefer this second distribution to the original distribution because this majority is better off on both selfish and altruistic grounds if they are so inclined. The logic can repeat itself and we are on the way to intransitivity.

We will next consider the case where the number of purely selfish people is $S < (N+1)/2$ and the remaining $N-S$ voters are altruistic.

---

[2] This cannot be the same X that beat X^* in the first place because there the median voter received more than the average.

PROPOSITION 4: *Suppose that $S < (N + 1)/2$. If $BC > N/[(N + 1) - 2S]$, then a voting equilibrium exists with all voters having the same income.*

PROOF: Consider the case where all S selfish individuals receive $x_W > Y/N$ and $[(N + 1)/2] - S$ altruistic people receive $D x_W \geq Y/N$. When given the choice between Y/N and $x_W > Y/N$, all of the S selfish individuals will vote for the distribution that gives them x_W. For the lucky $[(N + 1)/2] - S$ altruistic individuals to vote for this distribution, as well, the following must hold:

$$U^W = Dx_W + B\,Y/N - BC\,|x_W - Y/N|\,S/N - BC\,|Dx_W - Y/N|$$
$$\times[(N + 1)/2 - S]/N - BC\,|Y/N - [Y - x_W S - Dx_W[(N + 1)/2$$
$$- S]/[(N - 1)/2]|\,(N - 1)/2N > U^E = Y/N + B\,Y/N.$$

Again, we will take advantage of the fact that the sum of positive deviations from the average (the last two expressions in the first line) equals the sum of negative deviations from the average (the second line) by dropping the second line and multiplying the last two expressions of the first line by two. Hence,

$$U^W = Dx_W + B\,Y/N - 2BC\,|x_W - Y/N|\,S/N - 2BC\,|Dx_W - Y/N|$$
$$\times[(N + 1)/2 - S]/N.$$

We first show that this expression is linear in D so that U^W is maximized by either having the largest D possible or the smallest D possible. Taking the derivative of U^W with respect to D, we get:

$$x_W - 2BC\,x_W[(N + 1)/2 - S]/N = x_W[1 - BC\,[(N + 1) - 2S]/N].$$

For given values of BC, N, and S, this derivative is either always positive or always negative (when $BC > N/[(N + 1) - 2S]$). If the expression is always negative, then altruistic individuals will prefer D to be the smallest consistent with $Dx_W \geq Y/N$. That is, their highest utility would occur when they received Y/N; so, they would always prefer the perfect egalitarian distribution. Hence, if $BC \geq N/[(N + 1 - 2S]$, then the egalitarian distribution is weakly preferred to any other.

QED

We can see immediately that the transitivity requirements for BC are greater than when there are no selfish individuals and $S = 0$.

So far, I have not explicitly considered candidate motivation. However, it should be clear from the propositions that if an equilibrium exists, it will be an equilibrium for candidates who only want to win as well as for candidates who have similar altruistic preferences as the voters.[3]

---

[3] However, I have not considered the case where the candidates have different preference functions from the voters.

DISCUSSION

There is a significant body of work on positive theories of income distribution and redistribution when all of the voters are selfish (see, for example, work by Coughlin, 1986; Lindbeck and Weibul, 1987; Wittman, 1989; and Bishop et al., 1991). Unlike the analysis here, these papers have uncertainty built into their models – even though the candidates believe that a voter is getting more from candidate D than from candidate R, the voter may still vote for R.[4] Given the appropriate assumptions, probability creates enough voting inertia to guarantee an equilibrium.

There is an even more extensive and varied literature on normative criteria for income distribution and welfare (see, for example, Atkinson, 1976; Chakravarty, 1990; Roemer, 1996; and Jorgenson, 1997).

In contrast, here we have a positive theory of elections when some or all of the voters temper their selfish interests with some concern for the distribution of income. This combination of the positive theory of elections with norma-tively inclined voters is very rare, a major exception being Dixit and Londregan (1998).[5] In their model, one candidate prefers higher average income, while the other candidate prefers a more equitable distribution. They assume that income redistribution is costly and that richer people on average prefer less redistri-bution than poorer people do. The candidates are uncertain about the election outcome and maximize expected plurality. In order to ensure a pure-strategy equilibrium, the authors assume that the candidates' positions are not too close; they do this by assuming that the candidates themselves have strong preferences for the policies. Therefore the model that I presented here is quite different be-cause it does not assume probabilistic voting functions, preferences for equity being a function of the voter's pre-tax income, or taxes being uniform for peo-ple of similar pre-tax incomes. The results differ, as well. In particular, my model produces an egalitarian outcome when transfers are not costly, whereas in their model the median income voter gains the most. In my model, there is a clear demarcation between those parameter values that lead to a majority-rule equilibrium and those that produce intransitivity.

In the real world, the costless transfers assumed in this model do not occur. For example, taxes and subsidies may discourage effort and GNP. Therefore, full equality may not be achieved even if voters are altruistic because the incentive

---

[4] The uncertainty may also be modeled as voter uncertainty (see especially, Bishop et al., 1991).

[5] Roemer (1999) considers the case where the political parties choose A, B, and C in the equation $A^2X + BX + C$, subject to a balanced budget constraint, where X is pre-tax income and the equation is post-tax income. For any given pair of platforms, the probability of a party winning is uncertain. The political parties are composed of reformists, militants and opportunists. The militants and opportunists have concerns for wealth distribution (e.g., they want to help those with low pre-tax income), but each voter is solely concerned with his or her own post-tax income. Thus Roemer's model is quite different from the model considered here.

effects on effort might drastically reduce the overall size of the pie. People are only mildly altruistic – the rich are willing to be collectively taxed, but would prefer that the rest of the rich paid taxes and they personally avoided them. Because people are only mildly altruistic, the altruism benefit that rich individuals receive from their own taxes being redistributed to the poor does not compensate for the direct loss, and so the rich individuals may choose to work less hard. That is, a million dollars taken from one rich person only increases the average by $1.00 if there are a million poor people. While a rich person might agree to do this when there are 100,000 other rich people doing this as well, the rich person would still prefer that the 99,999 other rich people were contributing and the particular rich person was contributing not at all. As a result, when effort is voluntary, we would not see pure income equality even if everyone had altruism parameters $BC > 1$, because equality of income would reduce the size of the pie.

We have provided the critical values ($BC > 1$ and $C < .5$) such that (1) altruism produces equality in a pure income redistribution world, and (2) the distaste for inequality is not so severe that a person might be against Pareto improving outcomes. But what kind of tradeoffs are implied by these parameters, and how do these tradeoffs accord with our own sense of altruism?

First, consider the BY/N term. Suppose the following choice were presented to you: if your income were to go down by $10,000 a year, then average income would go up by $1,000 a year. Further assume that the overall variability in income does not change so that the $BC\Sigma(|x_i - \bar{x}|)/N$ term remains constant. If you live in Italy, then your sacrifice of $10,000 would result in an increase in per capita income of $1,000 for approximately 60 million people. Now such a tradeoff is unlikely, but if such a tradeoff were presented to you, would you be willing to take the sacrifice? If the answer is yes, then you weight $B > 10$.

Turning to the distribution term, suppose that total income remained constant, but that the richest 10 million Italians give $10,000 to the poorest 10 million Italians. Then the $\Sigma(|x_i - \bar{x}|)/N$ term is reduced by 10,000/3 (as 20 million out of 60 million Italians are affected). If you would be willing to sacrifice $10,000 to collectively achieve this outcome, then this means that for you $BC > 3$.

If you were the only rich Italian doing this, then the $\Sigma(|x_i - \bar{x}|)/N$ term would be reduced by only 10,000/30,000,000 (as only the equivalent of 2 out of 60 million Italians are affected by $10,000). To do this on your own would require BC to be greater than 30,000,000. Essentially, the requirement for a collectively altruistic act is much smaller than the requirement for an individually altruistic act.

Thus the "ties that bind" work at two levels: (1) the emotional caring for others and (2) the collective imposition of a charitable behavior. "Selfish" individuals can choose to be collectively altruistic.

REFERENCES

Atkinson, Anthony B. (1970) "On the Measurement of Inequality," *Journal of Economics Theory* 3: 244–263.

Bishop, John A., Formby, John P., and James W. Smith (1991) "Incomplete Information, Income Redistribution and Risk Averse Median Voter Behavior," *Public Choice* 68: 41–55.

Chakravarty, Satya R. (1990) *Ethical Social Index Numbers*. New York: Springer.

Coughlin, Peter J. (1986) "Elections and Income Redistribution," *Public Choice* 50: 27–91.

Dixit, Avinash, and John Londregan (1998) "Ideology, Tactics, and Efficiency in Redistributive Politics," *Quarterly Journal of Economics* 113: 497–529.

Jorgenson, Dale W. (1997) *Welfare, Vol. 2. Measuring Social Welfare*. Cambridge: MIT Press.

Lindbeck, Assar, and Jorgen Weibull (1987) "Balanced Budget Redistribution as the Outcome of Political Competition," *Public Choice* 52: 273–297.

Roemer, John E. (1996) *Theories of Distributive Justice*. Cambridge: Harvard University Press.

Roemer, John E. (1999) "The Democratic Political Economy of Progressive Income Taxation," *Econometrica* 67: 1–19.

Ward, Benjamin (1961) "Majority Rule and Allocation," *Journal of Conflict Resolution* 5: 379–389.

Wittman, Donald A. (1989) "Pressure Group Size and the Politics of Income Redistribution," *Social Choice and Welfare* 6: 275–86.

7

Democratic Resilience and the Necessity of Virtue

Alan Hamlin

"In a popular state, one mechanism more is necessary, namely virtue."

"A republic requires virtue; a monarchy, honour; despotic government, fear."

Montesquieu,
The Spirit of the Laws,
Book III, Chapters III and IX.

INTRODUCTION

The discussion of the rational foundations of democratic politics includes at least two senses in which democracy can be seen as *binding* individual agents, and these two senses pick out two aspects of democracy: an institutional aspect and a more human aspect. The institutional aspect focuses on the procedures, rules, and institutions that in one sense constitute democratic politics and which might be seen as binding, constraining, or otherwise structuring the political activity of individuals. The more human aspect focuses on the individuals who live in democratic societies, are *bound* together into a polity, and must make democracy work. Furthermore, the institutional aspect of democracy highlights one view of economic analysis, by emphasizing the analysis of rational individual responses to democratic institutions and rules, in much the same way as we might analyze individual responses to relative prices. However, the more human aspect of democracy highlights a different economic perspective, by emphasizing the analysis of individuals committing to a common enterprise that offers both intrinsic and instrumental rewards. Very often the former, institutional aspect dominates the economic discussion of democracy to the exclusion of the latter, human aspect – so much so that we often focus on the analysis

I am happy to acknowledge helpful comments from the participants in the Villa Colombella Group meeting on "The Binds of Democratic Politics," September 2000, Parma, Italy, and from Geoff Brennan.

of narrowly self-interested individuals in democratic settings without asking ourselves whether individuals of that sort have the resources to operate a fully democratic society. At a fundamental level, a key question prompted by the distinction between the institutional and the human aspects of democracy is, therefore, whether democratic institutions require any particular form of human agency or any particular human character, or whether democracy as a structure can be seen as "universal" in the sense that it can operate more or less successfully with any human "inputs."

Of course, this form of the question is insufficiently specific to be answered or even analyzed. On the one hand, *democracy* itself is hopelessly vague as a description of any particular political system. On the other hand, the criteria by which any particular form of government might be declared "more or less successful" are also vague – particularly if this is intended to be interpreted as "successful relative to other feasible forms of government." More specific and interesting versions of this fundamental question might then be: How might the performance of particular democratic institutions vary with different specifications of the character of the individual citizens? Or, how might institutional structures influence the characters of individuals that live within them?

As an example, consider the following thought experiment. Imagine a number of isolated island communities each facing identical physical and technological prospects and possibilities. The only significant difference between the communities lies in the characters (not the human capital, as normally defined in terms of skills and abilities) of the individuals who make them up. In each community political structures emerge – either by some evolutionary process or via some form of constitutional convention – and for the sake of argument, assume that the institutions arising in each community may be characterised as broadly democratic. How might we expect the detailed institutional arrangements to vary across the communities with variations in the character of the populations? How might we expect these institutions to operate in each community? And how might each community fare under the institutional regime adopted in some other community?

These questions point to the issue that I term the *resilience* of democratic political structures – resilience, that is, in the face of variation in the nature or character of individual citizens.[1] If particular democratic institutions are resilient in the sense that they can be expected to emerge in communities of different characters and operate similarly in those different communities, then this would count as a clear argument in favor of those institutions. But there is a slightly more subtle point here that should be made explicit. If resilience of the type outlined is valuable, then its value may be traded off against other dimensions of value. All things considered, we might prefer institutional arrangements

---

[1] The idea of resilience is deployed in a different context in Brennan and Hamlin (2001).

that are reasonably resilient across a relatively wide range of possible config-
urations of character (or other variables of interest), even if these institutional
arrangements are not optimal under any specific configuration. This simple
point has an immediate analytic implication: that we should be concerned to
analyse the operation of institutional arrangements in different contexts – and,
specifically, under different assumptions on the character of individuals – rather
than focussing on any particular context. Rather than optimising institutional
design under any particular description of the character of the human agents, we
should be concerned to explore the performance of institutions across different
specifications of individual character.

Also, I will examine here the more specific issue of the role of *virtue* in the
operation of democratic institutions. The quotes at the beginning of this chapter
from Montesquieu suggest a view – shared by Madison, Hamilton, and others –
that at least some element of virtue is an important, even a necessary, prerequisite of a well-functioning democratic system. In pointing to the respective roles
of virtue, honor, and fear in republican, monarchical, and despotic structures,
Montesquieu is attempting to identify the "springs," or sources, of political
action that are most naturally associated with each form of government. Despotism is characterised by the essentially arbitrary power of the despot, which
requires unquestioning obedience. Such obedience derives ultimately from fear
of punishment. Monarchy also grants power to a ruler, but monarchical power
is structured by the divisions and ranks of an aristocratic society. The considerations of honor that serve to ensure that individuals play out their roles in
such a society also serve to activate political life. In a passage that bears a striking similarity to discussions of the "invisible hand" operating within markets,
Montesquieu observes that, in a monarchy, "Honour sets all parts of the body
politic in motion, and by its very action connects them; thus every individual
moves toward the public good, while he has been thinking only of promoting
his own interests." (Book III, Chapter VII).

These two sketches of Montesquieu's account of the operation of fear and
honor are, I suggest, redolent of the modern analysis of the operation of democratic institutions in the rational actor tradition. In that literature, the spring of
political action is precisely self-interest informed by position within the political system (honor), and subject to the rewards, punishments, and sanctions
provided by political rules and laws (fear). By contrast, Montesquieu argued that
some form of virtue was the natural spring of action in a republican democracy.
His point here is simply that without virtue – on the part of both the governed
and the governors – the *form* of democracy is simply a façade, masking a more
despotic substance:

When virtue no longer exists, ambition enters those hearts capable of it, and avarice
becomes universal. The objects of desire are changed. What was once loved is loved no
more: citizens who formerly considered themselves as free because of their laws now

wish to be free from them. . . . What used to be accepted as a maxim of equity is now called rigour; what once was considered a rule is now called constraint; what was once considered the attention of the law-abiding now is called fear. (Book III, Chapter III)

These quotes provide a clear link back to the distinction between the institutional and human aspects of democracy. Montesquieu suggests in these passages that a defining element of democracy lies in its human aspect – an aspect that must include at least a modicum of virtue. Of course, Montesquieu is quick to recognize that, in practice, societies generally include a blend of different characteristics – virtue, honor, fear, and the like – and that such a blend must be recognized in institutional matters. And this observation leads to a second analytic implication. Not only should we analyze institutional arrangements in a variety of settings with respect to the character of individual citizens, but we should also examine the implications of heterogeneity of character within any population of citizens.

The interplay between the institutional and the human aspects of democracy has been the theme of much of my recent work with Geoff Brennan, specifically in our recent book *Democratic Devices and Desires* (Brennan and Hamlin, 2000). My intention in this chapter is to restate, extend, and develop ideas that may be found in that book to explore the two themes already identified. The next section provides a brief review of some ideas developed in *Democratic Devices and Desires* that are of relevance for the concerns of this chapter. The following section then attempts to develop these ideas in a particular case by presenting simple models of two-tier representation under different assumptions on the motivational character of individuals, to consider the issue of the resilience of a particular institutional arrangement. The intended outcome here is not so much a detailed analysis of the specific institution – although that may be of interest in itself – but an example of the type of analysis that seems to me to be required if we are to take the issue of the resilience of democratic institutions seriously. Some concluding comments that draw together the various themes are offered.

SOME IDEAS

The basic concern of *Democratic Devices and Desires* is to modify the standard Public Choice view of the human aspect of democracy, to gain a different perspective on the institutional aspect of democracy. In other words, we try to take seriously the two analytic points already identified concerning human character and its heterogeneity. The standard Public Choice or Constitutional Political Economy approach to the analysis of political institutions is that human agents should be modeled in strictly *homo oeconomicus* terms, and that all of the work to be done by democracy has to be done by institutional structures and procedures that can be both designed and operated by such persons. By contrast, we argue that a (slightly) more moral or virtuous conception of human agency is both justified and productive of a range of additional insights that modify both the analysis and the evaluation of specific democratic institutional arrangements.

It is important to note from the outset that the position we adopt is not one in which individuals are assumed to be fully moral in the sense that morality is the only, or even the major, element of their motivational structure. Rather, we take what we consider to be a minor step away from the orthodox Public Choice position by specifying that individuals have, among their basic desires, the desire to act as morality requires but that this is just one desire among many, and one that has no special priority relative to other, more self-interested, desires.[2] Behavior then depends on the interplay between the individual's full range of desires and the institutional and other constraints that apply. An individual may act morally in some circumstances and not others; an individual will weigh moral and non-moral arguments against each other, and the balance of argument may go in either direction. This motivational structure gives morality a foothold not a stranglehold, on the decision-making calculus of individuals.

In the remainder of this section I reprise two of the basic lines of thought developed in *Democratic Devices and Desires* that seem particularly relevant to the themes under consideration here: the idea of economizing on virtue and the idea that institutional mechanisms may employ virtue in a variety of ways. But first, it is appropriate to be a little more specific about my use of the term *virtue*.

Virtue

A first point to note is that I write of virtue in the singular, rather than virtues in the plural. The singular virtue that I consider relates to acting as morality requires. But this singularity should not be taken as an important limitation. In focussing on just one virtue, I do not mean to deny the existence, or the importance, of other virtues. Rather, I restrict attention to the case of one virtue for reasons of simplicity and to argue that the recognition of even a single virtue can make a significant difference to arguments about institutional design. Other things equal, I would expect the general line of argument to be still more powerful if a multiplicity of virtues are recognized,[3] so that the heterogeneity of individual characters spreads over more than one dimension.

If individuals are, as I suppose, motivated by a set of desires that includes the desire to act as morality requires, how are we to understand the idea of a virtuous individual? I will offer two types of answer to this question, which share a common structure, but differ as to the level at which that structure is

---

[2] I do not intend to imply a sharp distinction between self-interest and morality; see, for example, Schmidtz (1995), Smith (1994), Hampton (1997).

[3] Of course, some virtues may not be socially desirable in some situations – but my point is not that virtues are necessarily good, rather it is that recognising virtues in the design of institutional structures opens up new possibilities for social improvement.

applied. At one level, a virtuous person is simply one who acts as morality requires in a particular situation, and does so because morality requires it. The second part of that sentence rules out the view that "virtue is as virtue does" – that is, the view that behavior is all that matters, and that the details of motivation are an irrelevance. But the first part of the sentence indicates that a person may act virtuously in some situations and not in others – on this account it is this or that specific act that is virtuous, not the actor. At another level, a virtuous person is one who is disposed to act as morality requires in at least some domain of situations. Again, this definition includes the idea that the person must be appropriately motivated, or disposed, for any particular act to be truly virtuous; but the definition is now extended to a class of situations over which a particular disposition is relevant. So that the virtuous individual may now be regarded as having *bound* him- or herself to virtue rather than being open to debate on virtuous versus interested behavior on a case-by-case basis. This sort of dispositional virtue seems to come closest to the idea of a virtuous individual, as opposed to a virtuous act. I shall keep the possibility of both virtuous acts and virtuous individuals open.

While virtue is defined to include reference to the underlying motivation of the agent, the social value of virtue may be defined in such a way that the underlying motivation does not matter. The point here is that virtue itself should not be seen to be mainly of intrinsic value. From the point of view of institutional design, and of the design of political institutions particularly, our focus of attention must be on the impact of the recognition of the existence of virtue on the operation of political processes and on the outcomes derived from those political processes. In this sense, we should focus on the consequential rather that the intrinsic value of virtue. And in this sense, society may not recognise a significant difference between the value of a virtuous act and of a behaviorally identical but differently motivated act.

On the substantive question of the content of virtue – that is, the question of exactly what morality requires – I need not be precise. My discussion is more concerned with the *structure* of rational and moral choice than with the detailed content of morality. I shall make certain structural requirements on morality, most obviously that it should be broadly agreed in the sense that the content of morality is reasonably common across individuals – common enough for there to be a shared moral code covering at least the major aspects of moral behavior. I will underline two further structural points.

The first point concerns the distinction between morality and narrow self-interest.[4] For many writers this distinction is fundamental, with morality being

---

[4] Throughout, I use self-interest in the narrow sense of the individual's self-regarding interests. Of course, if the individual has, as we assume, a desire to be moral, then one could speak of morality being in the individual's self-interest in the broader sense that it is an interest that the *self* has. See also note 2.

characterized as a concern for others.[5] Of course, this characterization does not amount to a substantive theory of morality, since it leaves open the important questions of the form of the concern and the identity of the relevant others; but the contrast between self and others – between self-interest and altruism – seems to many to be the key step toward defining morality. This view is in sharp contrast with an alternative conception of morality that attempts to soften this contrast and to view morality and self-interest as mutually dependent. This alternative conception is most obviously present in the Aristotelian tradition in which the virtues are seen as indispensable and constitutive parts of the good life for any individual, but also in some parts of modern contractarian thought where morality is brought within the scope of interests.[6]

A second structural point relates to the authority of morality. On some accounts morality is taken as authoritative in the sense that moral arguments and moral reasons always outweigh or trump their non-moral counterparts. If morality requires you to undertake action *A*, then action *A* is what you *should* do, all things considered. But this can be true without morality actually motivating you to *do A*. The framework sketched here does not assume that agents do what they believe morality requires, either at the deep level of the choice of dispositions or at the level of the choice of action. In each case, the demands of morality are just one type of demand, which must be balanced by the agent against other demands. And different agents will weigh moral considerations differently. Some will be "more moral" in the sense that they grant moral considerations greater weight in their rational deliberations, and these agents are both more likely to select virtuous dispositions and more likely to act morally than their "less moral" counterparts. The weight placed on moral considerations by agents is part of the fine-grained detail of agent motivation and is not tied down by anything said here.

So, all that is required for my current purposes is that there is a roughly shared moral code that allows fine-grained, inter-personal differences in both the precise interpretation of what morality requires, and in the weight with which moral considerations enter into rational deliberation. This shared moral code does not reduce morality to individual interests but I *would* expect it to include a concern for the "public interest" defined in terms of the private interests of all individuals. Incorporating this idea of the public interest need not commit me to any simple utilitarianism – I have no need to insist that the public interest is defined as a simple sum of individual utilities, still less do I need to insist that the idea of the public interest constitutes the whole of morality. Rather I incorporate the specific idea of the public interest as a common element in moral motivation so as to provide a minimal substantive content to our moral structure in a manner that seems most appropriate to the study of democratic political

---

[5] This might be termed the Humean view, as expressed by Williams (1973).

[6] Most obviously, Gauthier (1986).

institutions. Democracy has many parts, but two that seem to be fundamental are that democracy involves both government *for* the people and government *by* the people. A shared morality that is at least sensitive to benefits and costs that arise *for* the people seems to be a sensible prerequisite for any account of the ways in which specific institutional devices operationalize the idea of government *by* the people.

A final point under this heading relates to the relationship between virtue and rationality. As I have already indicated, the basic feature of the account offered here is specified in terms of an "object of desire" (to use Montesquieu's term). Once the objects of desire are specified, the standard Humean notion of rationality seen as a relationship among desires, beliefs, and action is relevant. A rational action is that action, of those actions available, that best satisfies the agent's desires, given the agent's beliefs. I make no modification to this formula here. Clearly, a moral act may be rational on this account, given the role of the desire to act as morality requires. However, as has been noted by a number of writers,[7] the disposition of rational deliberation may be self-defeating in the sense that the direct calculation of the best action to take on a case-by-case basis may not, in fact, lead to the best possible outcome in its own terms. In this case, the choice of some other disposition (if only such a choice is possible) may be entirely rational. In this context, I simply note that the choice of a virtuous disposition may be entirely rational. I therefore offer no sharp distinction between the rational and the virtuous. The agents that I am concerned to model are both rational and (somewhat) moral.

Economizing on Virtue[8]

There seem to be two basic questions at stake in viewing the relationship between virtue and institutional design that are prior to the issue of resilience. We may think of them as the static and dynamic questions, or as the direct and indirect questions. The static, direct question is how best to design institutions given a particular distribution of dispositions (virtuous and interested, say) in the population. That is, holding dispositions and motivations constant, how best can we structure our institutions? The dynamic, indirect question then concerns the possibility of feedback effects from institutional design to dispositional choice. Do certain types of institution promote the choice or evolution of virtuous dispositions, while others undermine virtue? If such feedback effects arise, and are predictable, they too should be included in the overall analysis and evaluation of institutions. Here I will concentrate almost entirely on the first of these questions. Economizing on virtue identifies one family of strategies available to the institutional designer.

---

[7] See, for example, Parfit (1984).

[8] This subsection draws particularly on material in Chapter 4, Section 4.3, of *Democratic Devices and Desires.*

One thing should be clear from the outset. If all agents are wholly self-interested, there is no virtue to economize on; to put the same point in other words, economizing on virtue would be inevitable. Equally, if virtue were universal and abundant, there would be no need to economize on it. The strategy of economizing on virtue is only relevant in a world in which virtue exists but is scarce. To be sure, if most individuals are overwhelmingly self-interested, then institutions that make only modest demands on agents' virtue will be more crucial to a well-ordered society than if most people are virtuous most of the time. In other words, economizing on virtue is likely to be a more relevant consideration where individuals are more self-interested, but economizing on virtue must be an option of interest in any world in which virtue is scarce.

But what exactly does it mean for an institutional arrangement to economize on virtue? There are at least four different aspects to the idea of economizing that we wish to isolate. We will discuss each in turn. The first of these will be disposed of quite briefly. My main attention will be focused on the second and third aspects, because these are the aspects that we see as bearing most directly on the themes under discussion. The fourth aspect relates more specifically to the dynamic question of the impact of institutions on virtue and will therefore be mentioned only briefly here.

Economizing on a Stock

Consider a fixed stock of some good that can be used up or stored, like a quantity of a non-renewable resources such as coal or oil. Economizing on the stock of coal means saving coal now so that more will be available in the future. The application of this idea in the case of virtue might be that each person has a certain stock of *virtue*, and that when that virtue is used up, the person has to act selfishly or maliciously thereafter. A straightforward argument for arrangements that economize on virtue in this sense would then be that such arrangements – where they can be made – free up virtue to be used in other arenas.

However, we do not normally think of virtue as a stock that is consumed by use, and so I am not inclined to see this concept of economizing on virtue as a useful way to make sense of the metaphor. I mention it here only to dismiss it.

Economizing in Use

Consider some so-called virtuous act. By definition here, a virtuous act is one that not only has the appropriately moral content, but is also chosen for that reason. It is a matter of basic economic logic that this act will be undertaken more extensively (or will be more likely to be undertaken) if it is less costly to the actor in terms of other desired things forgone. That is, the demand curve for the virtuous act will be downward sloping. Economizing on virtue in this sense is simply a matter of relative prices, and a higher price of virtue – that is, a higher cost in terms of alternatives foregone – will lead us to economize on virtue in use in a manner that is essentially similar to the manner in which a higher price of sugar might be said to lead us to economize on the use of sugar.

When economists talk of economizing on virtue, it is usually this case of economizing in use that they have in mind. This fact may not be entirely obvious, however, because economists routinely discuss such issues in extreme settings where virtue is entirely absent from the motivational make-up of individual agents. In particular, in the context of pure invisible hand mechanisms based on selective incentives, agents can be expected to perform the act required by consideration of the public interest out of pure private interest – or not at all. In the famous case of Adam Smith's butcher and baker, the simple point is that the competitive market requires *no* virtue on the part of the baker to produce the wherewithal for the dinners of others. But the baker may still be virtuous. Smith does not rule out the possibility that the baker may delight in serving the dining needs of her community, and cannot do so on *a priori* grounds, because it is not possible to tell from the baker's actions what motivation is in place. The point here is that in the standard economic model, the market mechanism economizes on virtue absolutely – it offers a complete substitute for virtue – but our notion of economizing on virtue in use generalizes this same idea to point to the possibility of partial substitution, where a particular mechanism might economize on scarce virtue rather than replace absent virtue.

Economizing in Allocation

A critical element in any first-year undergraduate course in economic principles is the theory of comparative advantage – the idea, that is, that trade permits agents to specialize in things they are (relatively) good at. Indeed, this allocational issue is, on some views, the central consideration in any economizing ambition.

There is a direct application of this allocational idea in the context of economizing on virtue. Efficiency will require that virtuous individuals be allocated to roles that are particularly reliant on virtue – that individuals should be selected for roles, at least in part, by reference to their motivational dispositions; and further, that institutions should be designed and assessed with this in mind. Interestingly, however, this aspect of economizing is almost entirely absent from the economist's theory of institutional design. There are at least two possible reasons for this. One is that the focus on Smithian invisible hands has directed attention to incentive mechanisms almost exclusively. The second is that economists have been very reluctant to depart from the *homo oeconomicus* assumption and the attendant implication of motivational homogeneity. Only if there is some virtue in the population and only if that virtue is unevenly distributed across persons can there be any possibility of selecting the more virtuous agents for particular roles.

Economizing on virtue in this allocational sense might be thought of as an alternative to economizing in use – both attempt to extract the greatest value from a given level of virtuous motivation. But the ideas in play are very different and can be variously related. In some cases, the incentive aspects of an institutional device (focussing on "economizing in use") and the selection aspect (economizing in allocation) might operate in complementary fashion; while in other cases, the two aspects might operate against each other. It is an important element of the task of the analysis of particular institutions to view the nature of this interaction in specific cases, and where possible to choose institutional arrangements that minimize any conflict.

Economizing in Production

Economizing on virtue in production refers to the generation or supply of virtue, rather than its use or allocation. Any social process that inhibits the supply of virtue, other things equal, will not economize on virtue in production. It is at this level that the dynamic or indirect question identified above arises: Do some institutional arrangements reduce or erode virtue in production? Are there institutional arrangements that encourage the supply of virtue? And how do these institutional arrangements relate to those institutions that economize on virtue in use or in allocation? Since I do not intend to engage with this dynamic question here, I will merely note this aspect of economizing on virtue and move on.

To summarize, I have identified four possible senses in which we might speak of economizing on virtue. The first of these – the simple notion of economizing on a stock – I have dismissed from further consideration, but the remaining three are all of continuing relevance. Economizing on virtue *in use* requires us to make the best use of whatever virtue exists by reducing the effective cost of virtuous behavior. Economizing on virtue *in allocation* requires us to make the best use of whatever virtue exists by channelling or selecting virtuous individuals into those social roles that are particularly demanding of virtue. Economizing on virtue in either of these senses may be in conflict with the economizing on virtue *in production*. That is, institutions that economize on virtue in use or in allocation may erode the base of virtuous dispositions and so turn out to offer a false economy. But nothing we have said so far suggests that such conflicts are any more likely than are complementarities. Creating economic incentives to act in the way that virtue requires, and/or selecting relatively virtuous agents for roles where much virtue is required, seems at least as likely to encourage people to adopt virtuous dispositions as to discourage them from doing so.

Institutions That Employ Virtue[9]

In this subsection I mention five possible mechanisms that may operate in political settings – and focus on three that employ virtue in one way or another.

---

[9] This subsection draws particularly on material in Chapter 5 of *Democratic Devices and Desires*.

The two that do not employ virtue, and are the mainstays of the standard economic models of politics, are those that rely on sanctioning (a term I take to cover all incentive effects whether positive or negative) and on aggregating (as in the aggregation of preferences through voting mechanisms). Since these mechanisms are well understood, I will say no more about them here. The three types of mechanism that employ virtue will be termed *screening*, *virtue enhancing* and *virtue producing* mechanisms, respectively. I will concentrate on the first two of these, since the third relates primarily to the dynamic question of the impact of institutions on virtue.

Screening

We do not always think of an election – or of other political institutions – in terms of sanctions and aggregation, that is, as the means of disciplining or monitoring politicians or as the means of choosing preferred policies. And it does not always seem appropriate to reduce the discretionary power of a politician or official. The idea of representation, as opposed to delegation, captures the thought that an elected or appointed person is entrusted with discretionary power and allowed to display qualities of leadership and vision.

The idea of the screening mechanism revolves around the idea of sorting agents into social and political roles by reference, *inter alia,* to underlying criteria that pick out relatively virtuous dispositions. Screening devices of this type have not been much discussed in the economic literature on constitutional design, but it seems clear that this idea of screening is central to many of our social institutions, including the procedures used to select individuals for particular positions such as judges and civil servants, where direct private incentive mechanisms seem either inappropriate or ineffective for one reason or another.

The basic idea is simple enough. Once we drop the assumption of homogeneity of individual motivation, we open up a dimension in which screening may operate – that of agent motivations and dispositions. A motivational screening device would serve to allocate individuals to social roles in which their dispositions, as well as their talents, grant them a comparative advantage. In short, a screening mechanism attempts to institutionalize the idea of economizing on virtue in allocation by allocating discretionary power to those who are relatively trustworthy and virtuous.

Of course, it may be *desirable* to allocate individuals in one way or another across social roles, but we still need a practical mechanism which can achieve such an allocation (at least with some degree of accuracy greater than the random). Such matters will depend on particular details of any given setting. (I will offer an example in the next section under the heading, "The Partly Virtuous Case.")

It is important to note that screening effects can be negative as well as positive, and the recognition that institutional devices may carry screening implications may be as important in identifying institutional *failure* as it is in constructing institutional success. The possibility of "adverse selection" is widely recognized in a range of economic models – the basic idea being that under a particular institutional structure there may be a tendency for individuals of different types to act differently and in ways that adversely affect the overall operation of the institution.

Screening devices may complement sanctioning mechanisms in several ways. The introduction of screening may extend the range of the incentives in play. But more important, screening mechanisms are capable of offering institutional options in circumstances where incentive-based mechanisms may be weakest. If, for example, there is no basis for credible commitment, or no possibility for the discipline of continuous trading, or no opportunity for *ex post* monitoring of individuals, then it may be more appropriate to think in terms of the empowerment of appropriately selected representatives. At least, this will be so if there are available screening procedures that reasonably command some measure of confidence.

Virtue Enhancing

Screening attempts to sort the virtuous from the non-virtuous. A second type of mechanism may be identified that attempts to enhance or amplify the social effect of whatever stock of virtue there may be in society. The mere existence of virtuous individuals – at least beyond some critical number – may be enough to allow such mechanisms to operate. Here I merely wish to identify two distinct types of virtue enhancing mechanisms: one relating to the issue of enforcement, the second relating to the issue of aggregation.

The point in relation to enforcement is simple enough. In a world of un-relieved self-interest all enforcement has to be, in the final analysis, self-enforcement. Of course, this is not to deny than some enforcement may be possible within an institutional arrangement, but simply to point out that enforcement must itself be appropriately motivated and not simply assumed; in other words, enforcers have to be modelled. The key point that I want to make here is that the recognition of the *existence* of virtue can help to cut through the problem of "guarding the guardians." Imagine a simple situation in which an efficient co-operative equilibrium can only be supported by a threat of enforcement, but where there is no way to ensure that rationally self-interested persons will provide the required form of enforcement (i.e., if the power of enforcement is granted, it will be abused). However, if even a relatively small proportion of the potential enforcers are virtuous – in the sense that they act reliably in the way that efficient enforcement requires, rather than in the manner dictated by self-interest given the power of an enforcer – the possibility of virtuous enforcement may be sufficient to support the equilibrium in which everyone (virtuous and self-interested alike) acts co-operatively, so that actual enforcement is not called into play in equilibrium. In this way, the institution of enforcement can serve to magnify the impact of the limited virtue that is available, and make everyone act *as if* they were virtuous; that is, enforcement may be a virtue enhancing mechanism.

A second class of mechanism that may act to enhance virtue is illustrated by the "jury theorems" originally developed by Condorcet. The context in which these theorems were developed involved determining the truth or falsehood of a proposition – whether or not a defendant committed the crime – in circumstances where each individual's judgement is imperfect but more likely to be right than wrong. The theorems represent a version of the central limit theorem, or the law of large numbers. Specifically, if the probability of a randomly selected individual's judgement on the matter at hand being correct is greater than 0.5, then the probability that the majority of a jury of, say, n persons will be correct may be made arbitrarily close to 1 by increasing the size of the jury, n. Similarly, if the probability of, say, a politician being virtuous (and so supporting policies if and only if they are in the public interest, somehow defined) is greater than 0.5, then the probability that a majority decision within a legislature of, say, 100 such politicians will reflect such virtue will be large and may be made arbitrarily close to 1 by increasing the size of the legislature. This direct translation of the jury theorem to the political setting simply replaces the accuracy of a judgement of fact, with the normative desirability of a judgement of policy.

In this simple application of the logic of the jury theorem, majority voting acts as a virtue enhancing mechanism provided that there is a probability of virtue of at least 0.5 (equivalently, a majority of virtuous individuals). But the relevance of the jury theorem idea is not restricted to the majoritarian case. Most obviously, the same logic would operate in the case of qualified majority voting with appropriate stocks of virtue – two thirds majority voting in a large legislature will deliver virtuous policy if the stock of virtuous individuals is at least one third (so that the virtuous form a blocking coalition), and so on.

The point I wish to stress is just that the statistical theorem underlying the Condorcet analysis bears no less on issues of motivation than on issues of judgements of fact. In this sense, we may be able to institutionalize a reliance on virtue even when we believe virtue to be relatively scarce and difficult to detect. The law of large numbers ensures that we do not need everyone to be virtuous all of the time to develop arrangements that will produce desirable social outcomes much of the time. But equally, we do need there to be *some* minimal level of virtue (which may vary from case to case) for such institutional mechanisms to get off the ground at all. Such mechanisms can enhance virtue, but cannot completely substitute for virtue.

Virtue Producing

A virtue producing mechanism is simply an incentive mechanism operating at the dispositional level to encourage the adoption of virtuous dispositions. The obvious general point is that an institution will act as a virtue producing mechanism to the extent that it raises the attractiveness of virtuous dispositions relative to other dispositions, or it reduces the corresponding cost. There may be a wide range of social institutions that operate as virtue producing mechanisms, but I will not focus attention on this class of institutions or pursue the dynamic question of the production of virtue further here.

Given these ideas of alternative ways in which we might think of economizing on virtue, and alternative mechanisms that might be employed to these ends, I now turn to a particular case.

TWO-TIER REPRESENTATION

As an example of the type of analysis of institutional resilience that I am advocating, and as an example of the type of conclusion that might arise, this section is devoted to a simple modeling exercise. The intention is to take one simple but relatively specific part of a democratic institutional structure and examine how it might operate under different assumptions on the character of the individuals within the polity. I compare just two alternative assumptions on character: the pure *homo oeconomicus* case in which all agents are purely self-interested and a case of the sort previously discussed, where a proportion of agents are of a more virtuous disposition, so that both virtue and motivational heterogeneity are introduced. The models will display the various forms of economizing on virtue, and use both screening and virtue enhancing mechanisms, as well as more standard incentive based mechanisms.

The particular institutional structure that I shall consider is two-tier representation – a structure in which there are two levels of elected politicians within the overall democratic process. I do not want to limit the interpretation of this structure to particular cases at this stage, since it is a part of the aim of my discussion to flesh out the roles which such a two-tier structure might play, but examples of two-tier representation might include systems in which there are both regional and national elections to representative bodies, or where there are two elected houses of the legislature, or where there is an elected executive in addition to an elected legislature.

More formally, I shall simply specify that there are two levels of representation labelled L (lower) and H (higher), that there are $l > h \geq 1$ positions at each level, and that all positions are filled by competitive elections. In labeling the two levels lower and higher I want to indicate a relationship between them – that the lower level is the proving ground in which politicians establish themselves and their reputations before standing for election to the higher level. This is clearly a common feature of many real world systems in which it is unusual for candidates for "high" elected office not to have held some elected position previously. To emphasize this aspect of the model, as well as to simplify the discussion, I shall assume that *only* those who have served in office at level L can stand for office at level H. More specifically, potential politicians will be assumed to live for just two periods. In their first period they may stand for election to level L. If successful, in their second period they may stand for election to level H or stand for re-election to level L, or stand down. If unsuccessful in period 1, in period 2 they may again stand for election to level L (where they will compete against members of the next generation). So, those standing for election to level L at any given time will include both those who have no political or public experience and those seeking re-election (so that they will vary in their age), while all those standing for election at level H will all have experience at level L and so be of the same age.

The distinction between the two levels of politics will be taken to be potentially significant in at least two ways. First, from the perspective of society as a whole, the two levels will differ in their power or influence over policy choice and, ultimately, over the extent to which the government operates in the interests of citizens. Second, from the perspective of politicians, the two levels will differ in the opportunities that they offer for the extraction of private rents. I assume that both of these aspects of the relationship between H and L are, to at least some extent, matters of design. That is, the specification of further aspects of the overall constitution – the allocation of powers between H and L; the checks and balances that operate on H and L; the degree of monitoring of members of H and L; the salaries, prestige, or other rewards that flow to members of H and L; and so forth – will determine whether H or L is viewed as more powerful from the public perspective, or more desirable from a politician's purely private perspective. I shall take all four possible cases as worthy of consideration, so that it is important to note that while H and L are fixed in their relationship in terms of the political process of election, they are not fixed in terms of either their relative public importance or their relative private desirability. And neither are these two additional features fixed in relation to each other.

I shall also simplify the in-office behavior of politicians as much as possible. At each level, once elected, each politician will choose between two actions: one of which – action V (virtuous) – promotes the social value of government at that level, whereas the other – action S (selfish) – promotes the politician's private utility from office.

The *Homo Oeconomicus* Case

With this outline of the set-up in mind, I begin with the "standard" case in which all agents are taken to be purely privately motivated - so that all have the standard *homo oeconomicus* character. In this case, several points may be made immediately. First, since by assumption, all potential candidates have identical characters, there is no possibility of any *ex ante* screening or selection type of argument. As is usually the case in models populated by *homo oeconomicus* agents, whatever work is to be done by institutional design must be achieved by means of incentive effects of one sort or another. Second, given familiar arguments about issues of credibility and their link to the prospects of re-election, it is clear that it is the structure of the options available in the second (and final) period of a politician's life that will drive behavior in the first period. Third, given that all politicians are motivated entirely in terms of their private interests, the design of the institutions can attempt to manipulate the relationship between the private and social pay-offs to level H and L activity to achieve socially optimal outcomes (optimal, that is, relative to the feasible set of alternatives).

These points imply that, in the L level election, voters will always prefer a young candidate to an old one. This is simply to say that an old candidate will be impossible to discipline by any future threat of non-election; since in all other respects old and young candidates are identical by assumption, there can be no reason to prefer an old candidate to a young one, and some reason for the opposite preference. This logic applies regardless of whether the old candidate has experience at the L level, since even if the candidate had served at the L level, and had taken action V, this would make no difference to the predicted behavior as a second-term member at level L.

Of course, given that no old candidate will ever be elected (assuming only that there is a sufficient supply of young candidates), no one will ever stand at the L level in their second period. This result applies only weakly in the case where candidature is costless – so that relevant individuals will be indifferent between standing with a zero probability of winning and not standing – but is strengthened by the introduction of any cost of candidature. So, the only prospect for election for a second-period individual is at the H level.

Let H_p and L_p, respectively, denote the private pay-offs to successful candidates at levels H and L, respectively, normalising the pay-offs of the unelected to 0. Ignoring discounting, a first period potential politician will stand for election at level L if:

$$\text{prob}L\,L_p + \text{prob}L \cdot \text{prob}H\,H_p > 0 \tag{1}$$

where $\text{prob}L$ and $\text{prob}H$ denote the probabilities of being elected at each level, respectively (and recalling that only those that win at level L can stand at level H). Now, given the simple assumptions made, it is clear that all retiring L level representatives (all of whom are entering their second period) will be candidates for level H, provided only that $H_p > 0$, and that this condition is also sufficient for all potential candidates to stand for initial election to level L, provided only that $L_p \geq 0$. (Again, the introduction of costs of candidature would change the details in an obvious way, but would not affect the basic line of argument, so I continue to suppress such costs in the cause of notational simplicity). Since all candidates will be essentially identical in the initial L level election, it is clear that this election will be no more than a lottery, since no voter can have reason to prefer any particular candidate to any other. So that $\text{prob}L$ may be written as l/k where k is the total size of the generation of potential politicians.

We now need to consider the behavior of politicians in office. Trivially, in their second period, all those elected to level H will choose action S. This simply reflects their assumed character, and the fact that the institutional structure has no more leverage over them. This is just the same argument about final period behavior that led us to conclude that the electorate would never elect a second term representative at level L. H_p is therefore identified as the utility to the politician at level H conditional on action S. Given this, it is clear that the social pay-off to political action at level H will be relatively low.

At level L politicians face a slightly more interesting choice. As I have noted, the only impact on political activity that can be enforced in this structure is one that uses the second period election to discipline first period behavior. The obviously optimal strategy for voters is then to vote in the H level election for candidates who took action V at level L, not because this will influence the behavior of the level H assembly (since it will not), but simply to put in place the incentive to choose act V at level L. From the perspective of first period politicians at level L, this incentive will be sufficient for them to choose act V if (again, ignoring discounting):

$$(L_{p|S} - L_{p|V}) < \text{prob}HH_{p|S}. \tag{2}$$

That is, if the marginal cost in terms of the difference between the private pay-offs to selfish and virtuous actions at level L are more than compensated by the marginal benefits in terms of the expected private pay-offs if elected at level H.

We should also consider this from society's perspective. A baseline for comparison here is the social outcome if all politicians at all levels choose act S, so that the political system is entirely selfish in its operation. Relative to that case, the incentive structure that supports act V at level L offers a clear benefit in terms of the social performance of that level of government, but at the potential cost of increasing the private payoffs to politicians at level H to meet requirement (2). I shall assume that the benefit exceeds the cost, since otherwise the baseline case is optimal.

If we view the pure strategy equilibrium of the underlying game, in which all level L politicians will choose act V, and all will stand for election to level H, we must have, from (1):

$$l/kL_{p|V} + h/kH_{p|S} > 0.$$

The important points to be drawn from this sketch of a model are to recognize the roles of the various parts of the scheme, in both the private calculus of the politicians and the social calculus of institutional evaluation. Since the nature of the scheme is to use H_p as the ultimate incentive, it is clear that this will have to be significant. At the same time the social cost of the scheme can be reduced by ensuring, to the greatest degree possible, that the selfish action of politicians at level H does little social damage. At the same time, the social benefit of the scheme comes from the "virtuous" action of politicians at level L, so that it will be important to ensure that political functions or responsibilities where virtuous rather than selfish action is crucial are allocated to level L. All of this suggests that political careers within a two-tier structure operated by entirely self-interested politicians might best be organized – from a social perspective – if key political decisions affecting social outcomes are left to the relatively junior political ranks, who are also seen as competing for senior status, which carries considerable personal rewards and prestige but relatively little direct authority over key decisions.

The Partly Virtuous Case

I now turn to sketch the parallel analysis of the institution of two-tier represen-tation in the context of a society in which some fraction f of individuals are of a virtuous disposition, while the remaining $(1 - f)$ are of the *homo oeconomicus* character, as before. An individual's type is not public information. Virtuous persons, I stipulate, would choose act V over act S, if elected at either level of government, and regardless of the private incentives, provided only that in doing so they do not make themselves worse off than if they had not entered politics (so that there is a limit to virtue). This stipulation might be relaxed to the assumption that the virtuous person will choose act V rather than act S provided that the private cost is not greater than some specified value, without changing the essential nature of the discussion. The point is simply that I do not need to assume absolute virtue from those who are virtuous, any more than I need to assume that everyone is virtuous.

By assuming that the virtuous will only participate in politics provided that they are not made worse off in private terms, it is clear that society cannot screen between the virtuous and the self-interested by simply making the lot of politicians sufficiently unattractive to deter all self-interested individuals. Both the virtuous and the self-interested will require a participation condition of the general form of Equation 1 to be satisfied for them to enter politics at all. Nevertheless, the story will vary considerably from the standard case thereafter.

The basic point is that the virtuous will choose act V if elected in their second period, whether at level H or L. This fact offers the possibility of designing the political structure as a screening mechanism. Essentially, if the L level of politics can be used to distinguish the virtuous from the self-interested, it should be possible to ensure that the virtuous are over-represented at the H level so that socially desirable outcomes emerge at that level.[10] The basic mechanics are simple enough. Contrary to Equation 2, we now require:

$$(Lp_{|S} - L_{p|V}) > \text{prob}H \cdot H_{P|S}. \tag{3}$$

---

[10] Note that we do not require the screening to be perfect so that only the virtuous are present in the H level of politics.

In words, the level L differential between the private benefits conditional on act S and the private benefits conditional on act V must be larger than the expected value of the private benefits associated with election at level H. This will ensure that the self-interested reveal themselves at level L by choosing the selfish action. Voters can then adopt the same optimal strategy of voting only for candidates in level H elections who took action V at level L, but with a very different justification: in this case the strategy will ensure the election of virtuous individuals at level H, rather than enforce an equilibrium in which self-interested individuals will take action V at level L.

Note that this screening mechanism operates precisely because it rules out the case in which a self-interested individual will mimic a virtuous individual at level L to gain access to level H. Such mimicry is not incentive compatible, in that selfish individuals would make themselves worse off by such mimicry given the nature of the pay-offs at each level.

Such a screening mechanism carries with it implications for the further details of the constitution that are the exact reverse of those associated with the purely self-interested case. If we wish to design the political structure to amplify or enhance virtue in this way, we will need to allocate those political duties and responsibilities that have the most marked impact on the social value of outcomes to the H level, while limiting, to the greatest extent possible, the personal pay-offs available at that level. Equally, level L should be designed as a branch of politics in which private temptations are relatively high and social impact relatively low.

Of course, a number of other issues will arise in any fully specified model of this structure: There will be the issue of whether the fraction f of virtuous individuals is sufficient to allow a fully virtuous level H; the issue of the detailed specification of the probability of election of each type of individual at each level; the issue of the electoral choice at level L between a second-term virtuous person and a first term person of unknown character (if the screening mechanism is to work and supply a sufficient number of virtuous individuals for election at level H, not too many virtuous persons can be elected for a second term at level L); and so on. But is seems clear enough that the basic contrast between the *homo oeconomicus* case and the case with a modicum of virtue will withstand such further detailed modelling.

It should also be stressed that the mere presence of virtuous persons in society is not a sufficient condition for that society to wish to switch from the incentive based structure of the last sub-section to the virtue enhancing structure of this sub-section. One would properly have to compare the social benefits realisable under the two types of structure in a society that includes both virtuous and self-interested persons. The incentive based structure outlined in the previous sub-section would not cease to work simply because of the presence of the virtuous. Indeed it might work rather better in one sense, since a proportion (presumably the fraction f in the absence of any screening) of those elected to level H will be of a virtuous disposition, and this may improve social outcomes decided at level H. This comparison would be a relatively delicate affair and would demand much more detailed and specific modeling, since it will depend on the differential sizes of the social pay-offs associated with different political choices at different levels, the sensitivity of political decisions to the composition of the assembles at each level, as well as a number of other factors. But there are two points to stress here: First is that the introduction of a modicum of virtue opens up new institutional possibilities and may significantly affect the detailed institutional structure that best serves the public interest; and second that the presence of virtue puts more of the emphasis on the human aspect of democracy rather than the purely institutional.

OVERVIEW

In *Democratic Devices and Desires*, Geoff Brennan and I argue that a motivational structure that recognizes the possibility of virtue provides a good starting point for the re-examination of much of the analysis of the design of political institutions in the rational actor tradition. We suggest that many of the major institutional features of democracy – competitive elections, representation, political parties, the separation of powers – can be understood afresh from the perspective of a more morally motivated, and more motivationally heterogeneous, population. One impression that this discussion might give is that the institutions of democracy are robust or resilient to different specifications of the motivational character of the agents who live within them; that democracy may work better if at least some individuals are virtuous (which might not be taken to be too surprising), but that it works tolerably well either way.

One objective of this chapter is to limit and qualify this impression. I do not wish to deny that some form of democracy can be constructed that has good operating characteristics given any specific structure of motivational characters, but I do want to insist that the versions of democracy that might be supported by different structures of motivational character might be very different from each other in terms of both the details of the institutional arrangements and the manner in which they work. The extended example relating to two-tier representation is intended as no more than a demonstration of how two structures that might appear similar at first glance – with both operating the same sorts of electoral structure and both supporting the same sort of voting rule – are actually very different in their implications for the operation of the political structure as a whole. This example illustrates the idea that while democracy may be *flexible*, in that it can contain a wide variety of detailed institutional arrangements that in turn might accommodate a variety of motivational structures; this does not imply that any particular set of detailed democratic institutions will be robust or *resilient* to alternative specification of motivational character. In making this point, I hope to stimulate the thought that detailed democratic institutions may not be so resilient as we might imagine, or at least to stimulate the thought that the question of institutional resilience is worth pursuing.

A second objective of this chapter is to throw some light on the relationship between virtue and democracy. I began with a brief discussion of Montesquieu's idea that virtue was the natural and distinctive motivational element that relates to republican democracy, in the same way that honor relates to monarchy and fear relates to despotism. In the main body of this chapter I suggest that the recognition of virtue provides the basis for a very different approach to the design of the political institutions of democracy; opening the door to both new interpretations of the idea of economizing on virtue, and to the analysis of new institutional mechanisms. It is clearly not the case that in any literal sense virtue is a necessary prerequisite of democracy – the simple existence of the standard rational actor models of democratic institutions makes it clear that, in at least some settings, recognizably democratic institutions can work – and work tolerably well – without any virtue. The *homo oeconomicus* version of the model of two-tier representation illustrates this point.

Nevertheless, it is possible to argue that these models of democracy miss a vital aspect of democracy as it is more generally understood. That without at least some modicum of virtue, the human aspect of democracy is undermined so that there can be no sense in which citizens feel themselves to be bound together in a common enterprise, but must see themselves as merely bound by constraints and incentive effects.

REFERENCES

Brennan, G., and Hamlin, A. (2000) *Democratic Devices and Desires,* Cambridge: Cambridge University Press.

Brennan, G., and Hamlin, A. (2001) "Republican Liberty and Resilience," *The Monist*, 84, 47–62.

Gauthier, D. (1986), *Morals by Agreement,* Oxford: Oxford University Press.

Hampton, J. (1997) "The Wisdom of the Egoist: The Moral and Political Implications of Valuing the Self," *Social Philosophy and Policy,* 14, 21–51.

Montesquieu, C. L. (1748/1966) *The Spirit of the Laws* (translated by T. Nugent), New York: Hafner.

Parfit, D. (1984) *Reasons and Persons,* Oxford: Clarendon Press.

Schmidtz, D. (1995) *Rational Choice and Moral Agency,* Princeton: Princeton University Press.

Smith, M. (1994) *The Moral Problem,* Oxford: Basil Blackwell.

Williams, B. (1973) *Problems of the Self,* Cambridge: Cambridge University Press.

PART THREE

SOCIAL CAPITAL

8

The Optimal Level of Solidarity

Ronald Wintrobe

INTRODUCTION

This chapter looks at solidarity from a rational choice point of view. I begin with some puzzles about the meaning and significance of solidarity and its relationship to social capital, trust, and other concepts. The concept of social capital has been used to mean a number of things, and sometimes it means the same thing as solidarity and sometimes not. But perhaps this is the price for the new-found popularity of the subject. The heart of the chapter is a simple model of how solidarity, social cohesion, horizontal trust, or horizontal social capital – concepts that are interchangeable in this paper – is generated. I describe a production process for solidarity; that is, I explain one way in which it is created. This makes it possible to think more systematically than is usual about the conditions under which solidarity grows or declines. This model and some of its implications are described in the sections, "The Production of Trust" and "Trade in Beliefs."

The next two sections discuss the relationship of this model of solidarity to certain classical ideas about the formation and properties of group beliefs: Rousseau's "General Will" and the jury theorem of Condorcet. These works, with their emphasis on group decision making and the conditions under which various forms of group decision making are in the group interest, can be used to illuminate some of the social costs of solidarity. With the costs and benefits of solidarity in mind, I can then derive the optimal level of solidarity and show how this depends on various parameters. In particular, in the section "The Optimal Level of Solidarity," I discuss how the optimum varies among different kinds of organizations, including religious groups, political parties, business firms and universities.

The following section, "Contagion: Social Capital and Democracy," describes a complication: Solidarity, like other forms of social capital, is contagious. As a result, there tend to be two equilibria, one with high solidarity and one with low. So the optimum level of solidarity isn't necessarily or even typically the right level: We tend to either have too much or too little solidarity. Finally, the contagiousness of solidarity partly explains some interesting problems. For example, it explains how solidarity can decline so rapidly, as Putnam (2000) provides evidence has happened recently in the United States. And it provides a rationale for the existence of constitutional checks and balances (rules and restrictions on majority voting), just as the American Founding Fathers understood it: to prevent irrational decisions and instability. It follows that, as this section shows, one bind of democracy – solidarity or social capital – gives rise to another – constitutional protections. The concluding section completes the chapter.

SOCIAL CAPITAL AND SOLIDARITY

Putnam's work (e.g., 1993, 2000) on social capital has received a lot of attention and provides a convenient place to start our inquiry. Putnam believes social capital is good for democracy and for society. Indeed, he has said that "happiness is living in a society where horizontal trust is high." In *Making Democracy Work* (1993), he argued that social capital is beneficial for governing capacity. Social capital there is measured by the density of horizontal associations. He provides evidence that those regions of Italy that are well-governed have high social capital measured this way, while those that are badly governed have low. He also conjectures that social capital is amazingly durable, as shown by the apparent facts that the geographical pattern of good and bad government in Italy in the late 20th century appears to be the same as it was in the 19th century and, indeed, though with less certainty, similar to that which existed in the 15th century! Paldam (2000) presents some evidence that supports Putnam's thesis in general, while criticizing the idea that social capital is very long-lasting. In fact, he suggests that it lasts a few decades, which seems much more reasonable.

Putnam's latest book, *Bowling Alone* (2000), deploys a battery of indicators to show that social capital has been steadily falling in the United States since the 1960s. The evidence that social capital in the United States has fallen is compelling, but the analysis of why this has happened appears less so. The main reasons appear to be the growth of television consumption and "generational change" – a catch-all phrase referring to the passing of the "great civic generation" born in the years 1925–30, who became adults during the 1950s. There is no doubt that many of the correlations Putnam presents are fascinating, especially the ones between those who agree relatively strongly with the statement "TV is my primary form of entertainment" and various measures of civic engagement, such as the number of club meetings attended, whether the person worked on a community project, and even the mean number of times a driver "gave the finger" to another driver last year.

While there is little doubt that the book is a grand accomplishment, its underlying logic is not without its problems:

1. If social capital could have fallen so dramatically in the United States in a few decades, how could it have persisted in Italy for hundreds of years, as asserted in his previous book, *Making Democracy Work?*
2. At the same time as social capital is said to have fallen in the United States, macroeconomic performance has been spectacular. So, those who argue that social capital augments economic production might have a problem reconciling these two pieces of evidence.
3. Perhaps most important, here as elsewhere, the question arises, just what is "social capital"? The same term appears to be used to mean different things. For example, while the 1993 book on Italy is concerned with horizontal trust, and indeed draws a significant contrast between the properties of horizontal trust (which it is argued is good for democracy) and vertical trust (bad for democracy[1]), in the new book extensive reference is simply made to "social capital," and the distinction between horizontal and vertical trust seems to be lost.

The distinction between horizontal and vertical trust was first, to my knowledge, made in Breton and Wintrobe (1982) (and elaborated in Wintrobe and Breton, 1986, among other places) in the context of organizations like government bureaucracies and business firms. We argued that horizontal networks (T_h) lowered an organization's productivity; that is, no matter how beneficial they might be from the point of view of the personal well-being of subordinates, such networks tend to reduce the efficiency of the business firm or bureaucracy from the point of view of the organization's principals. The reasons are such things as the fact that horizontal networks make it easier for subordinates to distort information to their advantage, cover for each other, and so forth. However, vertical networks (T_v) raise productivity, for example, by improving communication between subordinates and superiors. Consequently, it is not the level of trust that is important for an organization's efficiency but its distribution.

While the trust concepts in Breton and Wintrobe and in Putnam are certainly similar, if not identical, it is interesting that their normative roles are reversed: In Breton and Wintrobe, vertical trust raises organizational productivity, while horizontal trust lowers it; in Putnam (1993), horizontal trust is good for democracy, while vertical trust is bad for it. Of course, one could reconcile the two positions by saying that one refers to politics, the other to bureaucracies or business firms, but this raises some interesting questions.

---

[1] Indeed it is emphasized that the problem of poor government in the Italian South is not due to the fact that the people in places like Sicily and Calabria have no or too few networks, but that they have the *wrong kind* of networks: vertical (patron client, mafiosi, etc.), as opposed to horizontal (voluntary associations).

In any case, it is worth looking at these concepts in a bit more detail. In Putnam (1993), the concept "horizontal trust" is used interchangeably with solidarity. The more general descriptive term appears to be "Networks of civic engagement" (p. 173, henceforth referred to here as NOCE). Putnam's central argument in *Making Democracy Work* about the beneficial effects of horizontal networks or NOCE is simple. He says:

The denser such networks in a community, the more likely that its citizens will be able to cooperate for mutual benefit (1993, p. 174).

The reasons are: NOCE (1) increase the potential cost to a defector in any individual transaction, (2) foster norms of reciprocity, (3) improve the flow of information about trustworthiness, and (4) "embody past success at collaboration which can serve as a culturally defined template for future collaboration" (1993, p. 174).

However, he says that "A vertical network, no matter how dense and no matter how important to its participants, cannot sustain social trust and cooperation" (p. 174). Vertical flows of information are less reliable, vertical bonds of clientilism "seem to undermine the horizontal group organization and solidarity of clients and patrons alike – but especially the clients (pp. 174–5). Among other things, Putnam says this is one reason democracy works better than autocracy and why capitalism is better than feudalism.

It follows that membership rates in hierarchically ordered groups like the Mafia or the Catholic Church should be negatively related to good government, and the 1993 book about Italy presents evidence that this is apparently the case with respect to the regions that are well governed versus those which are not.

As he also points out, his argument is exactly the reverse of Olson's famous proposition in his book, *The Rise and Decline of Nations* (1982), that small interest groups have no incentive to work toward the common good of society and every incentive to engage in costly and inefficient "rent seeking" (p. 176).

Neither Putnam nor Olson (nor Breton & Wintrobe) solved the problem of how to aggregate social capital. Whether for this reason or not, in the work of Knack and Keefer (1997), Fukuyama (1995), and Inglehart (e.g., in Warren, 1999) among others, there has appeared yet another concept of trust: "generalized social capital." Unlike Coleman's concept of social capital, or Breton and Wintrobe's or Putnam's T_v or T_h, this refers to the extent to which a person is willing to trust a stranger. One problem is that social capital in this sense and that in the sense of Breton and Wintrobe or Coleman are sometimes negatively related. That is, the more trust there is within a group, the more distrust there may be of outsiders. Hence the strange result in Fukuyama (1995), for example, that Italy and Japan are "low trust" countries. One explanation for this result is that in those countries, trust tends to be particularized within groups, and people are divided into "in-group" and "out-group." No matter how strong the level of in-group trust, such societies will score low on the Fukuyama-Knack and Keefer definition of trust. But maybe the classic instance of this kind of theorizing is Banfield's (1958) concept of "amoral familism," invented to explain the strange patterns he discovered in a small town in southern Italy. Again, (as in Putnam, 1993) the concept is invented to try and understand how Italian life and society work. Perhaps the right conclusion is that this is essentially a hopeless task for North Americans. But another big problem is China, where indexes of high levels of corruption seem to go hand in hand with high trust (see, e.g., Paldam, 2000).

As mentioned previously, in *Bowling Alone* (Putnam, 2000), there is much discussion of social capital but no mention of either horizontal or vertical trust. Instead, numerous correlations with an "index of social capital" are presented. This appears to be a composite measure which includes elements of all three types of social capital – horizontal, vertical and generalized. Thus, it includes "measures of engagement in public affairs" like turnout in presidential elections, "measures of informal sociability" like whether a person spends a lot of time visiting friends, "measures of community organizational life" and "measures of social trust" like the extent to which someone agrees with the statement "Most people can be trusted" (2000, p. 291). The justification is that these measures appear to be highly correlated with one another over the last 30 years or so. Perhaps it is true that, as Putnam in effect asserts, *all* forms of trust have been falling steadily in the United States, which would justify their inclusion in this manner. However, even if this was so, it is not obvious that the same thing can be said of other countries like Russia, China, or Italy, and perhaps this explains some of the strange and confusing results that people get when they try to apply concepts like this to other countries.

In sum, social capital appears to come in many variations: positive social capital, negative social capital, corruption, generalized trust, horizontal trust, vertical trust, solidarity, and so forth. It follows that, as Jean Cohen puts it, one basic issue is whether

"inherited social capital" is the right concept to use for six rather different things: interpersonal trust, social solidarity, general norms of reciprocity, belief in the legitimacy of institutionalized norms, confidence that these will motivate the action of institutional actors and ordinary citizens [social solidarity], and transmission of cultural traditions, patterns, and values. (Cohen, in Warren, 1999, p. 220)

Some of the concepts of trust are redundant: Corruption is just the inverse of honesty, which is really not much different from generalized social capital. Solidarity is just T_h. My own view is that all of them can probably be boiled down to three: horizontal trust T_v, vertical trust T_h, and the level of general social trust (the same thing as honesty or social capital). But let us move on to a deeper issue: How is trust produced?

THE PRODUCTION OF TRUST

If social capital is like other forms of capital, one should be able to describe the investment process by which it is produced and the conditions under which it depreciates. Breton and Wintrobe (1982) described one such process. In their analysis, a person invests in trust with another person by making an initial sacrifice or gesture on their behalf or by foregoing an opportunity to cheat that person. The amount that could have been earned by taking the lost opportunity to cheat or the size of the gesture measures the size of the investment. How much trust capital is produced for any given investment depends on a number of things, especially how well the "signal" given by foregoing the opportunity to cheat is received by its intended recipient(s), that is, on how easily the individuals communicate with each other, and so forth. It is no accident that secret and especially criminal organizations like the Mafia or youth gangs typically recruit members by presenting highly structured opportunities for newcomers. Salmon (1988) described another process involving conjectures and refutations. Coleman (1990) discusses the decision to extend trust in a number of social contexts.

In a similar vein, Uslaner (1999, pp. 145–6) argues that social capital is produced by participation in sports but not by visiting arts museums. He also discusses experiments done in the 1960s by Muzafer Sherif et al. (Uslaner, 1999, p. 145) where horizontal trust among two groups of campers was first destroyed, and then the issue was to see what could be done to rebuild it. The main finding appears to be that the only thing that worked was if the two groups were compelled to cooperate toward a common goal. For example, a field trip in a truck was organized for the groups in which it was arranged for the truck to break down. The two groups had to work together to fix the truck, and this seemed to rebuild social capital. No doubt such experiments could not be repeated in today's climate, possibly thankfully. In any case, illustrations like the sports example or the field trip experiment are easily seen as special cases of the Breton and Wintrobe framework, in that they provide plenty of opportunities for each side to make appropriate investments in trustworthiness and for these signals to be observed by the other group.

In Putnam and the work of many other political scientists and sociologists on trust or social capital, the investment process is mysterious and typically the amount available is described as the amount inherited (Putnam, 2000; Cohen in Warren, 1999). Putnam himself is very unclear on this point, but it looks as if he believes that trust is produced (or at least maintained) through participation in group activities. However, it seems unlikely that participation alone can create trust: For example, if there were serious disagreement among the participants, it is not obvious that social capital wouldn't be destroyed rather than created.

One point Putnam doesn't explore is the connection between trust and corruption. It would seem that corruption is the exact opposite of trust, that is, if corruption is observed, it means that that person could not be trusted, or it means a *breach* of trust. In the analysis of Breton and Wintrobe (1982), a person engaging in a corrupt act is simply one who is *taking* (rather than refusing) an opportunity to cheat. Hence trust is destroyed (depreciated) by corrupt actions. Della Porta (2000) argues and provides evidence from Italy that corruption destroys trust in government. She also shows in a cross-country analysis that the lowest satisfaction with democracy is reported for those countries that score high on the corruption index, like Italy, and the nations that are most satisfied with democracy are exactly those where corruption is lowest (Della Porta, 2000, p. 209).

As for the United States, it is not obvious that it is more corrupt now than it was in the 1950s. But it is certainly possible that it is perceived that way, possibly due to the growth of the power of the news media and their increased willingness to investigate and expose politicians. Note that this is an entirely different phenomenon from the growth in the consumption of sitcoms and other entertainment programs that preoccupied Putnam.[2]

In any case, in this chapter I am concerned with solidarity, so let us turn our focus on that. The essence of solidarity, as defined in the *Shorter Oxford Dictionary*, is:

> The fact or quality, on the part of communities, etc., of being perfectly united or at one in some respect, esp., in interests, sympathies or aspirations.

Other definitions all emphasize union, unity, or oneness: The *Random House Dictionary* defines it as "unity or unanimity of attitude or purpose, as between members of a group or class." Some antonyms are divisiveness, factiousness, or discord.

How is solidarity produced? One process is discussed in the next section.

TRADE IN BELIEFS

In Marc Galanter's (1999) fascinating book on cults, which sums up 15 years of his research on the psychology of charismatic groups, the power of group solidarity is described in the following manner by a heroin user who joined the Divine Light Mission:

> Once I got to know them, I realized they loved me. . . . When I wanted to take heroin, or even to smoke [marijuana], I knew they were with me to help me stay away from it, even if I was alone. And their strength was there for me. . . . I could rely on their *invisible hand*, moved by Maharaj Ji's wisdom, to help me gain control. (Galanter, 1989, p. 27, italics added)

Another, fictional, account of intense solidarity is provided by Arthur Koestler. In his famous novel, *Darkness at Noon* (1941), the hero ends by sacrificing the truth and ultimately his life for the good of the Party.

---

[2] Indeed, Putnam (2000) emphasizes that watching the *news* on TV, unlike watching other types of programs, is social-capital–*enhancing*.

The other remarkable feature about many situations where solidarity is particularly intense is the beliefs that people sometimes hold. To take an example suggested in the introduction to a recent book on extremism (Breton, Galeotti, Salmon, and Wintrobe, [2002]) how is it, for example, that a number of Americans, mostly members of paramilitary groups, would come to believe the view expounded in Mark Koernke's 1993 video, *America in Peril*, that "elements within the United States government are working with foreign leaders to turn the United States into a dictatorship under the leadership of the United Nations" (Karl, 1995, p. 69)?

To summarize, in many extremist groups, two remarkable features are the extremity of the beliefs and the depth of solidarity. I contend that neither of these two phenomena are necessarily irrational, and indeed that the key to understanding both of them is that they are related to each other. More precisely, they are the outcome of a process whereby beliefs are traded in exchange for solidarity or social cohesion. Thus, Galanter notes that many subjects experienced a decline in symptoms of psychological distress on joining the group, and that, in his statistical analysis of the reasons for this, 37% of this overall decline could be attributed to an increase in social cohesion (p. 32). Although Galanter, a psychologist, does not model this process, the basic elements involved seem straightforward. The person who gives up his beliefs loses something, which could be called his or her true "identity" or "independence of thought" or "autonomy" (following Breton and Dalmazzone in Breton, Galeotti, Salmon, and Wintrobe, (2002). However, he or she gains the experience of greater solidarity or social cohesion or "belongingness."

To sketch a model of how this process operates, assume that an individual is endowed with a certain set of beliefs, and, corresponding to this, a certain identity. If the person agrees to join a cult, the price of admission is, in part, that he or she adopt certain beliefs that are sanctioned by the cult. Additional requirements might be participation in cult activities or some other demonstration of sharing in the beliefs and goals of the cult. For example, at the bottom of Putnam's NOCE there appears to be a process of *participation* in civic events – going to a political rally or an interest group meeting, or writing a letter or other works about political issues or political or community philosophy.

The organization, in turn, supplies the individual with the sense of belonging to a community, by organizing events or activities that individuals can attend and participate in, meet and get to know others in the organization, by providing a framework of beliefs that the individual can adopt and identify with. The set of beliefs is common to all members to a greater or lesser degree. The more united the membership is in its beliefs, the greater the willingness of the members to sacrifice their time and energy and other resources in support of the goals of the organization, and the greater the organization's capacity for action or power.[3]

Now, it could be argued that there are other processes by which solidarity or horizontal social capital gets formed, and these do not necessarily involve conformity. But, to repeat, if there were disagreement – if the members of the group broke up into factions, say – it is not obvious that social capital or solidarity would be formed. That is, it is not obvious, at least to me, that social capital is formed through a process of vigorous argument ending in a stalemate of opposing viewpoints. So it seems to me that the process of agreement – which I model here as trade in beliefs – is essential for social cohesion or solidarity to be formed.[4]

There are four further aspects of the process that seem important:

1. Presumably, in order to be accepted for membership, a certain minimum sacrifice of beliefs and a certain minimum level of participation will be required.
2. The process of "indoctrination" (trade) typically does not happen all at once but takes place in small steps. Thus, initially, recruits are exposed to relatively innocuous ideas, and only as their involvement deepens are they treated to the full panoply of ideas, paranoid conceptions, and philosophical notions that characterize the cult's ideology.[5]
3. An important question, which so far has been left unanswered, is the problem of how trades are enforced. One cannot make a binding contract stating that person A will receive x amount of social cohesion in exchange for agreeing to subscribe to beliefs y and z. The reason is not only the issue of enforceability, that is, determining whether the social cohesion supplied was deficient, or whether A really changed his mind in the ways agreed to. The very making of the contract would imply that neither party was sincere and deprive A of his social cohesion and the group of knowing that A subscribed to the requisite beliefs. However, this doesn't imply that the trade cannot take place, only that the mechanism of enforcement is more subtle: It requires trust. In other words, the more trust there is between A and the members of the group, the more it will be possible for the trade to take place. So, it follows that groups with higher

---

[3] See Howitt and Wintrobe (1995) or Wintrobe (1998, Chapter 11), for a formal model of the proposition that a government's capacity for action is related to the similarity of beliefs of the groups within it. Here we are simply extending this idea to any organization.

[4] Another complication is that other rewards could be given out for conformity besides social cohesion. If the reward is cash, for example, this might be an instance of *corruption* and therefore of the destruction rather than the creation of trust.

[5] Other accounts of social interactions stress that involvement proceeds in small steps. For details see Wintrobe (2001).

social capital can come closer to having a more consistent viewpoint than those that have less. This appears to give rise to a chicken-and-egg problem: Trust is necessary for the trades to occur that establish trust. But the proper way to formulate this proposition is simply that groups that can communicate easily are more capable of building greater trust than those that cannot. It also follows that trust can sometimes get stuck in a low-level equilibrium, as may be the case for southern Italy and other places. However, this provides one reason why trust is contagious once it gets started (see number 4).

4. Note that implicitly there is the element of leadership. Who is it that determines the beliefs of the group? Who is that decides when these beliefs have to be changed? How is the minimum level of participation decided? Who decides whether cohesion is given out or withheld? The point is vital, because it suggests that in all groups with some degree of solidarity, there is always some element of hierarchy. So it is not clear that the distinction between horizontal and vertical trust can be completely maintained. Moreover, once there is leadership, it is no longer obvious that the goals of the members reflect the ideals of their members. Indeed, I have argued elsewhere (Wintrobe, 2002) that the greater the control of a leader, the more he can turn the organization to his own ends and the more likely the organization is to become extremist.

In so-called "charismatic" groups such as the Branch Davidians, the Scientologists, Divine Light Mission and the Aum Shinrikyu, Galanter found that social cohesiveness was tied to a charismatic leader whose flock "revered" him (p. 12). In the Branch Davidian cult, for example, compliance with the leader's (David Koresh) expectations was promoted by a series of reinforcements. According to Galanter, these produced a relief in depression and anxiety to the degree that a believer accepted the group's creed and its rules of behavior. By virtue of this relief effect, a member's mood became dependent on the degree of his or her commitment in the group. The consequence was that, as Galanter notes, "This emotional dependence on the group and its beliefs left the sect members fully responsive to Koresh's demands, which escalated to include beating young boys and engaging young girls in sexual activity" (Galanter, 1999, p. 170).

The importance of leadership is also often emphasized in works on extremist political movements. In Appleby's collection, "Spokesmen for the Despised" (1997), on Middle East extremism, the main theoretical message extracted is the presence of charismatic leadership. Thus, Appleby concludes the volume with the observation that "the various profiles confirm the centrality of strong male charismatic leadership in the formation and growth of the most powerful fundamentalist movements of the Middle East. . . . In each of these cases [radical Jews, Islamic fundamentalists, and the Protestant fundamentalist movements] the charismatic fundamentalist preacher is the catalyst for the hardening of resentment into organized opposition" (Appleby, 1997, p. 398). Chong (1991) also emphasizes the leadership factor in his study of the (by now usually viewed as entirely mainstream) American civil rights movement.

To sum up, there appear to be three elements involved in the formation of cult membership:

1. Leadership
2. Conformity
3. Solidarity

These three are characteristic of many other forms of social interactions (Wintrobe, 2001).

Similar propositions may be advanced for religious groups.[6] In sociology, perhaps the most celebrated recent work on this topic is Michael Hechter's *A Theory of Group Solidarity* (1987). Hechter, in turn, quotes Emil Durkheim on the subject of solidarity among religious groups:

[A religious group] does not unite men by an exchange and reciprocity of services, a temporal bond of union which permits and even presupposes differences, but which a religious society cannot form. It socializes men only by attaching them completely to an identical body of doctrine and socializes them in proportion as this body of doctrine is extensive and firm. The more numerous the manners of action and thought of a religious character are, which are accordingly removed from free inquiry, the more the idea of God presents itself in all details of existence, and makes individual wills converge to one identical goal. (Durkheim, 1897/1951, p. 159), quoted in Hechter (1987, p. 17)

Thus in one sense the motive behind religious attendance may be social interaction – people attend church to meet others, for example (Glaeser et al. 1996). More subtly, there may again be a trade involving *beliefs* – the individual receives the benefit of social cohesion in exchange for agreeing to beliefs sanctioned by the church.[7] Of course, the mechanism will seldom be perfect, and the Catholic Church, for example, has been plagued by the problem of heresy since its inception (Duffy 1997). The Church's response has been to supplement social cohesion with central control and direction, a formal hierarchy,

---

[6] Another, related approach to religious participation is provided by Larry Iannnaccone (1988, 1992, 1997), who suggests that the key distinction between church and sect is that between group and individually oriented religions. Iannaccone defines a *sectarian religion* in terms of the degree to which the religious group demands sacrifice and stigma, or the degree to which it limits and therefore increases the cost of non-group activities to its members (1997, p. 104). The purpose is to control free riding In his analysis, the membership benefits from these demands, because the utility of collective religious belief depends positively on the average level of participation in group activities.

[7] Pierre Salmon has remarked to me that in some cases, the trade may be exactly the reverse: The individual wants the belief rather than the social cohesion and supplies the social cohesion in exchange for participating in the Church's belief system!

approved dogmas, and a complex formal structure of bishops, popes, and so forth.[8]

In a particularly desperate moment (at the First Vatican Council in the 19th century), the Catholic Church introduced the notion of papal infallibility in order to solve this problem. (Duffy, 1997, p. 230). However, one surprising thing about papal infallibility is that it turned out to be a two-edged sword. For example, when Pope John XXII repudiated the teaching that Christ was a pauper, Franciscan theologians insisted that earlier popes had repeatedly accepted it. Thus, they argued that since true popes do not err, Pope John's rejection of the doctrine just proved that he was no longer a true pope (Duffy, p. 131).

Similar processes take place for admission to a youth gang (see Jankowski, 1991), or to the mafia (Gambetta, 1993; Hess, 1973), where, because of the nature of the group, further demonstrations that the person has given up some of his autonomy and identified with the organization may be required. In the same way, but perhaps to a lesser extent, political parties may make similar requirements. Marx thought that the working class, interpreted as a group, could attain consciousness by itself, but that idea turned out to be wrong, as Lenin showed, essentially because of the free rider problem. Lenin argued that leadership was essential for the working class to obtain consciousness of its predicament. The Communist Party required complete agreement with its ideology and participation in its activities as a condition for continued membership, and periodically removed people from its membership lists who did not fulfill this requirement. Indeed the doctrine was, and continues to be, updated by a process where once the new doctrine was propounded everyone had to follow the "party line." Of course, other political parties are more flexible, but they all demand acquiescence to their platforms and ideology to a considerable extent.

To the extent that this process of trade takes place, the person who holds a belief that appears on the surface to be irrational is not behaving irrationally: The rationality consists not in the content of the belief, but in the reason for holding it. On this reading, the person who believes there is a U.N. plot to take over the U.S. government is no more irrational than the professor who states to the officials in the administration of his university that all the members of his department deserved to get tenure: In both cases, the reason for the belief may be solidarity or social cohesion, not the coherence of the belief itself.

One advantage of the present formulation is that we are able to show some implications. The basic proposition of the model is that social cohesion (solidarity) and conformity (unity of belief) are positively related. A second proposition is that social cohesion will tend to be positively related to the extremity of beliefs.

---

[8] Mario Ferrero (2000) discusses a related problem of how the Church continues to survive in a centralized fashion and how it motivates its followers. He suggests that the "competitition for sainthood" provides one important mechanism which explains how the Church has been able to thrive for so long.

The reason is that if the views are really extreme, people typically have to give up a lot in the way of their original (more mainstream) identity to adopt them. Hence they will demand more social cohesion in return for adopting them. Other propositions may be derived if we ask what happens when the price of a belief or of social cohesion changes. One interesting variable here is the relationship between the true preferences of the population and the preferences of the leader. It seems reasonable to suppose that the closer the true preferences of the group are to the preferences of the leader, the easier it should be to give them up in favour of the leader's preferences. It follows that the price demanded in terms of loss of autonomy is lower in such cases, and the outcome should be that the organization's membership is likely to have a more consistent point of view.

A third proposition concerns individuals with "weak" identity or low autonomy. Our model suggests that such individuals will be giving up less by joining relatively extreme groups than those with strong identities and will therefore be more likely to do so, *ceteris paribus*. So the membership of such groups should be composed usually of people with weak identities.

A fourth proposition has to do with the decline of solidarity (Putnam's hypothesis). The most natural interpretation of this is that either the value of solidarity has fallen, or the price of solidarity (agreeing with the beliefs of the group) has risen. I have suggested elsewhere (Wintrobe, 2000) that the first proposition is true, at least as far as business firms are concerned. But the second proposition is also interesting. The next two sections pursue this point.

THE GENERAL WILL

One implication of my model is that the more trade in beliefs there is, the more that the group will have a unified point of view. Consequently, it may be tempting to interpret the outcome of the trading process described in the previous section as suggesting one way to generate a common "will" along the lines originally put forth by Rousseau. Of course, many now think the idea of a group will seriously misplaced. For example, Hardin says that "there can be no common will of a people numerous enough to constitute a nation. It is a fallacy of composition to suppose that there is a common will" (Hardin in Breton, Galeotti, Salmon and Wintrobe, 2002, p. 14).

Runciman and Sen (1965) suggest that one way to provide a modern interpretation of Rousseau is to employ the Prisoners' Dilemma. They interpret the general will as the cooperative solution to the game and point out that this differs from the equilibrium outcome, where people have a tendency to defect. They suggest that the equilibrium or defection solution may be likened to Rousseau's "will of all," whereas the cooperative solution represents the "general will." They also argue that this supplies a meaning to the phrase "forced to be free": In the case of the two prisoners in the Prisoners' Dilemma, they would both be ready to appoint an agent who would see to it that neither of them confessed.

From their arguments, and many other examples, it is apparent that the notion of democracy in Rousseau's sense (as opposed to the Schumpeter-Downs conception of it as essentially meaning electoral competition) continues to appeal to many scholars of politics. On these accounts, democracy is a system that somehow implements the "will" of the people – that is, it is a means to collective ends, rather than just a method of for aggregating narrow interests (see, e.g., Arblaster, 1987; or Grofman and Feld, 1988). Normally, in such accounts, it seems to be accepted that, as Grofman and Feld put it, "democracy works better when individuals try to see beyond their narrow self-interests to see the collective good" (p. 572).

Trade in beliefs provides one way to get a uniform viewpoint in a group, though it is hard to imagine the process of trade going on at the national level. Still, even at that level, political parties could "logroll" among platforms. Of course, the process is more likely to take place in small groups. The result could be that every member of a group could be 100% in favor of a proposition or policy even though many of them have traded away their original beliefs.

What is the relationship between the formation of social capital and the formation of the general will? The general will is not capital – it is a policy or an opinion. Apart from showing one way it could be developed, the model suggests that it may be difficult to maintain the conditions required by Rousseau: Either the members will tend to develop solidarity among themselves, in which case their views may not remain independent, or they will break up into factions. This point is pursued further in the next section.

CONDORCET

In a fascinating article, Grofman and Feld (1988) interpret Rousseau's general will as meaning the same thing that Condorcet asserted in his famous jury theorem. Condorcet's theorem says that if voters are addressing a common question with only two possible answers, one of which is correct and one incorrect (such as the guilt or innocence of an accused criminal), and if the average probability of each voter choosing the correct answer is greater than .5, the probability that the answer chosen by a majority of them will be the correct one increases to certainty as the size of the group increases. (Condorcet 1976, 33–70).

The theorem is really a consequence of the law of large numbers and does not attribute any magical power to group decision making. The best way to see this point is to note that if the probability of an individual choosing the correct answer falls below .5, the probability of getting the correct answer for the group as its size increases goes to zero. Changes in group size can have other consequences. For example, as the group increases in size, it may become more difficult for each one to identify with the group, as Grofman and Feld (1988) put it, "in such a way as to prevent their decision making being distorted by bias and interest" (p. 1323).

Still, the theorem is inviting, and a welcome corrective to the negative view of group decision making based on the Arrow problem that groups are necessarily prone to instability. However, there is a third condition necessary for the theorem to hold: The individuals must decide independently. To the extent that they do not, that is to the extent that they form a herd or a faction where each individual decision is based on the decisions of others rather than his own private information, the power of the group process to reach the right decision is lost.

It follows that, in terms of the conditions required for group processes to reach optimal judgements, the conditions suggested by Condorcet are exactly the opposite of my trade in beliefs! That is, precisely to the extent that someone makes a decision based not on his or her own information but because someone else is deciding that way, so the conditions for group processes to improve decision making are violated. That is exactly what happens with the trade in beliefs described previously. It follows that Condorcet's theorem is a nice way to show the costs of conformity. As in the model of Banerjee (1992), there is an externality when an individual changes a belief not on the basis of his or her own information but because someone else holds that belief: The externality is that the benefit of that person's own information to the group is lost.

Perhaps this suggests a different explanation for Putnam's evidence about the decline of solidarity in the United States. It's worth recalling after all that the great civic generation of the 1950s was noted also for its conformity. The year 1947 saw the release of the film, *Gentleman's Agreement*, which described the process by which Jews were excluded from the mainstream of American society. The 1950s witnessed little in the way of attempts to break up discrimination against blacks. American society presented a homogeneous front, it was pre-occupied with the fight against communism (in which Elia Kazan, the director of *Gentleman's Agreement*, took part by testifying to the House Un-American Activities Committee), and dissent or alternative lifestyles were not particularly welcome.

In social science, perhaps the most famous work of the time was William Whyte's *The Organization Man*, which described the conformity of life in the American business firm. At one point, in a chapter entitled "The Fight Against Genius," Whyte asks the reader to do a "mental exercise" and imagine what would happen if science were to be organized like a business firm. Among the results would be, he suggests,

1. Scientists would now concentrate on the practical application of previously discovered ideas rather than the discovery of new ones.
2. They would rarely work by themselves but rather as units of scientific cells.
3. Organization loyalty, getting along with people, etc., would be considered just as important as thinking.
4. Well-rounded team players would be more valuable than brilliant men, and a very brilliant man would probably be disruptive. Lastly and most important, *these things*

would be so because people believe this is the way it should be. (Whyte, 1957, p. 225, italics added)

Today the popular notion of the workplace is possibly expressed best by the TV show, *Survivor*, in which, as the critic Natalie Southwork in the *Toronto Globe and Mail* put it,

"the show's scheming, backstabbing and fragile alliances are all features of the modern workplace. . . . The participants on the television hit bear a striking resemblance to a group of middle managers trying to avoid a downsizing hit list at a not-so-profitable company." (*The Globe and Mail,* August 22, 2002, p. R1).

On this view, people in the 1950s were more conformist than people now. Recall that on our analysis all forms of solidarity imply some kind of control, if only in the form of peer pressure. One can point to things like the growth of the counterculture, the Vietnam War, and the exposing of the private behavior of heroes in authority like John F. Kennedy in the 1960s, all of which have made Americans more skeptical than before. The fall of communism in the late 1980s and 1990s removed a major cause of American solidarity. The information revolution has also turned out to favor freedom. Whatever one thinks of these events, the increased distrust in authority and skepticism about social pressures are, in my view, not necessarily bad. However, it is hard to be salutary about the decline of trust in the workplace, as the downsizing revolution has meant that firms increasingly are dispensing with trust in their employees (Wintrobe, 2000).

THE OPTIMUM LEVEL OF SOLIDARITY

From an organization's point of view, one cost of solidarity (in my sense) is the suppression of true information that gets lost in the process of conformity. Or, looked at in Condorcetian terms, the number of independent votes is smaller whenever a group forms into a herd. So the cost is that its decisions are not as good.[9]

What is the benefit of solidarity to the organization? Solidarity implies unity of belief and purpose. With all agreed on the goals of the group, this raises the possibility of and the gains to collective action, as discussed previously.

It seems reasonable to assume that the marginal benefits of solidarity *to the organization* (not to the individual – the costs in terms of the individual's loss of autonomy don't play any role here) are positive but diminishing, that is, $B = B(S)$, $B'_s > 0$, $B''_s < 0$. Marginal costs $C(S)$, which arise from the reduced quality of organizational decision making are positive and increasing, as is usually assumed for damage functions, $C'_s > 0$, $C''_s > 0$. The optimum level of

---

[9] Perhaps it is worth emphasizing that it is also possible to have suppression of information that does *not* create solidarity. An obvious example is communism; it is not obvious that every repressive act of the system created more solidarity.

solidarity to the organization is therefore where the marginal benefits (increased collective action) are equal to marginal costs, that is where $B'_s = C'_s$. It follows that the larger the costs of solidarity *to the organization*, and the smaller the benefits, the less solidarity there will be.

To illustrate, consider the case of religious groups, a particularly interesting example. It would seem that here, unity in belief is paramount, because the good (or "service") that the church sells is a pure credence good. If competing views are allowed to be heard, then the church's message may suffer a loss in credibility, and credibility is everything in the case of a pure credence good. However, the actual truth of church doctrine is not the result of a voting process or group judgement but is "revealed." For doctrines like this it would seem that the cost due to the loss of true information from the individuals within it is not that large. For both these reasons the optimal level of solidarity in the case of religious groups is high.

Political parties bear some resemblance to the church, the more so, the more they are ideologically based. However, for a business firm, truth is "revealed" through the balance sheet, in terms of the purchases of its customers or the expectations of the capital market about the firm's future profits. Unity is not important unless it bears on the credibility of the firm's product. So business firms can dispense with solidarity whenever it is not in their interest. Within the firm, Becker argued in his early work on human capital (1994) that, to motivate employees to accumulate firm specific human capital, business firms would want to be a party to implicit contracts with their employees. In these contracts employees are typically paid wages beneath their marginal products in early years and compensated by above-marginal-product wages in later years. However, more recently firms have reneged on these contracts to appropriate the investments in firm specific capital for their executives or for their shareholders, as I have argued elsewhere (Wintrobe 1999).

What about a university? It would appear that unity in this case is relatively unimportant, while independence of thought is most important. The optimal level of solidarity would appear to be low in this case. Indeed, organizations like universities do not have formal requirements that people subscribe to a certain set of beliefs to be hired (accepted as a member). The model would predict that the result is that social cohesion or solidarity is low in these cases. However, informal pressures along these lines, especially within departments of disciplines with a strong paradigm can be quite high. The careers of individuals often hinge on their publication in certain places defined as correct by some group of their peers. It follows that if the optimal level of solidarity is to be kept low, institutions should be put in place to assure independence of thought. This provides a rationale for tenure.[10]

---

[10] Of course, tenure is a two-edged sword: It guarantees intellectual freedom once you have it. But by forcing you to follow the paradigm of your elders while young and untenured, it causes

CONTAGION: SOCIAL CAPITAL AND DEMOCRACY

There is one proposition about social capital which has not yet been noted: Social capital, like any other form of network externality, is contagious (Katz and Shapiro 1985; Becker 1996): its value is larger, the larger the stock. This implies that it gives rise to another bind of democracy, the constitution.

The contagion property is particularly important in politics, where genuine information is weak and the incentive to collect it is not there because of the free rider problem. Indeed, it is well known that ideas and political support are contagious, hence the name *bandwagon* effects. Our model explains things like bandwagons and fads in terms of the desire for social cohesion. People adopt an idea in order to be "in," that is, to be either in the vanguard of or at least a part of the group or movement that promotes the idea. It need have nothing to do with the logical case for the idea (if any) at all. Thus, there has never really been a case on esthetic, medical, or logical grounds for hula hoops in the 1950s, tie-dyed T-shirts in the 1960s, disco culture in the 70s, backward baseball caps (the 80s), or wearing earrings in your tongue (the 90s and beyond).

One might object that where there is lots of social capital, that is, lots of horizontal associations à la Putnam, this acts as a bulwark against instability. But that may be exactly wrong: There is evidence that the more social capital there is, the more *unstable* the polity. The classic example is the Weimar Republic. It was thought Hitler rose because Germany was an "atomized" society with few individuals who were members of groups or voluntary associations, but in fact exactly the opposite was true: Germany was particularly rife with horizontal associations, that is, there was lots of social capital in precisely Putnam's (2000) sense in Weimar Germany![11] Indeed, many organizations joined the Hitler movement *as a group*, encouraged by their leaders.

It follows that one of the binds of democracy gives rise to another: The more social capital there is, the greater the demand for constitutional protections in the form of checks and balances. One important application of these ideas is to the reasoning of Madison and others in *The Federalist Papers* about the design of the American Constitution. There the case for a constitution is made on grounds of the instabilities caused by passions. And one big source of instability was said to be bandwagon effects, especially under the influence of the wrong kind of political leaders.

---

young academics to devote the years when they have the greatest energy to conform, generally speaking, to the paradigm of their elders, since this is normally the only way to get out enough publications to earn tenure. Still, it means that the relatively old at least have some freedom, wheareas in the absence of tenure no one would.

[11] See Wintrobe (1998) and references therein.

The Founding Fathers were especially worried about demagoguery: the notion that citizens could be "misled by the artful misrepresentations of interested men," or by the "wiles of parasites and sycophants, by the snares of the ambitious, the avaricious, the desperate."[12]

Another implication of the analysis is that it shows one reason why the decline of social capital in the United States could have been so precipitous as it appears in Putnam's charts: Since it is contagious, once it starts to decline, the process sets up expectations that are self-fulfilling. And there are applications to other societies. Thus, in Russia, the fall of the communist system left lots of social capital, now unconnected to the Communist hierarchy, and these horizontal connections gave birth to the "antimodern society" of contemporary Russia, to use Richard Rose's (1999) phrase.

CONCLUSION

Alexis de Tocqueville's classic *Democracy in America* (1835, 2000) is often referred to in studies of social capital. Indeed, Putnam (2000) refers to him as its "patron saint" for the way in which he glowingly spoke about the American proclivity to join associations. However, de Tocqueville also described America as "the most conformist society he had ever seen." In our view, these two observations are related. The central proposition of this chapter is that there is a positive relationship between social capital, interpreted as solidarity, and conformity in the sense of uniformity of beliefs. This chapter sketches a model in which people trade their beliefs in exchange for social cohesion or solidarity. Thus the same process that produces trust or social capital also produces conformity. No doubt there are other ways in which trust can be produced that do not have this effect, and I have in fact mentioned some in the chapter. However, I suggest that uniformity of belief will be especially characteristic of organizations or groups where social cohesion is deep.

The model developed here can be used to show the optimal level of solidarity for a number of different types of organizations, including political parties, religious groups, and business firms. One can also predict some of the situations in which social capital would rise or fall (depreciate). Thus, if Putnam's provocative evidence that social capital has been declining in America since 1970 or so is accepted, one can look for an explanation in the costs of social capital as well as in its value and a primary cost of solidarity is the costs of conformity. Moreover, if social capital is contagious, as I have argued, it is possible to understand how it could have declined so precipitously in the United States.

---

[12] Federalist Paper no. 71, p. 432, quoted in Page and Shapiro (1989), p. 57.

REFERENCES

Appleby, R. Scott, ed., *Spokesmen for the Despised: Fundamentalist Leaders of the Middle East.* Chicago: Chicago University Press, 1997.

Arblaster, Anthony, *Democracy: Concepts in Social Thought.* Minneapolis: University of Minnesota Press, 1987.

Banerjee, Abhijit V., "A Simple Model of Herd Behaviour," *Quarterly Journal of Economics,* 107(3) (1992), 797–817.

Banfield, Edward, *The Moral Basis of a Backward Society.* Glenfield, IL: The Free Press, 1958.

Becker, Gary, *Human Capital,* 3d edition. Chicago: University of Chicago Press, 1994.

_____, *Accounting for Tastes.* Cambridge, MA: Harvard University Press, 1996.

Breton, Albert, Gianluigi Galeotti, Pierre Salmon, and Ronald Wintrobe, *Political Extremism and Rationality.* New York: Cambridge University Press, 2002.

_____, and Silvana Dalmazzone, "Information Control, Loss of Autonomy, and the Emergence of Political Extremism," paper delivered at the Villa Colombella seminar on Political Extremism, Vichy, France, May 1998. To appear in Albert Breton, Gianluigi Galeotti, Pierre Salmon, and Ronald Wintrobe, *Political Extremism and Rationality,* Cambridge University Press, 2002.

_____, and Ronald Wintrobe, *The Logic of Bureaucratic Conduct.* New York: Cambridge University Press, 1982.

Chong, Dennis, *Collective Action and the Civil Rights Movement.* Chicago: University of Chicago Press, 1991.

Coleman, James S., *Foundations of Social Theory.* Cambridge, MA: Harvard University Press, 1990.

Condorcet, Marquis de, *Selected Works.* English, Indianapolis: Bobbs-Merrill, 1976.

Della Porta, Donatella, "Social Capital, Beliefs in Government and Political Corruption," in Susan J. Pharr and Robert D. Putnam, *Disaffected Democracies: What's Troubling the Trilateral Countries?* Princeton, NJ: Princeton University Press, 2000.

de Tocqueville, Alexis, *Democracy in America,* translated by Henry Reeve, 2000 [1835], New York: Bantam Classic.

Duffy, Eamon, *Saints and Sinners: A History of the Popes.* New Haven, CT: Yale University Press, 1997.

Durkheim, Emile, *Suicide.* New York: Free Press, 1951 (originally published 1897).

Ferrero, Mario, "Competition for Sainthood and the Millenial Church," paper delivered at the European Public Choice Society Meetings, Siena, 2000.

Fukuyama, Francis, *Trust: The Social Virtues and the Creation of Prosperity.* London: Hamish Hamilton, 1995.

Galanter, Marc, *Cults: Faith, Healing and Coercion,* 2d ed. New York: Oxford University Press, 1999.

Gambetta, Diego, *The Sicilian Mafia: The Business of Private Protection.* Cambridge: Harvard University Press, 1993.

Glaeser, Edward, Bruce Sacerdote, and Jose A. Scheinkman, "Crime and Social Interactions," *Quarterly Journal of Economics* 111 (1996), 507–548.

Grofman, Bernard, and Scott Feld, "Rousseau's General Will: A Condorcetian Perspective," *American Political Science Review,* 82 (1988), 567–576.

Hechter, Michael, *Principles of Group Solidarity*. Berkeley: University of California Press, 1987.

Hess, H., *Mafia and Mafiosi: The Structure of Power*. Lexington, MA: Lexington Books, 1973.

Howitt, Peter, and Ronald Wintrobe, "The Political Economy of Inaction," *Journal of Public Economics,* 56 (1995), 329–53.

Iannaccone, Lawrence R., "A Formal Model of Church and Sect," *American Journal of Sociology,* 94 (1988 supplement), S241–S268.

_____, "Sacrifice and Stigma: Reducing Free Riding in Cults, Communes and Other Collectives," *Journal of Political Economy,* 100 (1992), 271–291.

_____, "Towards an Economic Theory of Fundamentalism," *Journal of Institutional and Theoretical Economics,* 153 (1997), 100–121.

Jankowski, Martin Sanchez, *Islands in the Street: Gangs and American Urban Society.* University of California Press, 1991.

Karl, Jonathan, *The Right To Bear Arms: The Rise of America's New Militias.* New York: Harper Paperback, 1995.

Katz, Michael, and Carl Shapiro," Network Externalities, Competition, and Compatibility," *American Economic Review,* June, 75 (1985), 424–40.

Knack, Stephen, and Phillip Keefer, "Does Social Capital Have an Economic Payoff?" *Quarterly Journal of Economics* 112 (1997), 1251–1289.

Koestler, A., *Darkness at Noon*. Translated by Daphne Hardy. New York: Macmillan, 1941.

Page, Benjamin, and Robert Y. Shapiro, "Restraining the Whims and Passions of the Public," in Bernard Grofman and Donald Wittman, eds., *The Federalist Papers and the New Institutionalism.* New York: Agathon Press, 1989.

Paldam, Martin, "Missing Social Capital and the Transition in Eastern Europe," paper presented at the IMAD conference on Institutions in Transition, Portoroz, Slovenia, June 2000.

Putnam, Robert, *Making Democracy Work*. Princeton, NJ: Princeton University Press, 1993.

_____, *Bowling Alone: The Collapse and Revival of American Community.* New York: Simon and Schuster, 2000.

Rose, Richard, "Getting Things Done in an Antimodern Society: Social Capital Networks in Russia" in P. Dasgupta and I. Serageldin, eds., *Social Capital: A Multifaceted Perspective.* Washington, DC: World Bank, 1999.

Runciman, W.G., and Amartya K. Sen, "Games, Justice and the General Will," *Mind* (New Series) 74 Issue 296 (1965), 554–562.

Salmon, Pierre, "Trust and Trans-Bureau Networks in Organizations," *European Journal of Poltitical Economy,* 4 (Extra Issue), (1988), 229–52.

Uslaner, Eric M., "Democracy and Social Capital," in Mark Warren, ed., *Democracy and Trust.* New York: Cambridge University Press, 1999.

Warren, Mark E., *Democracy and Trust*. New York: Cambridge University Press, 1999.

Whyte, William, *The Organization Man*. New York: Doubleday, 1957.

Wintrobe, Ronald, *The Political Economy of Dictatorship*. New York: Cambridge University Press, 1998.

_____, "Downsizing Trust," in Gianluigi Galeotti, Pierre Salmon, and Ronald Wintrobe, eds., *Competition and Structure: The Political Economy of Collective Decisions: Essays in Honor of Albert Breton.* New York: Cambridge University Press, 2000.

_____, "The Economics of Group Social Relations," *Journal for Institutional Innovation, Development, and Transition,* vol 5, 2001.

_____, "Leadership and Passion in Extremist Politics" in Albert Breton, Gianluigi Galeotti, Pierre Salmon, and Ronald Wintrobe, *Political Extremism and Rationality.* Cambridge: Cambridge University Press, 2002.

_____, and Albert Breton, "Organizational Structure and Productivity," *American Economic Review,* June 1986.

9

The Bonds of Democratic Politics – An Economic Perspective

Stefan Voigt

INTRODUCTION

The welfare state that co-emerged with industrialization and democratization can be interpreted as an attempt to make the fate of the worst off independent of their personal bonds, that is, the ability and the willingness of their personal environment to help in times of need. Majoritarian – democratic – politics tend to be redistributive. Thereby, they reduce the potential value of personal bonds. Economists could thus argue that democratic politics can be expected to lead – at least in the long run – to a loosening of personal bonds. On the other hand, an extended welfare state seems only sustainable if those who are net-payers feel some sort of general solidarity for those they are supporting. In other words, majoritarian decision-making seems to drive out personal bonds but depends on the existence of more general anonymous ones.

It has become fashionable to criticize economic thinking for being too individualist. Some communitarians claim that the individualist approach of economics drives out civic virtue (e.g., Etzioni 1988). Among public choice scholars, a new trend to criticize the simplistic behavioral assumptions of *homo oeconomicus* seems to be emerging: Frey (1997) states that a constitution for knaves crowds out civic virtue and Brennan and Hamlin (2000) argue in favor of a behavioral model that allows for motivational heterogeneity. In their arguments, the possibility of being interested in the public good plays a central role. Within the confines of this chapter, this could be a bond toward the community.

On the one hand, economists usually do not deal with concepts such as "bonds." On the other, over the last couple of years, quite a voluminous literature

This chapter was written while the author was a Fellow at the Institute for Advanced Study in Berlin (Wissenschaftskolleg zu Berlin) and a member of its AGORA group. He thanks all his co-Fellows for numerous discussions on this and related topics. Thanks are also due to Roger Congleton, Andrea Eisenberg, Alan Hamlin, Margaret Levi, and two anonymous referees for helpful suggestions.

concerning values and norms, trust, the relevance of communication, and civil society has emerged, sometimes by scholars at the edge of the discipline, sometimes by scholars considered to belong to the core. This chapter attempts to make the term *bonds* tractable within the logic of economics. Bonds can be analyzed both as exogenous variables that determine other variables, such as transaction costs, distribution, or growth, and as endogenous variables determined by other variables that would have to be identified. We look at bonds from both angles. Bonds can be directly relevant in that they reduce transaction costs incurred to secure voluntary exchange on a private law basis. Our main concern here, however, is with issues of collective choice, that is, issues that are relevant for a large group of people, possibly the entire community. If bonds influence the valid political institutions – and are possibly also influenced by them – then this will have indirect effects on the costs of transacting if we assume that the political institutions constitute a framework for economic transactions. More specifically, we will set out to compare the bonds of democratic politics with those of non-democratic politics. Here, a chicken-egg problem almost suggests itself: Are bonds – of whatever sort – a precondition for establishing sustainable democracy, or is democracy a precondition for certain bonds to evolve? On a methodological level: Are bonds subject to deliberate choice? If not, how do they emerge and – even more important – how are they transferred?

Hayek's insight that "a group of men can form a society capable of making laws because they already share common beliefs which make discussion and persuasion possible and to which the articulated rules must conform in order to be accepted as legitimate" (1960, 181) points to various aspects involved. Building on that insight, it is hypothesized here that – on top of making laws – only some groups who have at their disposition certain bonds will be able to establish democratic regimes.

The remainder of the chapter is organized as follows. In the section, "Concepts," the basic concepts, that is, "bonds" and "democratic politics" will be delineated. The section on "Conjecture" presents some conjectures on the relationship between bonds and democratic politics. In its first part, the focus is on the preconditions that have to be fulfilled for a group of people to establish sustainable democracy. In the second part, bonds will be assumed as endogenous to the political (democratic) process. The last section, "Open Questions," concludes the chapter.

CONCEPTS

Bonds

Homo oeconomicus does not know any bonds. He is modeled as neither benevolent nor malevolent but as completely uninterested in the well-being of others.

In his simplest version, he is furthermore modeled as trying to maximize his individual utility in every single instance. It is well known that these attempts can be futile and that such a (myopic) utility maximizer might end up being worse off than somebody who adopts a more long-term stance or who follows a rule of thumb (Sen 1977; Heiner 1983). It can therefore be in the rational self-interest of a utility maximizer to bind himself against short-term temptations. The ability to credibly commit can make oneself better off and can therefore be rationally striven for. This consideration has often been transferred on the collective level: An entire group – in a sane moment – tries to bind itself against short-term temptations that might occur in less sane moments. This can be done, for example, by restricting the domain to which majoritarian decision-making can be applied. This alternative interpretation of the topic of the bonds of democratic politics, however, will not be pursued here.

Instead, we will name three categories of observable behavior that are difficult or impossible to reconcile with the assumption of *homo oeconomicus*. Before proposing a delineation of bonds, some methodological issues involved with a modification of *homo oeconomicus* and rational choice theory will be briefly touched upon.

Three Categories Difficult to Reconcile with Homo Oeconomicus

1. *To help somebody out.* Three subcategories are suggested: (a) To help somebody who is part of the family, (b) to help somebody who is known to the person helping, and (c) to help somebody who is not known to the person helping.

   With regard to the first two subcategories, it could be argued that an infinitely repeated game is being played. Helping others can be perfectly rational if one calculates that one has a positive chance of being in need in later periods. If reciprocity is enforced – if I can only expect to be helped if I have helped others in previous rounds – then it might be perfectly rational to help over a number of periods without any short-term compensation. If actors expect to find themselves in repeated interactions, reputation and reciprocity might be very powerful constraints. It is no problem to incorporate them into traditional rational choice models (see, e.g., Axelrod 1984). But it is difficult to explain the behavior in the third subcategory. Why should anybody rescue someone who is about to drown in an icy river without knowing her and with low odds of ever seeing that person again? Yet behavior like this can be observed daily on a large scale (Frank 1988).

2. *To make a point.* Whereas the category "to help somebody out" aims at an identifiable person, the category "to make a point" includes deviations from rationality attributed to some anonymous concept or attitude. Again, a subcategorization is offered: (a) Deviations due to a concept of

fairness, (b) deviations due to a concept of decency, and (c) deviations due to a concept of civic loyalty.

There is vast evidence from experimental game theory as well as from descriptive decision theory that actors are willing to incur some costs if they perceive others as offending their concept of fairness. The ultimatum game introduced by Güth, Schmittberger, and Schwarze (1982) has been played dozens of times. It has been observed (a) that, very often, splits close to 50:50 are proposed and (b) that proposals that give less than a third to the respondent are often rejected. This is even the case with very substantial stakes as, for example, in Cameron (1999) who has played the game in Indonesia with stakes that constituted approximately three times the average monthly expenditures of the participants. These observations are often explained by drawing on notions of fairness, although this interpretation is anything but generally accepted.[1]

Following Frank (1988), the concept of fairness generally refers to a transaction between people. A transaction is said to be fair if the difference between the buyer's and the seller's reservation prices is split approximately equally (ibid., 164ff.). If would-be buyers reject a transaction in which the surplus is split unequally although the offered price is below their reservation price, they are assumed to be willing to make a point. An example can frequently be observed at gas stations when the major brands are trying to increase the price for fuel: Long queues will build up quickly at so-called unaffiliated stations, with consumers waiting a long time just to save a couple of cents. Decency, on the contrary, is referred to by Frank to cover a variety of circumstances, including such different acts as returning lost wallets, helping people who have fallen ill in the subway, and responding favorably to requests like "tell me how to get to Times Square" on the street (ibid., 212ff.). An example for the subcategory "civic loyalty" would be the "voter's paradox." Economists in general and public choice scholars in particular have trouble explaining why people bother to vote. The chance that a citizen will cast a decisive vote in an election is obviously very low. We claim that citizens want to make a point and do incur some costs to do so.[2]

3. *To further the common good.* The category is conceptually not always clearly separable from the "to make a point" category. It includes voluntary contributions of both time and money to non-profit organizations. They constitute voluntary contributions to the production of public

---

[1] In a "personal review," Güth (1995) warns his fellow game theorists against modifying an assumption here and there because that would lead to a "neoclassical repair shop."

[2] See also Brennan and Lomasky (1993), who describe voting behavior that not only aims at the improvement of one's own position, but that also has the common good in mind as "expressive voting."

goods, an observation that must be stunning for representatives of the narrow view of rationality, since the latter would predict that everybody had an incentive to free ride, and the private provision of public goods would therefore fail in most cases.[3]

After having presented these categories, which serve to question the universal adequacy of the *homo oeconomicus* assumption, an extension of the narrow model seems warranted. Before dealing closer with just one – but very broad – aspect, namely the possibility that bonds can play a role in individual decision-making and can thereby also influence the collective level because they are the result of individual interaction, we will shortly deal with some methodological issues involved.

Some Methodological Issues

If economists observe that values, norms, trust, and the like do play a role in decision-making, they usually try to explain their emergence, maintenance, and modification over time as a consequence of rational choices. Then, even seemingly irrational behavior can be made plausible as rational on a more abstract level. Yet the "super-rationalization" of seemingly irrational behavior can lead to an infinite regress.[4] Choice can only be rational within a given structure. If that structure is itself analyzed within the confines of rational choice theory, at a certain point it is difficult to see how it could be rational itself. Denzau and North (1994) propose to take explicitly into account the mental models upon which people act. Thus, they do not part with the concept of rationality but propose that there is more than a single version of it. The interesting question then is how one can explain the diversity of mental models that people hold. [5]

---

[3] Two additional aspects in which people can be interpreted as deviating from their rational choices are, first, their *limits of computational capacity*. Economic actors might err in calculating expected values, might misperceive or forget information, remember or re-interpret it wrongly, etc. They might also use some rule of thumb in decision-making, based, e.g., on previous experience, thus not using their computational capacity because the opportunity costs are perceived as being too high. And second: *Weakness of will*. Economic actors might deviate from their rational choice due to some short-term temptation. This will not be treated further here, because people are taken to have made a rational decision but just to lack the willpower to stick to it.

[4] Trivers (1971, 35) notes: "Models that attempt to explain altruistic behavior in terms of natural selection are models designed to take the altruism out of altruism."

[5] As far as I can see, no economist is willing to give up the notion of rationality in its entirety. Heiner (1983) and the subsequent literature, e.g., propose rule rationality in which what is rational is not every single choice but rather the choice of a rule that is applied to a sequence of choices later on. But notice that arguing in favor of rule-rationality is not as innocent as it might appear on first sight: if actors are assumed to be boundedly rational, why should they be sufficiently rational to select utility-maximizing rules, given that the complexities connected with the decision are very high? Vanberg (1994, ch. 2) points to learning, trial-and-error, and adaptive behavior as a possible alternative. Giving up the notion of rationality would be equivalent to giving up the entire project of economics.

Others seem to argue that the weight of bonds are partially hard-wired: Robert Frank's (1988) "commitment model" can be read as an approach to solve the commitment problem by recourse to emotions. He argues that emotions like anger or guilt can serve as signals about the type of person one is. If they are costly to fake, they can become a valuable clue in predicting other people's behavior. The benefit of being a cooperator would lie in being able to selectively interact with other cooperators.

But are hard-wired commitment mechanisms subject to deliberate choice? If not, are we genetically determined to become cooperators or defectors? We enter into similar problems once we adopt a Humean stance on norms, as, for example, Robert Sugden (1986, 152) does: "Our desire to keep the good will of others ... is more than a means to some other end. It seems to be a basic human desire. That we have such a desire is presumably the product of biological evolution." One could criticize the assumption that individuals have an inherent desire to keep the good will of others as a dogmatic and unjustifiable rupture of the causal chain. This procedure can, however, be justified by using conjectural history and some group-selection mechanism. One can conjecture that biological evolution has negatively selected those groups of persons that were not endowed with genes striving for the approval of others. This argument is prone to lead directly to an impasse, though: The differences in the bonds shared among the members of different groups are too large to be explained *exclusively* as the result of genetic disposition. Moreover, it should be recognized that the human desire to gain the respect of others works within groups of variable size. It seems that the composition and thus the relevant size of the group within which the approval of others is striven for depends on cultural factors, that is, factors not based on biological evolution.

We have thus identified a fundamental problem: if (the theory of) rational choice is confined to deliberate choice, mechanisms based on hard-wired constraints or biological evolution could not possibly be part of the theory, because they are not chosen by individuals but by "nature." With regard to the evolution of norms, Boyd and Richerson (1994) try to take a mediating position by drawing on three forces of evolution, namely, biased transmission, which is based on explicit choices by the actors; unbiased transmission, which takes place during a person's childhood; and natural selection, which functions just as genetic variation. Biased transmission is described in analogy to the diffusion of innovations. Just as a person has the choice to adopt an innovation, a person has the choice to adopt those memes (Dawkins 1989) for which he has preferences. In our view, the assumption that norms are subject to deliberate choice is mistaken. Norms structure our interactions even if we explicitly refuse to accept them individually – or do not perceive of the necessity to choose at all. The analogy is mistaken, because the adoption of an innovation is subject to deliberate choice, while norms are not. Due to the systems perspective prevalent in evolutionary approaches, the social interactions by which norms are diffused remain unspecified. This, however, should be the very essence of an explanation if norms are to structure social interaction.

Evolutionary game theory is the analytical tool used by many representatives of an evolutionary approach. Compared with standard game theory, it has the advantage of not making such demanding assumptions concerning the computational capacity of the players. A bird or a rat that structures its behavior using trial and error will do. This, however, can also be seen as a disadvantage: It remains unclear what role the human capacity to reason, to conjecture, or to hypothesize is to play in such models. Majeski (1990, 277f.) notes that most empirical work on the evolution of strategies rests on a biological birth–death mechanism. "This is not surprising since it is the only approach that can be formalized and tested without developing a model of individual cognition. It is, however, the least persuasive approach for explaining the effects of norms on social behavior. . . . A rejection of a biological perspective leaves only approaches that have some form of human cognition."

If we are able to identify instances (or circumstances) in which bonds do influence behavior systematically, then the quality of predictions (and/or explanations) that economists can make will improve, if they are taken into account explicitly. This improvement of predictive quality, however, does have its price, namely the increased complexity of the models. In their recent book, Brennan and Hamlin (2000, 23) argue that it is an old methodological principle to choose a weak – instead of a strong – assumption if that will do. With this argument, they hope to make a plea for the possibility of motivational heterogeneity. Until now, motivational homogeneity was presumed: People were supposed to be atomistic and rational utility-maximizers. Now, Brennan and Hamlin claim that the actions of many people might be modeled within such a model correctly many a time, but that some individuals might be motivated by other dispositions – at least some of the time. But allowing for motivational heterogeneity surely reduces parsimony – another hailed principle of modeling. One could possibly respond that "parsimony" has been overvalued, especially when compared to another principle, namely, "congruence of theory and facts," and that such a re-evaluation should take place.

Delineating Bonds

Instead of trying to come up with arguments for more elaborate trade-offs, we propose a pragmatic position here: If we repeatedly and consistently observe behavior that is hard or even impossible to reconcile with the assumptions of *homo oeconomicus*, it might be appropriate to modify or broaden the concept.

We propose to begin with the following utility function:

$$U_i = f(\alpha p_i + \beta p_j) \tag{1}$$

Actor i's utility not only depends on his bundle of private goods p_i, but also on the goods bundle of some other actor j. Traditionally, β is assumed to be zero, that is, the utility somebody else draws from having at her disposal some goods does not influence my utility – neither positively nor negatively. Theoretically, β might well be negative. We propose to talk of bonds only when β takes on a positive value.

This first approximation of what we mean by bonds leads to a host of new questions. As it stands, the equation only seems to hold for a two-person setting. It might, however, be the case that the fate of more than one person is important to i:

$$U_i = f(\alpha p_i + \beta p_j + \chi p_k + \delta p_1 + \cdots) \tag{2}$$

It would seem plausible that the coefficients become smaller, the farther away a person is: a member of the family, a friend or acquaintance, and finally an unknown person. But it might also be possible that positive coefficients not only exist with regard to (known or unknown) individuals, but also with regard to groups of people or even with regard to abstract principles such as one's polis, the state, a certain regime, and so forth. The state is often described as the sole organization endowed with the legitimacy to use violence (Max Weber). Since we are especially interested in the role of bonds with regard to democratic politics, that is, a specific form of running the state, it is here proposed to distinguish between horizontal and vertical bonds: Bonds are horizontal if the entity whose utility increases my own utility is on the same level as I am, that is, if we deal with each other on the basis of private law. We will talk of vertical bonds where the entity has the potential to use violence, that is, if it is (a representative of) the state. To make things even worse, we propose to distinguish between procedural and substantive bonds with regard to vertical entities (Figure 9.1).

Another aspect is whether there are additional limits to the size the individual coefficients can take. This might be especially relevant with respect to the relative sizes of horizontal and vertical coefficients: One can conceive of complementary as well as of competing relationships between these two kinds of bonds. It seems obvious that the size of the coefficients will influence the weight of transaction costs in both their vertical as well as their horizontal variants: Horizontally, exchanges will be less costly because one does not have to secure against all possible contingency, simply because one can count on the other side acting within the "spirit" of the agreement.[6] On the vertical level,

---

[6] Supposing, of course, that the persons one transacts with have a similar utility-function. The question then becomes how one can know the structure of the utility-function of others. If at

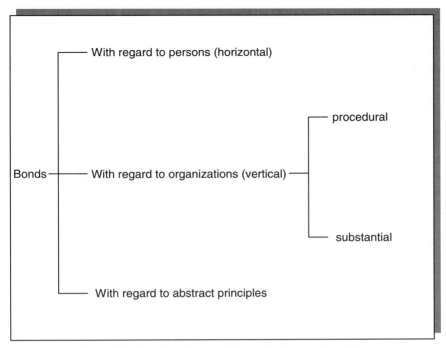

Figure 9.1. The role of bonds with regard to democratic politics.

positive coefficients lower the costs of governing: if taxes are paid more or less voluntarily, the costs for tax collection will be lower; if citizens voluntarily comply with most of the regulations, enforcement costs will be lower, etc.[7] Translated into game theoretic language, actors who are connected by bonds – no matter whether horizontally or vertically – might be able to reduce the

least some arguments of the utility-function are subject to deliberate choice – a question to be discussed in a minute – one could conceive of "networks" of utility-functions. Over a number of years, actors learn by experience to evaluate the weight their own utility takes in the utility-functions of others – and to correspondingly modify their own. Depending on the value of the coefficients, it is, of course, also conceivable that the prices agreed upon – and not only the costs that have to be incurred to exchange goods successfully – will be influenced. Actually, large positive coefficients may even constitute a problem: If actors are known to be benevolent toward others, these others might exploit that benevolence (Samaritan's Dilemma, see, e.g., Buchanan 1975a). Rational benefactors can therefore have an incentive to delegate the provision of social security to the state in order to protect themselves against their own exploitability.

[7] Behind a veil of ignorance or uncertainty (i.e., *ex ante*), rational individuals of the standard *homo oeconomicus* type might very well be ready to agree to a system of state-provided social security. *Ex post*, however, at least those individuals who do not expect to ever profit from such a system would have incentives not to pay their share. In such a case, positive coefficients with regard to some abstract entity such as "the common good" can help to decrease enforcement costs.

conflictual element in mixed motive games, at the limit so far as to transform the structure of the game.[8]

A second group of questions that comes to mind when considering the proposed utility-function is concerned with the determinants of the coefficients. It almost suggests itself to assume that closeness translates into higher values in the coefficients (only chosen, or also given closeness?). The frequency of interaction (exchange of goods) or communication (exchange of opinions) seems to be highly relevant. In Prisoners' Dilemma experiments, it has been shown time and again that (cheap) preplay communication considerably increases the likelihood that the players will cooperate (Bohnet 1997). This could be interpreted as a form of bonds: After having talked cheaply, one knows that one's opponent expects one to cooperate. Of course, it can be argued that the disappointment that the opponent displays after one's own defection decreases one's own utility. But why should one care about the good will of others? We are thus back to Hume's point, already alluded to above. Furthermore, the implicit hypothesis of the topic seems to be that the coefficient in democracies could systematically be different from that in non-democratic regimes.

A third group of questions is concerned with whether the size of the coefficient is subject to deliberate choice. Recently, some economists have argued as if it were: Buchanan (1994), in a paper on meta-preferences, seems to assume that one is able to "choose what to choose." Likewise, Brennan and Hamlin (2000) assume that one can choose one's "disposition," that is, one can choose whether one wants to be a stubborn egoist, a naïve altruist, or somewhere in between. To make the notion of bonds empirically relevant, we are in need of hypotheses that tell us exactly under what circumstances we can expect actors to have substantial bonds either with other persons or with organizations or abstract concepts. We will have to deal with this issue later on.

---

[8] An example could be a Prisoners' Dilemma that is transformed into the game of stag hunt. Suppose the following matrix:

	C		D	
C	3	3	1	4
D	4	1	2	2

Further assume that α is 1 and β is .6 for both players. This leads to a transformation of the game, which is now described by the following matrix (for simplicity, we assume that β is independent of the strategy chosen by one's opponent although this seems to be a highly unlikely assumption):

	C		D	
C	4.8	4.8	2.4	4.6
D	4.6	2.4	3.2	3.2

The game has been transformed from a PD to a game of stag hunt and now has two equilibria. It is by no means certain that (C,C) will emerge as the outcome of the game, but (D,D) is not a certain outcome either.

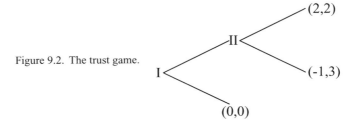

Figure 9.2. The trust game.

On Bonds and Related Concepts

After having described our concept of bonds, it might make sense to demarcate this concept from related ones. In doing so, we might overemphasize commonalities and correspondingly undervalue differences. Granovetter (1992) has introduced the notion of "embeddedness" into economics. His aim is to find a middle ground between the undersocialized actors of economics and the oversocialized ones of sociology. The notion of a generalized morality that some economists have started to use is too broad for him. Instead, he argues that "the role of concrete personal relations and structures (or 'networks') of such relations in generating trust and discouraging malfeasance" have to be taken into account (ibid., 60). Translated into our equations, he seems to argue against a constant positive coefficient that would hold for each and everybody one deals with, but in favor of various coefficients depending on the history of a concrete personal relationship.[9] In that sense, his concept seems to be completely compatible with the concept of bonds proposed here.

Over the past few years, quite a few papers on trust have appeared (see, e.g., Zak and Knack 1998). Often, a trust game of the kind illustrated in Figure 9.2 is the starting point of the analysis.

When deciding whether to enter the game, player I will conclude that if player II gets to choose he will defect, which means that player I will realize a payoff of −1. If he does not enter the game in the first place, he can be certain to reach a better payoff, namely, 0, which is why we would not expect player I ever to enter the game. Yet, if player I could trust player II to cooperate, both players would be better off, both realizing a payoff of 2. This simple two-person game can easily be translated into the notation we introduced above. To cooperate, player II needs to weigh the disutility that he would cause to player I so heavily that it will make him better off to cooperate.[10] Trust and bonds are not identical, but complementary concepts: trust is concerned with the expected behavior of another person, bonds are concerned with the utility function of just one person.

---

[9] The difficulties of ever achieving a general theory following this procedure seem so obvious that they need not be spelled out in detail here.

[10] In the example, this will be the case if the coefficient is at least one. As soon as the game is played repeatedly, externalities between games – e.g., reputation – might lead to different equilibria.

Yet, a specific structure of the utility-function, that is, a specific form of bonds, is a precondition for trust to yield better payoffs. Bonds of a specific kind are therefore a precondition for trust to emerge.

In his seminal work, "Exit, Voice, and Loyalty," Albert Hirschman (1970) defines loyalty as "considerable attachment to a product or an organization" (77). In case the quality of a product decreases (Hirschman's paradigmatic case), the presence of loyalty can make voice more likely in comparison to exit. Loyalty thus means that an actor is somehow not only bound to the product or organization as it is currently available or as it currently stands, but that he has developed some bonds to the product as it used to be or to the principles of the organization that he still endorses. Without overstretching the case, it could probably be said that the utility function of a loyal person contains an argument that puts some positive weight to the utility of those producing the good. It is worth noting, however, that Hirschman describes exit and voice as very different kinds of action: Whereas exit is neat, impersonal, and indirect, voice is described as messy, involving the articulation of critical opinions, and direct and straightforward. If loyalty increases the chances of voice, that is, political action, then loyalty might be a precondition – but also a consequence – of democratic politics in which critical opinions can be freely expressed.

Values have been defined as " conceptions of the desirable, influencing selective behavior" (*International Encyclopedia of the Social Sciences*, entry values). Norms for conduct are sometimes differentiated from values: "Values are not the same as norms for conduct. . . . Values are standards of desirability that are more nearly independent of specific situations. The same value may be a point of reference for a great many specific norms, a particular norm may represent the simultaneous application of several separable values" (ibid.). If values and norms influence behavior, they must somehow enter into a person's utility function. Similarly, breaking a norm must somehow reduce the actor's utility. Two questions arise: How can norm-conforming behavior be explained, and how can one explain that where a norm has been broken, some people are willing to incur costs in order to sanction deviating behavior?

Norm-deviating can be costly if one has internalized following values and norms as "the right thing to do," that is, in the words of Max Weber, if not only purpose-oriented rationality but also value-oriented rationality is admitted. Recognizing the possibility of internalization means breaking with the notion of traditional instrumental rationality. If actors have a capacity to learn, it makes sense to model them not only as forward- but also as backward-looking. They take into account the experiences they have had in previous rounds. Dennis Mueller (1986, 9) writes: "More generally, an effort to model human behavior based on realistic assumptions about 'how men think' as opposed to 'how they would think if they were rational' would place more emphasis on the experience of the individual in relationship to the context in which the decision is posed, and less on the consequences of the decision." Mueller thus pleads for a model of "adaptive egoism" (instead of rational egoism) that takes path-dependence explicitly into account.[11]

Let us now turn to the question why costly sanctioning of norm-deviating behavior should ever occur. If interdependent utility-functions are introduced, it can be made plausible. If the utility of my little brother enters as a positive argument into my utility-function, I could increase my utility by sanctioning my little brother's playing partner. My decision to sanction will depend on the costs involved, that is, on the available sanctioning technology.[12]

Bonds can be the outcome of deliberate choice. But they can also be the outcome of "human action but not of human design" (Ferguson 1988/1767). Norms belong to the latter category. The influence of any individual on their content and the way they are enforced is marginal. Yet, an individual can still choose whether to comply with the norms or to renege. It has been argued that, beginning with industrialization and accelerating with globalization, the dominant forms of bonds have changed: Norms have become relatively less important in comparison to freely chosen bonds (such as friends).

Closely related to values and norms is the topic of shared cognition or beliefs. Shared values imply shared conceptions of the desirable. To share conceptions of the desirable, that is, of the *ought*, the group that is sharing those conceptions

---

[11] Mueller (ibid.) proposes an orientation of economics toward behavioral psychology. He argues that actors who have been educated to cooperate in many situations can be predicted to cooperate even if they no longer get the immediate reward they got when they were children. If this is taken into account, it almost suggests itself to model human behavior in a two-step procedure. The first step consists of a decision rule that tells the actor how to classify the problem: if a cooperation norm is involved and the monetary stakes are rather low, the actor will supposedly stick to the behavior he or she was taught, i.e., instrumental rationality in the economic sense of a cost-benefit calculus will not come into play. As monetary stakes are gradually increased, more and more actors will at least begin to classify the problem in which costs and benefits have to be weighted in a rational, future-oriented manner. Supposedly, only a small number of decision problems are totally immune from ever becoming subject to an explicit cost-benefit calculus. As long as this switch in the treatment of a specific decision problem does not exhibit any regularities, this model is of little help for the economist. The research task would thus consist in developing hypotheses concerning the "switch" (see also Kliemt 1991, 199). Lindenberg (1992) is a first step in that direction. He claims that three instrumental goals exist universally: gain, norm-conformity, and loss avoidance. Depending on the framing of the situation, one of them will be more important to the actor than the other two, even though the latter two do not vanish. If one is able to influence the way people structure various interaction situations, one can influence the way they behave.

[12] Suppose I have two little twin brothers whose utilities enter my utility-function with equal weights. If I sanction one of them, I therefore increase and decrease my utility simultaneously. Within the logic of economics, I would sanction only if I would be better off afterward. The example shows that it might make sense to introduce conditional arguments into the utility-function. Another person's utility might increase mine only *given* that he acts within the valid behavioral norms.

must have achieved some shared perception of the *is* as well. This might not seem to follow straightforwardly but since values are supposed to influence a person's selective behavior, it follows that in a certain situation a person who has internalized some value will consider only so many different possible ways to act in this situation and will exclude other theoretically possible ways from closer consideration right at the outset. If a second person who shares the same value acts in one of the ways excluded by the first person, then she must have perceived a different situation. We will therefore assume that shared values imply not only shared normative conceptions but also shared cognitive perceptions. This is so because we do not consider it useful to assume that two persons sharing the same value act differently in a situation apparently identical. A society that is bound together by a set of shared norms can therefore be assumed also to be bound together by shared cognition.

To sum up: The concept of *bonds* as here presented is very broad indeed. Aspects of networks, ties, trust, loyalty, norms, and even cognitive beliefs can all be subsumed under the concept or at least closely connected to it. It will be our task in section three of this chapter to enquire whether certain institutional arrangements – democratic ones – are affected by bonds or have an effect on them. Our delineation of bonds has been very broad. They can apply to persons and to concepts, to neighbors and the state. To test the relevance of the concept empirically, not only does one need hypotheses concerning the effects that various kinds of bonds will have on social outcomes, one also needs tools to ascertain them. As economists, we are not interested in knowing the exact weights of a utility-function of a specific person, but rather in knowing whether on average a group of persons has a utility-function different from another group, possibly as the consequence of facing a different set of restrictions.

Surveys are one possible instrument. The World Values Survey has been conducted repeatedly, and it not only contains information on the general level of trust that citizens display vis-à-vis each other, it also shows that systematic differences exist between members of different societies. (Inglehart 1997 contains a good introduction to the survey; La-Porta et al. 1997 is one example of economists making use of it.)

Another instrument to ascertain the weights attributed to other persons, organizations, or concepts would be to count membership in civil associations, for example, as done by Putnam (1993) in his study on democracy in Italy. Similarly, one could count time and effort spent on contributions to the voluntary production of public goods.

Constitutional Democracy

When we use the term *democratic politics* here, we want to confine ourselves exclusively to constitutional democratic politics, that is, democracies in which the domain to which majoritarian procedures can be applied are limited. A

Table 9.1. Role and Effect of Bonds: 4 Cases

	Democracy	Non-Democracy
Rule of Law	1	2
Non-Rule of law	3	4

constitution can be defined as the rules based on which a society makes its decisions concerning the provision and financing of public goods. Stated in more simple terms: The choice of a constitution is a choice of how to choose subsequently. A democratic constitution contains specific procedures concerning the choice (and the substitution) of those who are to make decisions concerning the provision of public goods and who have the power to tax even those who are not in favor of a specific bundle of public goods being provided.

Two implications might be worth noting: Theoretically, one can think of a rule-of-law state that is not democratic (and vice versa). One could then distinguish four cases, as shown in Table 9.1.

In our assessment of the role and effects of bonds, we will constrain ourselves to cases 1 and 4. A second implication that we will have to deal with more explicitly later on is that the criteria used here refer to organizational aspects of the state. Bonds might, however, well exceed the borders of states.

CONJECTURES

On the Preconditions for Establishing Sustainable Democracy: Bonds as Exogenous Variables

Hayek's insight that "a group of men can form a society capable of making laws because they already share common beliefs which make discussion and persuasion possible and to which the articulated rules must conform in order to be accepted as legitimate" (1960, 181) was already quoted here previously. It is hypothesized here that certain kinds of bonds are prerequisite for a specific procedure of making laws, namely, a democratic one. In other words, it might very well be the case that sustained democracy depends on preconditions that it is not capable of producing or bringing about itself.

It has often been observed that behavior is not only channeled by formal institutions (where rule-breaking is sanctioned or its sanctioning at least threatened by the state) but also by informal ones (where rule-breaking is sanctioned informally by other members of society). It has been argued (e.g., Kiwit and Voigt 1995) that many informal institutions are very stable and not subject to deliberate change. Since incompatibilities between formal and informal institutions will greatly increase the cost of governing, it can be concluded that the formal institutions that can be set and modified at will should not be completely at odds with the prevalent informal institutions. If this conjecture is correct, then the prevalent informal institutions should be by and large compatible with those characteristic of constitutional democracy. In the following paragraphs, I will attempt to make this general claim more concrete with regard to the concept of bonds as delineated above.[13]

Elsewhere (Voigt 1998), I have attempted to identify the preconditions for a viable rule-of-law constitution, namely (1) individual attitudes compatible with it,[14] (2) the possible relevance of organized interest groups, and (3) the possible relevance of "constitutional culture" (referring to the perception of the constitution either as merely a "book of hopes" or as a legally enforceable document). Since here we are only interested in constitutional democracies (i.e., those conforming with the rule of law), all those preconditions should be relevant for our case of interest. However, it is possible that we have to extend our list, since we are interested here in a *democratic* rule-of-law state. We are, however, not interested in preconditions in general, but only in those that can be expressed in terms of bonds.

Democracy is an unlikely form of state organization. At least historically, autocracy has been much more prevalent. Some economists argue (Barzel 2000) that democratic institutions were set up by autocrats as a consequence of their strength: Handing over some competences to a state organ different from themselves could make their own pronouncements more credible and thereby make themselves better off. Granting a bit more power to other organs, however, always entails the danger of kicking loose a dynamic process that the autocrat cannot control anymore (Przeworski 1991). We therefore propose the opposite hypothesis, namely, that participatory (democratic) rights will be granted only as a consequence of changes in the bargaining power of various groups. Groups whose cooperation is not needed for a regime to remain in power will not be granted any rights, whereas groups whose cooperation is crucial will have a better chance of being granted democratic rights. Democracy is thus only likely to emerge as a "negotiated universal" if a multitude of groups are organized and have at their disposal some bargaining power in the sense that their

---

[13] Cooter (2000, 20) argues that two cases through which law can become especially effective should be distinguished: (1) If it is in alignment with pre-existing morality – this is the case we have just described as the congruence between formal and informal institutions. (2) If some citizens regard lawmakers as moral authorities, or citizens believe that law as such deserves respect. Here, the relationship between formal and informal institutions would be turned on its head: citizens modify at least part of their moral convictions because the law is changed or because the lawmakers are seen as representing some higher form of moral authority. The empirical relevance of this second case seems doubtful. Were it to exist on a broad scale, it would constitute incentives for lawmakers to misuse the trust that many citizens have toward them. Democracy does seem sustainable, however, if a major part of the citizenry believes that the law deserves respect *as long as it was passed using procedures deemed to be fair or just.*

[14] Subjects believe that it is not fate determining their lot, but, at least to a certain degree, their individual action. Further, they should not hold an organicist concept of the state that attributes to the state goals such as the determination of truth, etc.

non-cooperation will make life worse for those who are already cooperating with the regime.

If we observe that democracy has been brought about as the result of domestic interest groups fighting for participatory rights against the existing autocrat, we can infer that some bonds within these groups and possibly also among them must exist. From this, we infer the hypothesis that democracy will prove more sustainable if it has resulted from a domestic struggle then if it was introduced by an outside force or if it was unilaterally imposed by an autocrat (Weber 1922/1947).[15]

Suppose a society has given itself not only a constitution compatible with the rule of law, but also one that mandates periodic elections of those who are to determine the exact composition of the public goods bundle to be provided. Under what conditions will such a constitution become effective? We propose to distinguish two levels here, in both of which bonds play a crucial role. The first is concerned with the candidates and parties competing for office or, in short, the elite. Assume that the hitherto governing party has just lost the elections. Why should its members leave office and hand the government over to the winning party instead of simply holding on to it? Economically speaking, one would expect the losing party to leave office only if the expected utility of that action is higher than the expected utility of not leaving office. If the losing party expects that the representatives of the (now) winning party would never leave their offices after a (future) defeat, the representatives of the (now) losing party would not have a good reason to leave.[16] Trust that the opposing party will play according to the rules in the future is therefore a prerequisite for a functioning democracy. Expressed differently: If some of the crucial actors are bound to the functioning of democracy *per se* and attribute some utility to its preservation

---

[15] With regard to Central and Eastern Europe, Offe (1997, 65) observes the following: "Instead of an incremental growth of free economic and political institutions which, in the West, were promoted over an extended period of time by various social and political forces that typically valued these institutions for their own sake, the method of introduction of these institutions in the East was elite-dictated and instrumental." Although we do not agree with Offe's presumption that these institutions were fought for in the West primarily due to their intrinsic value, it is certainly true that they emerged organically over an extended period of time. Offe (ibid., 66) continues by conjecturing that a "civic ethos" is needed "generating among the participants in political and economic life the confidence that 'all others' . . . are not to be suspected as 'enemies', and which beyond that, also leads sufficiently large parts of the political community to take collective concerns into consideration and to develop some measure of 'positive external preferences'." Translated into our lingo, he identifies bonds as a necessary precondition for sustained democracy. With regard to the question whether anything can be done in order to speed up this emergence of bonds – possibly even from the outside – Offe arrives at pessimistic conclusions very similar to the ones developed here (ibid., 67): "The rise of a robust 'civil society' cannot be initiated from the outside."

[16] Inglehart (1997, 172) advances a similar argument: a government losing elections must moreover trust the former opposition that it will not imprison or execute the former government once the former opposition takes over office.

even if it is not they themselves who hold office at that time, the likelihood that democracy will be sustainable is higher (see Przeworski 1991).[17]

A second level on which bonds play a role is concerned with the population at large or mass participation. It is here conjectured that horizontal bonds are a necessary condition for vertical bonds, which are a prerequisite for sustainable democracy.[18] Suppose there are no vertical bonds, that is, the voters do not feel bound to the governing at all. In that case, we would expect them to act according to the traditional *homo oeconomicus* model: If given the chance to cheat the state, they will; if given the chance to act opportunistically, they will; and so forth. It now seems extremely unlikely that vertical bonds exist where horizontal ones do not. It seems plausible, rather, to assume that a group that has developed a high degree of trust on a horizontal level will be more likely to attribute trust even to those who have the power to tax and to threaten the use of force.[19]

Suppose a government has just lost elections and considers staying in office anyway, thus breaking the rules of democracy. As already mentioned, it is less likely to do so if that does not promise a utility exceeding that of leaving office in an orderly way. Now, the expected utility will depend not only on the actions of the winners of the elections but also on the reaction of the media, organized interest groups, and the public in general. If serious opposition against the move is expected because the media heavily criticize government and crucial interest groups announce they will not cooperate with government any more, then the expected utility of leaving office now (and hoping to regain it after the next elections) might be higher than that of breaking with the rules of the game. We are here dealing with the capacity to produce the public good "opposition" spontaneously. This capacity will be greatly enhanced if horizontal bonds are present: before opposing government, there must be consensus that government is indeed trying to break the rules. A shared perception of what is going on will greatly enhance this possibility. We are thus referring to bonds and their connection to shared beliefs. But agreeing on the evaluation that government is breaking the rules of the game does not suffice to stop it from doing so.

---

[17] It would be interesting to deal with the question whether it is possible to induce such bonds by creating respective institutional arrangements (e.g., by exchanging hostages and the like). This, however, does not belong here.

[18] But notice that horizontal bonds are by no means a sufficient condition for vertical bonds. It is quite conceivable that citizens trust each other, but not their government. In 1958, 24% of the U.S. public expressed distrust in the federal government; by 1992, that figure had risen to 80%. Yet, levels of interpersonal trust (horizontal bonds in this paper's language) have remained stable (Inglehart 1997, 207).

[19] This relationship has recently been observed by pollsters with regard to surveys carried out in Latin America. Those describing the results of "Latinobarómetro 2000" write: "Those who do not trust their neighbors are unlikely to trust their political leaders and state institutions in general." (Frankfurter Allgemeine Zeitung, May 23, 2000)

Opposition really needs to be produced. We hypothesize that the spontaneous production of opposition will be more likely if a number of latent interest groups have managed to overcome the problems of collective action described by Olson (1965).

Bonds are here doubly relevant: Between the members of factually organized interest groups, some kind of bonds must be present, otherwise they would not have been able to get factually organized in the first place. But suppose that the opposition of one single interest group will not impress those who govern and only some sort of common action between a number of groups will. In that case, the interest groups face the free rider problem on a higher plane: It is not the question whether to get organized (or become members of an organization), but rather, whether to make a – possibly risky – move against government. If bonds between the members of the various groups exist, then it will presumably be easier to produce opposition.

Traditionally, organized interest groups have met with skepticism from economists; they were always suspected to be rent seeking, which is, in turn, suspected to decrease general welfare. In two other papers, I have tried to establish a more favorable view of organized interest groups: In Voigt (1998), it is argued that, through the working of an invisible hand, organized interest groups can become the unintended watchdogs of the rule of law; in Voigt (1999), it is argued that the rule of law itself can be reconceptualized as the unintended consequence of competing interest groups seeking rents. Here, it is argued that the way democracy was brought about in a given group will influence its sustainability.

Again referring to Hayek's conjecture quoted here previously and taking into account our reflections on collective action, the question of the size of the group to which most individuals feel close bonds becomes relevant. A society that consists of a plurality of groups who feel strong intragroup bonds, but no overarching intergroup ones will have more difficulties in setting up and sustaining democratic institutions. Communication between the groups will be costly, the readiness to incur costs out of solidarity with other groups might not be sufficient, and so forth. From this, we can infer that a society with bonds consistent with democratic institutions is more likely to make them stay if strong intergroup bonds exist or if it is made up of just one homogenous group.[20] John Rawls (1993) has observed that the "factum of pluralism"

---

[20] This is surely a politically incorrect statement but its relevance might be grasped by looking at former Yugoslavia, Northern Ireland, etc. With regard to Central and Eastern Europe, it has been observed that: "A high degree of social cohesion early in the transition – that is, a consensus within society on the broader goals of transition – eased the implementations of reforms and weakened any subsequent pressures for reversal or backlash. Lack of cohesion, demonstrated by a polarization of the political preferences of the electorate, created significant obstacles in the reform process. Politicians in polarized systems were often forced to make greater compromises to win support from their opponents for a reform package" (EBRD 1999, 107).

is here to stay. Now, if that is interpreted to mean that people have different values – and that heterogeneity in societies has increased in the long run – and that their substantive bonds have become less important than they used to be, this means that the sustainability of democracy in modern societies depends on procedural bonds, that is, that a large majority accepts the outcome of democratic decision-making not because they necessarily like the substantive results, but because they believe that they have been brought about by a fair procedure.

To sum up, bonds that can be expressed in terms of interpersonal trust are primordial not only for the development of vertical bonds but also for sustainable democracy. The level of interpersonal trust also seems crucial for the emergence of organized groups, which are another important precondition. Democracy will be more easily sustainable in homogenous societies. Last, it will be more easily sustainable the larger the portion of the citizenry that values democracy for the underlying decision-making mechanisms rather than for the substantive outcomes brought about by drawing on them.

On the Repercussions of Democracy: Bonds as Endogenous Variables

In the previous section, it was hypothesized that there might be certain bonds that are crucial for a (formally) democratic constitution to become effective. Now, if that was the end of the story, little could be done to speed up the development toward democracy. If the bonds are not supportive of democracy, little could be done to implement it. This seems to be, for example, Putnam's (1993, 183) position: "The civic community has deep historical roots. This is a depressing observation for those who view institutional reform as a strategy for political change."

Yet, few scholars would dispute the claim that bonds are also subject to change, at least in the long run. If one understands the mechanisms that cause them to change, one could use this knowledge to foster the spread of democracy.[21] Looking for such possibilities is not identical to what Inglehart (1997, 206f.) has dubbed "institutional determinism," namely, the position that the level of interpersonal trust (bonds) is determined by the prevailing institutions. Institutional determinism is rejected by Inglehart.

In this section, I ask whether institutions that are assumed to be given can have effects on the prevailing bonds that the members of a society display toward each other, their government, and certain general principles. Special

---

[21] Traditionally, economists have been rather agnostic toward democracy. Democracy was perceived to be of instrumental value – namely, as a collective decision rule – but not of value in and of itself. There are, of course, exceptions, the most noteworthy probably being Sen (1999). But notice that most questions that economists who are critical about the functioning of democracy would ask are not dealt with by Sen. What should be the scope of collective decision-making and what areas should be restricted to private decision-making?

emphasis is placed on the potential differences in bonds that could be caused by democratic as opposed to non-democratic institutions.

It has often been mentioned that the willingness to help one's neighbors was substantial in East Germany under the socialist regime and that this willingness has rapidly decreased since 1989. These changes are supposedly one of the major reasons for the apparent nostalgia many East Germans display toward the former regime. It thus seems clear that political institutions can induce certain forms of behavior and that changes in these institutions will induce changes in behavior. But it seems doubtful whether this behavior can be explained by the incentives set by non-democratic, non-rule-of-law institutions. Rather, it seems to be a consequence of the general shortage economy. If one family somehow received a dozen oranges, it was willing to share on the assumption that those it was sharing with would be willing to share in return later on. It is thus not even clear that one needs to take recourse to the concept of bonds at all to explain the behavior observed: For actors who expect to be part of an infinitely repeated game, it can be in their narrow self-interest to establish reciprocal links with a number of other actors. As soon as one could count on always being able to buy oranges, bananas, and so on, those loose exchange networks broke down. This shows that actors rationally adapted their behavior to the changed circumstances.

But it could be argued that not only the shortage economy but also the unpredictability of state action induced solidarity amongst the subjects: if anybody could be the target of discretionary state action, the emergence of solidarity among potential targets seems plausible. Yet, if such solidarity meant complaining about state authorities, it could have a very high price. State action with regard to potential opposition was quite rational: on the one hand, the state was interested in giving its subjects the impression of being left undisturbed as long as they behaved reasonably (i.e., the state was interested in adhering to certain rules in order to make its own behavior predictable), and on the other, it had to create the impression that it was omnipresent, that it would immediately acquire knowledge of any behavior not in line with that expected; this it did by means of the extensive *Staatssicherheit*. Thereby, it was able to induce what Kuran (1995) calls preference falsification consisting of publicly lying about the preferences one really holds.

At the beginning of this chapter, it was hypothesized that an extensive welfare state could lead to a loosening of personal bonds. This hypothesis is exactly in line with the observation on solidaric networks observed in the shortage economies of the formerly socialist countries. There, the accidental availability of goods led to a sharing of those goods among small circles. An extensive welfare state can be interpreted as going one step further: Here, even if I am unable to earn my own income, the state will secure that I will not starve. Being a member of a voluntary network of people who help each other will therefore be less crucial. Over time, we can expect membership to decrease and networks to dissolve. Again, this is a rational response to changed circumstances. Yet, the welfare state is not necessarily based on a set of democratic institutions. Majoritarian – democratic – institutions tend to favor redistribution, but redistribution is not confined to democratic states. The changes in bonds induced through the institutions of the welfare state are therefore not necessarily connected with the bonds of democratic politics.

Earlier in this chapter the distinction between horizontal bonds – to other persons – and vertical ones – to the state and its representatives - was introduced. Now suppose a democratic constitution is passed and many individuals consider the process by which it was brought about as "fair" (or the rules of the document itself as fair); then it might generate vertical bonds to the document (*"Verfassungspatriotismus,"* "Civil Religion") in the sense that actors are willing to accept substantial outcomes that are not in accordance with their own preferences because they have been generated using procedures with which they agree. It is thus argued that a congruence between values and norms, on the one hand, and formal rules, on the other, can induce bonds that make governing less costly. It might be worth noting that, at least in principle, this sort of bonds does not depend on democratic institutions, either. Here, we focus on the rule of law and constitutionalism. It is, however, conceivable to have a rule-of-law constitution, yet not a democracy.

So far, we have identified a couple of institutional arrangements that could possibly influence the kinds of bonds between subjects, but we have not identified any differences in bonds depending on whether democratic or non-democratic institutions prevail. In other words, we are led to hypothesize that the causal chain does not go from (democratic/non-democratic) institutions to bonds but rather the other way round, as argued in the previous section.[22] Nevertheless, we want to go one step further and ask whether the *kind* of democratic institutions in place could have any effects on the prevalent bonds that can be found in a society.

From experimental games we know that communication increases the likelihood of cooperation even in games in which defection is the dominant strategy. It therefore seems reasonable to assume that communication broadly understood increases bonds. If that is the case, then "communication intensive" institutions will *ceterus paribus* lead to closer bonds than "communication non-intensive" institutions. If we assume that geographical proximity makes

---

[22] This observation, however, in no way excludes the possibility that the state (whether democratic or not) can have substantial effects on the bonds prevalent in a society. In games with multiple equilibria, the state surely has the capacity to make one of the possible outcomes more salient and thus create a bias in favor of it. Drawing on Hume again, the induced behavior will create expectations that the same behavior will also be displayed in the future. In that sense, induced conventions can lead to the emergence of norms (Schelling 1960; Hardin 1989; Ordeshook 1992; Ullmann-Margalit 1977; Sugden 1986; Voigt 1999).

communication easier (with the secular decrease in communication costs, this assumption could well be challenged) and further that the number of actors involved in communication processes is negatively correlated with the influence any individual expects to command, then some hypotheses can easily be derived:

1. *Bonds should, ceterus paribus, be more relevant in federal than in unitary states.*

   With a given size of territory and of the population, there are more collective decision-making units in federal than in unitary states. This might lead to greater satisfaction with the bundle of collective goods provided, because it allows a more fine-grained supply that takes the specific situations, for example, of geography, into account. But it might also be the case, and this is the argument put forward here, that it will be much easier to have a public discourse concerning the exact composition of the public goods bundle. This will not only make individual citizens more influential, but will also increase their propensity to take their fellow citizens' utility explicitly into account.

2. *Bonds should be more relevant in regimes that have direct-democratic elements than in those who rely exclusively on representative choice-mechanisms.*

   This is basically an extension of the first hypothesis. The case of Switzerland, where announced referenda regularly lead to society-wide discussions concerning the implications of the decision, seems to be a good example.

3. *Bonds should be more relevant in regimes with proportional representation than in those with plurality rule.*

   We know that plurality rule will regularly lead to a two party system (Duverger's Law). Parties in such systems will be more heterogeneous than parties in a system of proportional representation. The interests of many citizens will therefore only be represented in a loose fashion. As Breton and Galeotti (1985) observe, the plurality rule is the institutional foundation for the view that representation primarily serves to choose the government, whereas proportional representation provides the foundation for the view of representative government. If this leads to a more intensive public discourse, bonds might become more important than in plurality-rule systems.[23]

Hence, we come to the somewhat paradoxical conclusion that the prevalent bonds are not influenced by whether the formal institutions of a society are

---

[23] For this hypothesis to hold, we have to assume that discussions within parties (which will probably be more intensive with plurality rule) have smaller effects on the development of bonds than discussions between parties.

democratic or not, but that the kind of democratic institutions in place might
very well have an impact on the bonds to be found.[24]

OPEN QUESTIONS

This chapter has been between the anecdotal and the conceptual. Nevertheless,
a host of possibly relevant questions have not even been mentioned. Here, we
want to allude to at least some of them.

How does the concept of legitimacy enter into the picture? Economists have
drawn on it when trying to legitimize certain rules or organizations (Buchanan
1975b) but have seldom applied it to positive or explanatory theory. Can we
observe that the legitimacy of democratic regimes is regularly higher than that
of non-democratic ones? Is legitimacy a relative concept in the sense that the
legitimacy of non-democratic regimes is the lower, the higher the number of
democratic regimes (a) in its neighborhood or (b) on a worldwide scale? What
does this mean with regard to bonds? Does a high degree of legitimacy increase
the probability of a closely bound community? A closer look at these questions
seems promising.

What relevance does the nation state have for bonds? Earlier, we noted that
our approach of dealing with bonds heavily depended on the nation state. Yet,
the nation state has not always existed – and it will probably not exist *ad in-
finitum*. Loyalty to the nation state – that is, a specific kind of bonds – has
been deliberately created. What does this mean with regard to democracy? Are
bonds to democratic regimes deliberately creatable in an analogous way? If
the nation state is indeed to lose some of its importance, as many observers
claim, does this also mean that the bonds to the nation state will become
less tight? If so, would that imply that the amount of bonds is simply decreasing or would it mean that some other concept could attract bonds toward
itself?

These questions and the ones dealt with in a little more depth in the last
section of the chapter promise to be highly relevant on two levels: the theoretical
level and on the policy level. On the theoretical level, they go to the very core
of the discipline, namely, the behavioral model used by economists, including
the rationality assumptions. The standard assumption of constant preferences

---

[24] The next logical step of inquiry is to ask where the propensity to cooperate comes from,
i.e., to endogenize trust. Putnam (1993) conjectures that hierarchical organizations – especially
the Catholic Church – are obstructive to the emergence of trust and reciprocal cooperation.
La Porta et al. (1997) operationalize the importance of hierarchical religion by measuring the
percentage of the population belonging to a hierarchical religion defined as Catholic, Eastern
Orthodox, or Muslim. They find (ibid., 336f.) that "holding per capita income constant, countries with more dominant hierarchical religions have less efficient judiciaries, greater corruption,
lower-quality bureaucracies, higher rates of tax evasion, lower rates of participation in civic activities and professional associations, a lower level of importance of large firms in the economy,
inferior infrastructures, and higher inflation."

is likewise touched upon. If preferences might be subject to change because they are discussed in open debate, this touches the core of economics.

But these questions are also relevant on the policy level: It is often argued that the European Union is not ready for more directly established democratic choice procedures because functioning democracy depends on the existence of a united public in which debates of common interest could be had. The multitude of various European publics is then seen as an argument against further democratization of the European Union. We do not make any evaluations on the adequacy of such statements but simply stress that this is an area hitherto largely neglected by economists.

REFERENCES

Axelrod, Robert (1984), *The Evolution of Cooperation*, New York: Basic Books.
Barzel, Yoram (2000), "Property Rights and the Evolution of the State," in: *Economics of Governance* 1(1):25–51.
Bohnet, Iris (1997), *Kooperation und Kommunikation*, Tübingen: Siebeck.
Boyd, R., and P. Richerson (1994), "The Evolution of Norms: An Anthropological View," in: *Journal of Institutional and Theoretical Economics* 150(1):72–87.
Brennan, Geoffrey, and Hamlin, Allan (2000), *Desires and Devices*, Cambridge: Cambridge University Press.
Brennan, Geoffrey, and Lomasky, Loren (1993), *Democracy and Decision – The Pure Theory of Electoral Preference*, Cambridge: Cambridge University Press.
Breton, André, and Gianluigi Galeotti (1985), "Is Proportional Representation Always the Best Electoral Rule?" in: *Public Finance* 40(1):1–16.
Buchanan, James (1975a), "The Samaritan's Dilemma," in: E.S. Phelps (ed.), *Altruism, Morality and Economic Theory*, New York: Russel Sage Foundation, 71–85.
Buchanan, James (1975b), *The Limits of Liberty – Between Anarchy and Leviathan*, Chicago: University of Chicago Press.
Buchanan, James (1994), "Choosing What to Choose," in *Journal of Institutional and Theoretical Economics*, 150(1):123–135.
Cameron, L. (1999), "Raising the Stakes in the Ultimatum Game: Experimental Evidence from Indonesia," in: *Economic Inquiry* 37(1):47–59.
Cooter, Robert (2000), "Do Good Laws Make Good Citizens? An Economic Analysis of Internalizing Legal Values," Working Paper 2000–8, U.C. Berkeley Law and Economics Working Paper Series.
Dawkins, Richard (1989), *The Selfish Gene*, New Edition. Oxford: Oxford University Press.
Denzau, Arthur, and North, Douglass (1994), "Shared Mental Models: Ideologies and Institutions," in: *Kyklos*, 47:3–31.
EBRD (European Bank for Reconstruction and Development) (1999), *Ten Years of Transition: Economic Transition in Central and Eastern Europe; the Baltic States and the CIS.*
Etzioni, Amitai (1988), *The Moral Dimension*, New York: Free Press.
Ferguson, Adam (1988/1767), *Versuch über die Geschichte der bürgerlichen Gesellschaft*, Frankfurt: Suhrkamp.

Frank, Robert (1988), *Passions Within Reason*, New York: Norton.

Frey, Bruno S. (1997), "A Constitution for Knaves Crowds Out Civic Virtues," in: *The Economic Journal*, 107:1043–53.

Granovetter, Mark (1992), "Economic Action and Social Structure: The Problem of Embeddedness," in: Mark Granovetter and Richard Swedberg (eds.), *The Sociology of Economic Life*, Boulder et al.: Westview, 53–81.

Güth, Werner (1995), "On Ultimatum Bargaining Experiments – A Personal Review," in: *Journal of Economic Behavior and Organisation* 27:329–44.

Güth, Werner, Schmittberger, Rolf, and Schwarze, B. (1982), "An experimental analysis of ultimatum bargaining," in: *Journal of Economic Behavior and Organizations* 3:367–88.

Hardin, Russell (1989), "Why a Constitution?" in: Grofman, Bernard and Wittman, Donald (eds.), *The Federalist Papers and the New Institutionalism,* New York: Agathon Press, 100–20.

Hayek, Friedrich (1960), *The Constitution of Liberty*, Chicago: University of Chicago Press.

Heiner, Ronald (1983), "The Origin of Predictable Behavior," in: *American Economic Review*, 73:560–95.

Hirschman, Albert (1970), *Exit, Voice and Loyalty – Responses to Decline in Firms, Organizations, and States*, Cambridge, MA: Harvard University Press.

Inglehart, Ronald (1997), *Modernization and Postmodernization*, Princeton: Princeton University Press.

Kiwit, Daniel, and Voigt, Stefan (1995), "Überlegungen zum institutionellen Wandel unter Berücksichtigung des Verhältnisses interner und externer Institutionen," in: *ORDO*, 46:117–47.

Kliemt, Hartmut (1991), "Der Homo oeconomicus in der Klemme – Der Beitrag der Spieltheorie zur Erzeugung und Lösung des Hobbesschen Ordnungsproblems," in: Esser; Hartumut and Troitzsch K. G. (eds.), *Modellierung sozialer Prozesse* Bonn: Informationszentrum Sozialwissenschaften, 179–204.

Kuran, Timor (1995), *Private Truths, Public Lies: The Social Consequences of Preference Falsification*, Cambridge and London: Harvard University Press.

La Porta, Rafael, Lopez-de-Silanes, Florencio, Shleifer, Andrei, and Vishny, Robert W. (1997), "Trust in Large Organizations," in: *American Economic Review*, 87(2):333–8.

Lindenberg, Siegwart (1992), "An Extended Theory of Institutions and Contractual Discipline," in: *Journal of Institutional and Theoretical Economics* 148:125–154.

Majeski, S. (1990), "Comment: An Alternative Approach to the Generation and Maintenance of Norms," in: K. Cook and M. Levi (eds.), *The Limits of Rationality*, Chicago: Chicago University Press, 273–281.

Mueller, Dennis (1986), "Rational Egoism versus Adaptive Egoism as Fundamental Postulate for a Descriptive Theory of Human Behavior," in *Public Choice* 51:3–23.

Offe, Claus (1997), "Cultural Aspects of Consolidation," in: *East European Constitutional Review* 6(4):64–8.

Olson, Mancur (1965), *The Logic of Collective Action*, Cambridge, MA: Harvard University Press.

Ordeshook, Peter (1992), "Constitutional Stability," in: *Constitutional Political Economy*, 3(2): 137–75.

Przeworski, Adam (1991), *Democracy and the Market – Political and Economic Reforms in Eastern Europe and Latin America*, Cambridge: Cambridge University Press.

Putnam, Robert (1993), *Making Democracy Work*, Princeton: Princeton University Press.

Rawls, John (1993), *Political Liberalism*, New York: Columbia University Press.

Schelling, Thomas (1960), *The Strategy of Conflict*, Cambridge, MA: Harvard University Press.

Sen, Amatya (1977), "Rational Fools: A Critique of the Behavioral Foundations of Economic Theory," in: *Philosophy & Public Affairs*, 6:317–44.

Sen, Amatya (1999), *Development as Freedom*, Oxford: Oxford University Press.

Sugden, Robert (1986), *The Economics of Rights, Co-operation and Welfare*, Oxford: Basil Blackwell.

Trivers, R. (1971), "The Evolution of Reciprocal Altruism," in: *Quarterly Review of Biology*, 46:35–57.

Ullmann-Margalit, Edna (1977), *The Emergence of Norms*, Oxford: Clarendon Press.

Vanberg, Viktor (1994), "Rational Choice vs. Adaptive Rule-Following: On the Behavioural Foundations of the Social Sciences," in: *Rules & Choice in Economics*, London and New York: Routledge, 25–41.

Voigt, Stefan (1993), "Values, Norms, Institutions, and the Prospects for Economic Growth in Central and Eastern Europe," in: *Journal des Economistes et des Etudes Humaines* 4(4):495–529.

Voigt, Stefan (1998), "Making Constitutions Work – Conditions for Maintaining the Rule of Law," in: *Cato Journal*, 18(2):191–208.

Voigt, Stefan (1999), "Breaking with the Notion of Social Contract: Constitutions as Based on Spontaneously Arisen Institutions," in: *Constitutional Political Economy*, 10(3):283–300.

Weber, Max (1922/1947), *The Theory of Social and Economic Organization*, ed. with an Introduction by Talcott Parsons, New York: The Free Press.

Zak, P., and Steve Knack (1998), *Trust and Growth*, downloadable from www.SSRN.com.

PART FOUR

THE ROLE OF CONSTITUTIONS

10

Voting Rules: A Constitutional Quandary

Gianluigi Galeotti

INTRODUCTION: STABILITY AND CHANGE
OF ELECTORAL SYSTEMS

Civic and economic freedoms depend on the competitiveness of a political system, a competitiveness fostered by the constitutional division of powers, the rule of law, and the contestability of the elective positions. Regarding the last issue, this chapter deals with the citizens or representative relationship and moves from the factual remark that the rules governing the appointment of the members of legislative assemblies are not sanctioned in any contemporary constitution. Leaving the framing of people's consent to statutory laws amounts to entrusting the regulation of political competition to the very ones who should be regulated. Notwithstanding the whims of partisan politics, however, those rules prove to be remarkably stable. Hence a first question, why so much stability? If we agree with Roger Myerson (1999) that political leaders meeting and negotiating in the halls of government cannot be exempt from Adam Smith's remark on the risk of conspiracies against the public, we face a subtler question: Is any trick behind that stability, often accompanied by apparently minor innovations consented to by incumbent representatives?

As often occurs, it is the subtler question to have attracted scholars' attention when discussing political opportunism. The first question, however, remains unasked and political economists resort to *assuming*, explicitly or implicitly, the constitutional status of electoral rules (see, e.g., Buchanan and Tullock, 1962; Mueller, 1996). A weak assumption indeed in a relationship where it is the agent more than the principal who has the whip-hand.

Following the due order, the chapter starts addressing the first question to introduce the logic of those very ones who control the method of registering electoral consensus. In that light, the section that follows this introduction deals

I am indebted to Vani Borooah and Luisa Giuriato for comments and suggestions and to an anonymous referee for healthy criticism that led me to clarify some passages of an early version.

with the constitutional status of the voting rules, whose stability rests on the transaction costs of re-coordinating on different ones, unless changes are somehow imposed by external shocks. That proposition is supported by the historical evidence and it is shown that the plurality rule asserted itself as the focal point of an unequal coordination game. It was the extension of the franchise, and the threat of exclusion from power, that prospected the advantages to shift to a proportional rule potentially less risky for the incumbents' stance. The section on the "Paradox of Delegation" addresses the second and main concern of the chapter, the representative exchange. A neglected comment by Anthony Downs on the irrationality of delegating political decisions leads to the point that a latent tension features that relationship, a tension exploited by incumbent representatives in ways that no electoral rule seem able to tackle in a stable and smooth way. That tension is eased in a setting where representatives' uncertainty on citizens' vote is an efficient spur to make the multiple principals' authority effectual at the end of agents' term of office. Incumbent politicians, however, find that setting uncongenial and try their best to reduce the effectiveness of that spur and to bind voters' to their own choices through the cultivation of political loyalties or by making themselves indispensable.

That leads to poorer performances and periodic, minor but still worrying crises in the life of a representative democracy. The next section, "Stages of Representative Democracy and Asymmetric Mistrust," describes the different stages of that life, depending on how much voters consider incumbents dependable and how much incumbents are confident about voters' support. Thus, a deceptive setting where a high incumbents' confidence combines with voters' low reliance on the incumbents can be followed by a weak setting made of both voters' and incumbents' low reciprocal reliance. That weak stage underpins the restoration of asymmetric and time consistent reciprocal attitudes, internalizing the line of mistrust that led to representative democracy.

The focus of the section on reducing incumbents' uncertainty via voters' entrapment appeals to empirical evidence showing how voters' entrapment tend to occur under both the plurality and the proportional rule since they convergence in producing long incumbencies and high cost of entry for contenders. If no voting rule is impervious to rational incumbents' exploitation – with the elapsing of time they are always able to manipulate or to bypass the margins inevitably left under their control – it would seem that only a change of rules *as such* would be apt to keep the required level of agents' uncertainty. Hence the constitutional quandary of reconciling stability and change. In this vein, the next section, "Efficient Uncertainty and Political Responsiveness," explores by way of exercise a manageable reinterpretation of a proposal put forward by Henry Theil apt to combine permanence and variations of the rules superintending the votes/seats transformation. A conclusion section, "The Quandry of Stability vs. Change of Rules," completes the analysis and hints to a more general proposition concerning the political property rights where the agents (politicians and bureaucrats alike) enjoy a more effective authority in applying the terms of the incomplete contracts supposedly constraining their action.

THE CONSTITUTIONAL STATUS OF VOTING RULES: WHOSE CALCULUS OF CONSENT?

Buchanan and Tullock's *Calculus of Consent* made clear that the rules superintending the election of representatives are an integral part of a country political constitution.[1] Yet, real-world constitutions do not deal with the matter, although they define the number of representatives and the election of the head of the State, however ceremonial its duties. In a fifth only of the 131 constitutions reported and updated by Albert P. Blaustein and Gispert H. Flanz (1984), general criteria are mentioned (for example, in terms of the proportional principle or with regard to the design of electoral districts). Yet, electoral systems prove to be rather stable, apart from apparently minor formal changes dealing with district redesign, term limits, public funding of political campaigns, politicians' financial disclosure, or procedural decision rules. Why that substantial stability? Do those adjustments rise out of collusive or competitive pressures? By deferring the latter question to later, we start with the former to show how the constitutional status of the voting rules is a matter of substance, somehow paradigmatic of the stability and evolution of the constitution itself.

Following Russell Hardin (1989), we maintain that a constitutional order[2] represents a "massive act of coordination" among power-holders backed not "by external sanctions . . . [but] by default, by the difficulty of re-coordinating on an alternative arrangement" (p. 102). Therefore, it is the costs of changing the standing coordination rules that make acquiescence more important than agreement in generating a strong equilibrium based on stable and self-enforcing expectations (Ordeshook, 1992). It follows that not all that is included in the formal constitution is strictly constitutional (think of the many rhetorical propositions aiming to legitimate the new drafters in citizens' expectations) and, vice-versa, several institutions of constitutional nature are not included in the formal constitution.

Power-holders are not indifferent to the solution of that coordination so that focal points – be they historical precedents or, more in general, Joseph Stiglitz's

---

[1] They refer to the "four essential constitutional variables" of political representation: the *degree*, the *basis* of representation, and rules for *choosing* representatives and for *deciding* issues in legislative assemblies.

[2] With that expression we refer to a reality wider and deeper than that regulated by the formal constitution. It represents the set of socially recognized rules, behaviors, and expectations that identify political leaders (power-holders and political entrepreneurs) and structure their relations in view of the provision of what is expedient to the public action (see Galeotti, 2000).

"natural irreversibilities associated with the creation of knowledge" – are required to stabilize expectations. A useful analogy is provided by the road networks that the Romans built in several European countries two thousand years ago. Observing the lasting survival of that network scheme, people could admire Roman ingenuity. But it is clear, first, that in most of the cases the Romans just improved older footpath networks and, second, that whoever followed could only maintain, extend and technically update the system, given the prohibitive costs of any radical change. Third, stability does not mean immobility, as external shocks can cause the disappearance of towns, the foundation of new ones or the expansion of small villages, with the need of new roads inevitably related to the standing network. Out of the analogy, Galeotti (2000) shows how both the stability and evolution of the constitutional order are based on the competitive and evolving agreements of power-holders in a changing social and economic environment. Constitutional flexibility rests on old leaders' consent as well as on the cost of entry of new leaders able to voice people's dissatisfaction, so that any change requires either the unanimous consent of all those who count (constitutional adjustments) or the respect of predetermined procedural rules when that unanimity is lacking (constitutional changes).

Origin and Evolution of Electoral Rules

In the case of the voting rules, the focal point was represented by the process which led to the adoption of the plurality rule, today followed by more than half of the countries enjoying a more or less effective representative democracy. If we go back to the thirteenth century when in Europe, as a matter of royal convenience, "a multitude of conciliar bodies . . . the great political invention of the middle ages . . . [were called] to give consent to but also – by the same token – to exert some control over their rulers" (Finer, 1997, p. 1024), we have to remember that attendance at Parliament was a chore and a duty reluctantly performed. It was only with the passage of time that parliamentary representation began to be used as a device for furthering local interests. A detailed account of the electoral evolution of the British Parliament in the period 1620–1680 shows how the rules for polling and counting voters were gradually standardized, often thanks to legal battles where Court decisions played a great role (Mark Kishlansky, 1986). In addition, for centuries the issue of liberty was not related to individuals but to social groups along geographical (towns, counties) or social lines (trade or professional associations) and because of that the passage from some kind of "organic" choice (illustrious citizens, rotation among noble families) to the election by plurality presented itself as immediate.[3] The plurality rule – or

---

[3] Proportionality was relevant to determine the *degree* of representation, as it happened in 1789 France with the convocation of the General Estates or with the U.S. Constitution, silent on

the dual ballot rule of Imperial Germany – was consistently adopted across the democratic countries until the last century.

It was with the uncertainty generated by the extension of the franchise during the 20th century that the proportional rule came into the political scene, as a strategic decision by the political elite to prevent social unrest and protect their own legislative positions (Rokkan, 1970, and, more recently, Acemoglou and Robinson, 2000). That occurred when the old parties were uncertain on the strength of new entrants and on their own ability to gather the consensus of the new voters.[4] *Ex post*, that resulted to be the case in most countries of continental Europe which switched to the proportional rule before or after the First World War. Conversely, the weakness of the new entrants (as in the United States) or the strength of the two-party domination (as in the United Kingdom) would explain the survival of the traditional plurality rule.[5]

Politicians' preferences on the voting rules are not discussed within the normative paradigm: Neither in the rational choice version concerned with voters' rationality and strategic behavior (implicitly assuming politicians' passivity), nor in the Leviathan version deferring those rules to far-sighted Founding Fathers and enforced by fiat. Yet, the tendency of party-politics to prefer the proportional rule can be explained because it encourages more ideologically oriented platforms that appeal more strongly to the loyalty of subsets of voters thus providing the party leaders with more leeway (Breton and Galeotti, 1985).

Granted that constitutional rules are based on the short-term interests of the politicians constrained by or drafting them (Mueller, 1996), we have to take into account the interaction between voters' and politicians' calculus in molding the effective evolution of any electoral system. The incumbent politicians play their cards when regulating their own competition, and to understand the main features of the learning process through which they find new strategies to adjust their behaviors underneath the apparent stability of the rules, we have to consider the nature of the voters or representative relationship more closely. Our analysis will focus on the latent conflict between voters and representatives, with the former interested in holding the incumbents' fate under their control, and the latter interested in keeping their permanence in office shielded as much as possible from that control.

---

the election rules of the Congress but dealing with the "3/5 compromise" (slaves counted as 3/5 of a person *for the purpose of determining the number of representatives* of each State).

[4] According to Charles Boix (1999), "under conditions of very high uncertainty about the structure of the electoral arena, the ruling elite will select the electoral system mostly to minimize risks – and therefore it will lean toward a mixed or pure PR system." Needless to say, women's enfranchisement did not create any partisan unbalance.

[5] We cannot review here the many adjustments and the few bigger changes that occurred during the last century: For details within a systematic reflection, see Taagepera and Shugart (1989).

THE "PARADOX OF DELEGATION" AND THE INNER TENSION
OF THE POLITICAL PROXY

The study of features and issues characterizing the political proxy is far from new. Swiftly cleared out by Schumpeter through the competitive struggle for people's vote, it had been discussed at length by John Stuart Mill when he asked whether "pledges" ought to be required from the members of his Congress of Opinions.[6] A century later, Anthony Downs stressed the problems posited by voters' information costs and by the congruence of voters' and representatives' goals. The issue of voters' rational ignorance and political sloth raised a vigorous debate,[7] but the issue of congruence was neglected although it prospected a more serious paradox. Downs maintains that the dissonance of goals makes the delegation of political decisions irrational:

> The crux of the matter lies in the assumption of common goals necessary for rational delegation. According to our hypothesis, party officials are interested only in maximizing votes, never in producing any particular social state *per se*. But voters are always interested in the latter. Therefore a rational voter who is not a party official himself cannot assume members of any party have goals similar to his own. But without this assumption, delegation of all political decision to someone else is irrational – hence political parties[8] can never be the agents of rational delegation. (Downs, 1957 p. 234)

Before the "intellectual revolution" of information economics that proposition appeared indeed to fly in the face of the self-interest assumption and to be inconsistent with the distinction between individual motivations and outcomes of interaction. Downs, however, softens the point when he hurries to mention the case of candidates seeking the consent of specific groups of the electorate. Still, any member of those groups must verify the congruence between his own goals and those of the group so that he has "to incur some of the costs of information about policies anyway" (Downs, 1957, p. 234). If congruence is a matter to be ascertained, information costs and delegation costs are tangled up. We can unravel them, however, if we follow the interpretation suggested by Alghion and Tirole (1997) in dealing with the authority that results in any

---

[6] Galeotti and Breton (1986) show the merits of following Mill in interpreting political relationships as centered around the representation of opinions, defined as general orientations or attitudes toward policies against which views with respect to "old" and "new" issues are formed. Those opinions replace the notion of citizens' definite preferences and help to underpin politicians' reputation.

[7] See Mueller (1988) for a review of the early literature on the paradox of voting, though the interest on the theme has not decreased since. Important contributions are found in Riker and Ordeshook (1968) at an individual level, and in McKelvey and Ordeshook (1985) and Palfrey and Rosenthal (1985) at an aggregate level. For an important shift of emphasis on expressive voting, see Brennan and Lomasky (1993).

[8] This term is a synonym of *political representatives* since Downs defines a political party as a team whose members are all identical since "they agree on all their goals."

organization from the implicit contract allocating the right to decide to an agent. They model a two-way interaction between the distribution of information costs and an authority structure, spanning from integration – where the principal may always overrule the agent's decision – to non-integration or delegation, where the decisions of the agent are not overruled by the principal.

The case of a formally integrated structure is that of a direct democracy, and Michele Grillo (1997, p. 59) shows how different levels of real non-integration can occur even there.[9] The application of the model to the representative case is less immediate, because now the formal authority to decide is allocated to the agent over a pre-definite span of time, at the end of which the principals regain the instantaneous and simplistic power to confirm or to change the agent.[10] Two issues seem to be the main ones at stake: the discontinuity of that power that deprives the political delegation of the required flexibility and the level of goals congruence. When the *ex ante* probability that principals and agents share the same decision criteria at the time of a decision is expected to be low, the loss of control offers the agent larger opportunities to pursue her own benefits. The conflicting pressures – the asymmetry of information thrusts the principals upon the agent's initiative, but lack of congruence presses for less delegation[11] – express themselves in terms of a latent tension, the solution of which impinges on the effectiveness of the multi-principals power exerted on the election day, that is, is on its being or not the "Day of Judgment" dreamed of by Karl Popper.

Political Bond versus Voters' Controlling Power

Galeotti and Breton (1986) stress the role played by party organization and political ideologies in providing a substitute to the Millian "pledge," indirectly solving Downs's problem of delegation. More specifically, they submitted that political parties support the political proxy by *tightening the bond* between incumbents and footloose voters and by *enhancing the control* that voters can exercise over representatives.[12] Here we investigate how those control and bond

---

[9] Grillo (1997) shows that the formal authority of the assembly of people does not preclude the exercise of actual authority by those in charge of implementing the decisions when the actual control of all the people would imply an inefficient waste of resources.

[10] Alghion and Tirole (1997) offer many valuable insights in terms of factors fostering the delegation of formal authority to the agents' initiative and of those influencing the costs of delegation, such as problems of performance measurement and the presence of multiple principals who may themselves have imperfectly aligned objectives.

[11] Democratic elections accomplish the dual role of signaling voters' general orientations with regard to public action and choosing those who should represent those orientations and, if in the majority, run the appropriate policies. Voters' criteria of choice may be different in a Millian world of representative government and in a Schumpeterian one of responsible government. The issue of congruence, however, is common to both approaches.

[12] The longer life of political parties motivates them to control lame-duck representatives (Barro, 1973), and political ideologies supply a common language helping a coordination (Calvert,

dimensions come to underpin and undermine each other at the same time, so that the life of the representative relation undergoes dialectical ups and downs. The emphasis is on the strength of the bond dimension which softens the issue of congruence at a cost, that of making less effective the control exerted on the election day. Keeping the paramount importance of that day intact requires an asymmetric mistrust (voters can rely on the incumbent only when the latter is unsure about voters' reaction), the failure of which can explain the occasional flailing around of political representation.

If uncertainty on the electoral outcome is the leverage disciplining the incumbent over her term of office, incumbents do not like it, and they have a common interest in resorting to all available devices to establish stronger bonds that trap the voters in their own choice, thus reducing that uncertainty. Those devices can be of an affirmative nature – nurturing loyalty through reputation or ideology – or of a negative one: making themselves the only credible option or otherwise indispensable. Common to both are the specific features of goals congruence and reputation as relevant to the political proxy. Alghion and Tirole (1997) treat that congruence as an exogenous parameter and mention only in passing the various methods through which the principals could improve it. The opposite seems to occur in politics, where the agents are in a better position to influence congruence for reasons related to the nature of political reputation.

Incumbents' performance is not easily verifiable in presence of soft information, but that does not preclude delegation thanks to the garrison provided by a party caring of its reputation. Building up of a representative's reputation requires time and its testing presents two sides: fulfilling the electoral platform and showing the skill and power to deliver. Those sides should complement each other, ideally: What is the use of a loyal accomplisher if it leads to nothing? However, in the real-world politics they can be used as substitute, thus leading to equivocal and, at times, wrong signals. More specifically, the ability to deliver is made of political power, and that power has its own momentum. Suppose that the issue at stake is the construction of a bridge at an important junction. If there is general agreement on the importance of the bridge, getting it approved can be easy. By the same token, however, that comes to be a weak signal of power, or at least a signal weaker than the one that would be provided by getting an extra bridge built at a junction already well provided with bridges. The latter result, more difficult to achieve just because of its superfluity, would be a clear signal of effective power.

In this way an ambiguity comes in, an ambiguity implicit but not addressed in the career concerns discussed by Persson and Tabellini (2000, pp. 83–85).

1995): Both those features substantiate a reputation mechanism supporting a self-enforcing incomplete contract along the lines later expanded by David Kreps (1990) in relation to "corporate culture."

Mixing up effective accomplishments with symbolic performances is a device used to focus popular attention on what is more convenient to the incumbents. When the voters become aware of that ambiguity (how can a more or less costly pork-barrel present be distinguished from a far-sighted welfare-improving program?), to confirm an incumbent can be a risky choice, because a higher expected yield is accompanied by greater expected losses in terms of opportunistic behavior: Will not the experienced representative be tempted to use her skill to feather her own nest? At the same time, the alternative of voting for the challenger may not look that much better, since here a lower loss comes to be accompanied by a much lower expected yield. In this way, the voter can find himself trapped in his choice.

The situation is not different from the ploy adopted by company managers to avoid to being replaced. Andrei Shleifer and Robert Vishny (1989) show how managers can entrench themselves in their position by exploiting their informative advantage over the firm by making specific investments that make themselves indispensable, thus reducing the probability of being replaced while allowing them to extract larger perquisites from shareholders[13]. In both instances, agents are motivated to please their principals instrumentally, since their main aim is to compel them to keep their consent. The trick is somehow easier in the political case, because the incumbents can appeal to the bond dimension, manufacture congruence and exorcise the challenger to reduce the impact of the control dimension.

STAGES OF REPRESENTATIVE DEMOCRACY
AND ASYMMETRIC MISTRUST

The ability of the incumbent to look "too good" amounts to making a valuable hostage of herself in the eyes of voters, and that makes the threat of punishment less credible (and enforcement by punishment is always weak when compliance is not assessable easily: Kreps, 1990). That means that the principals' only safeguard – the certainty of holding the incumbent's fate under their control – can be at times reduced to a blunted knife. When voters can only keep voting for the incumbent as the less worse alternative, they find themselves in the hands of the incumbent, and they cannot rely any more on her because of the fear that she enjoys too much leeway to *ex post* opportunism.

What we are presenting can appear as a rather extreme case: After all, voters' exit is always available, and other formal and informal institutional remedies are present.[14] Those considerations, however, have to be read within a more complete picture of the dialectical ups and downs of the life of the representative proxy. More precisely, we have to consider how information and delegation

---

[13] See also Edlin and Stiglitz (1995). For the analogy between corporate and political control, see Wintrobe (1987) and Wittman (1995).

[14] Of the kind discussed by Congleton (1984), Breton (1996), and Grillo (1997).

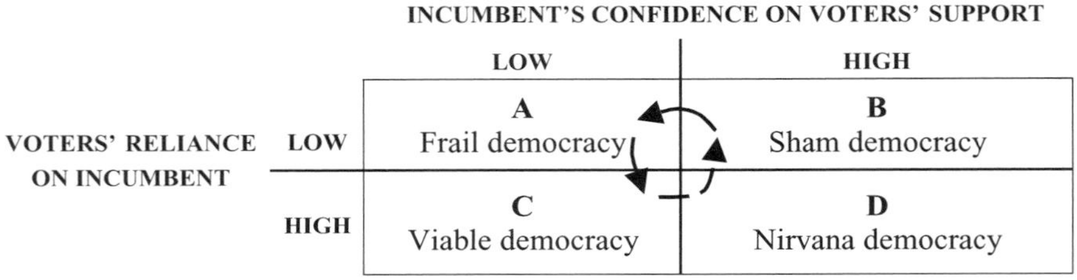

INCUMBENT'S CONFIDENCE ON VOTERS' SUPPORT

		LOW	HIGH
VOTERS' RELIANCE ON INCUMBENT	LOW	**A** Frail democracy	**B** Sham democracy
	HIGH	**C** Viable democracy	**D** Nirvana democracy

Figure 10.1. Four polar combinations

costs combine with those bonds at the time of the intermittent "renegotiation" occurring at the end of the term of office. To present in a systematic way the different situations, let us distinguish sharply between the incumbents' low and high confidence on voters' support[15] and the voters' low and high level of reliance[16] on their representatives.

The matrix in Figure 10.1 summarizes four polar combinations, which can be read either as different democratic settings or as *snapshots* expressing recurring stages of the voters/representatives relation. For expository convenience, we stay with the latter interpretation and start with the combination C, made of high voters' reliance on the incumbent and the latter's low confidence on voters' support. It could be the hypothetical first stage of a new representative democracy, labeled as *viable* democracy because of a set of fully compatible incentives: The agent fulfills her job to the best of her ability so as to keep the support of her constituency, and the principals are ready to dismiss her should she go astray. If everything works properly, the system should reach the almost ideal combination D, where both sides of the relationship can trust each other. But in a more realistic perspective we have to consider how those fiduciary exchanges evolve along consecutive elections in terms of the factors previously discussed. In such a light, it is easy to show that D is an incentive inconsistent setting doomed to instability. Once the incumbent succeeds in making her ability clear, in building the proper bonds and in making herself indispensable, voters know that the incumbent deems her position safe and they can start having doubts about her reliability. Once their vote is taken for granted, the threat of dismissal becomes devoid of its biting value and her responsiveness can be expected to be weak: elections would become a "fake" auction.

Therefore stage D should be seen more properly as an imaginary one (hence the *Nirvana* label) so that, with voters somehow trapped in their own choice, sooner or later the system reaches combination B, with representatives quite confident on their supporters' vote and voters' reliance on them decreasing

---

[15] A confidence necessary in itself to protect the incumbent against the risk of voters' whimsical attitudes.

[16] *Reliance* is the term used by Anthony Downs, and we have seen how it is not a synonym of blind faith.

progressively.[17] The label of *sham democracy* appears to be the appropriate one: Incumbents confide in the support of voters who do not rely on them and some sort of crises can occur, for example, in terms of party fragmentation or of the success of populist leaders able more to express people's discontent than to offer effective political alternatives. Ian Buruma (2001) interprets in that way what has occurred in countries like Austria, India, and Italy (with Japan following suit, in his view) where traditional political elites "have been sewn up for too long." When politicians discover their royal nakedness in terms of voters' attitude, the system lands at stage A, a *frail setting* where a low reliance of voters combines with a low level of politicians' confidence in their potential supporters. Yet, it is a necessary stage to restore the stage C where representative democracy regains its health. As already suggested, it is a *viable* combination where a low level of confidence makes the incumbent's behavior more cautious. Credible fiduciary relationships are supported by congruent incentives in a setting able to compel incumbents to nurture voters' reliance by fearing their reaction. At first sight, the conclusion could appear an odd one – voters can trust an incumbent more, the more they know that she cannot be fully confident on their vote – but it is an asymmetry far from rare[18] within the logic of efficient contracts. In our case, it is required by the institutional features (periodic elections, secret ballot, recall normally unavailable, etc.) underpinning the life of the political proxy: A constrained delegation where the principals are provided with a necessary, but not sufficient spur and where political bonds soften the issue of congruence at the cost of making less effective the authority exerted on the election day.

More in general, what can be defined as an efficient level of mistrust is the key for understanding both the origin and the working of representative democracy. Indeed, a feeling of trust – or of a moral obligation to obey the authority – represents a behavioral primitive (Berg, Dickhaut, and McCabe, 1995), a notion related to Sam Finer's three preconditions for political stability (1997, pp. 28–29). From the Runnymede meeting onwards, however, modern democracy developed from a variable degree of mistrust towards the legitimate authorities, the same mistrust we can read in the institutions of Athenian democracy and republican Rome.[19] Mistrust, again, accompanied the reflection

---

[17] Some years back a well-known Italian journalist, worried about the victory of the Communist Party, invited people to hold their nose and keep supporting the Christian Democratic Party. As many people followed that advice, we have an instance of voters not trusting incumbents who could still count on their support.

[18] See the paradox of compensation in the economics of the contract law (Cooter and Ulen, 1998, p. 201).

[19] In Athens the elected magistrates had to undergo a threefold scrutiny (before their election, before their effective appointment once elected, and at the end of their term of office). In Republican Rome the setting was more complex: Finer (1997) speaks of an explicit system of checks and balances. Let us only mention how the traditional *cursus honorum* represented a progressive testing of the appointees and a way of favoring the needed degree of goals congruence.

on democracy of people like David Hume and James Madison, whose marks
we live with in terms of checks and balances constraints. It should not sur-
prise, therefore, that in contemporary representative democracies the political
proxy is based on asymmetric mistrust, somehow internalizing what Wintrobe
(1998) calls the dictator's dilemma: voters can trust their appointee insofar
as they are reasonably certain that she does not count on their unconditional
support.

If democratic politics is built on mistrust – the key variable of the representative proxy – the crucial passage is to test the effectiveness of the risk of
going from stage C to stage B. Is there any instance of voters getting trapped in
their own choices? In the following section we appeal to evidence provided indirectly by other research – works showing, first, how incumbents of all stripes
seem to be able to control their constituencies and, second, how different voting rules converge in terms of length of incumbency and seat/votes ratios. Our
proposition on the latent conflict between voters and representatives not being disproved, we face the constitutional quandary discussed in the last two
sections.

REDUCING INCUMBENTS' UNCERTAINTY VIA VOTERS' ENTRAPMENT: A CONVERGENT PATH

Rather than discussing the country-specific devices through which incumbent
politicians try to shield themselves from the risk of the polling box,[20] let us see
whether they succeed. Neglecting what for our purposes are minor differences
(such as those in terms of district magnitude, legal thresholds and other adjustments), let us contrast the proportional with the plurality rule. The conventional
view holds that that former rule tends to score better in terms of (Mill's) opinion representation. A better fitting of voters' opinion and lower costs of entry
in the political arena should be the prerequisite of a more competitive political environment: dissatisfied 'customers' would face more 'suppliers' ready to
oblige. As a consequence, we should expect that the proportional rule lead's
to greater volatility of the vote, as measured in terms of variations of party
vote shares occurring between two consecutive elections. Bartolini and Mair
(1990) considered a century of European elections and found, contrary to their
expectations, that not only is the volatility of the vote independent of the degree
of proportionality, but that "those elections which produce extremely proportional results . . . are characterized by the lowest level of volatility" (p. 164).[21]
An explanation of that outcome is provided by Galeotti (1994), who shows how
that alleged virtue of the proportional rule is lost because of the stronger ties

---

[20] The interested reader is deferred to Michael Wohlgemuth (1999), who makes an interesting
distinction between "innocent" (in the sense of spontaneous) and "strategic" barriers.

[21] Unfortunately, no empirical test is available on whether that stability increased in time. Bartolini
and Mair are inclined toward a negative reply, although the evidence they provide is inconclusive.

it fosters with the preferred party. As happens with monopolistic competition, platforms fitting well the preferences of subsets of voters make it more difficult for them to switch from one party to another – voters find themselves trapped in their own choices – up to the point that political competition decreases with the number of political parties.[22]

As for the plurality rule, let us refer to the apparent paradox occurring in the United States where limiting the number of legislative terms seems to be favored by three quarters of the American voters, who still keep re-electing their incumbents. In terms of the present analysis, we are in presence of a kind of cognitive dissonance consistent with voters' uneasiness assigned to case D. The entrapment could be due to a prisoner's dilemma situation in which voters enjoying a skilful senior representative do not like to lose her services, however aware of the risk of that skill, unless all other constituencies adopt the same limitation: the explanation suggested by Dick and Lott (1993).[23] Daniel Friedman and Donald Wittman (1995) provide a slightly different one, as they consider it as a referendum against the long terms of the other district representatives. Whatever the case, both explanations are consistent with the chancy feature of combination D and they support the view that voters feel the loss of something in presence of representatives, long incumbencies (turnout tended to increase after the introduction of term limits: Grofman, 1996).

Although through different routes, under both rules incumbent representatives seem able to achieve the aim of trapping their supporters in their own choice. And the ensuing latent conflict filters through somehow when voters are allowed to express themselves in referendums. That is the case with the term limits in the United States and with the electoral reforms introduced in Italy and New Zealand (against the opposition of the main political parties).

The results just described shed a light on the related issue of the role played by the institutional devices regulating internal competition and making the bargains among members of legislative assemblies enforceable. That is the focus of Barry Weingast and William Marshall's (1988) analysis of the internal organization of Congress based on clear-cut committee domains and the promotion by seniority to the more valuable positions. After discussing the virtues of that system in promoting the stability of Congress decision-making, Weingast and Marshall (p. 159) observe that in the case of party government strong political parties "provide an alternative means of enforcing agreements" and "they yield considerable influence over the distribution of legislative [read: useful in electoral terms] benefits." It is an observation fully in line with

---

[22] Galeotti (1994) tests that hypothesis with the postwar electoral results of 18 countries and finds that vote volatility decreases significantly with the proportionality of the political system.

[23] They submit that term limits are preferred collectively by constituencies, even though no constituency would independently oust its own incumbent representatives since senior representatives provide "better services."

Schumpeter's early assimilation of political parties to cartels aiming at reducing politicians' competition. In my words it shows how what secures the stability of those bargains helps the incumbents to make themselves indispensable to their constituencies.

Incumbents' Tenure

If the incumbents succeed in their endeavor to protect themselves from voters' control, rather long incumbency should follow. Empirical evidence shows how the length of incumbency – remarkably high and increasing in time – is not significantly different under either rule. In a comparative study aimed to assess the relationship between political tenure and rent-seeking, Patrick McNutt (1997) computed a tenure variable as the percentage of incumbent politicians (lower House) returned at the last general elections (for the countries he could collect data). He found no significant difference: on average 81.6% of the incumbents kept their seat under the proportional rule and 84.2% under the plurality rule. Moreover, he weighted the above variable in terms of voter turnout and regressed the result on a number of independent variables, including an index of proportionality whose coefficient was not statistically significant.

The Convergence of the Seat/Vote Ratio

There are many innovations agreed upon by the incumbents for the purpose of improving the regulation of elections that reduce political competition either by encouraging more habit oriented choices or by discouraging citizens' participation.[24] As for the latter, it is recognized that a low turnout tends to help the success of the incumbents (Powell, 1981). What is less noticed is how the impact of a lower turnout, although different under the two rules, leads then to an unexpected convergence. After all, the rules superintending that transformation of votes into seats are far from neutral and with the elapsing of time they mould voters' and representatives' reciprocal attitudes in a convergent way.

Those who abstain from voting represent a kind of stabilizing reservoir, the size and implications of which are affected by how the rules combine with the credibility of contenders. Under plurality, think of the British Liberal voter in a constituency where the Liberal candidate has no chance of winning: If he decides to stay home on the polling day instead of voting for the more serious contender, he helps the incumbent while reducing the disproportionality of the eventual seats/votes ratio (in the 1929 elections, the British Liberal party

---

[24] Think of financial disclosure and limits to campaign expenditures or laws governing election broadcasts, as well as partisan attempts to increase or to lessen the cost of voting (e.g., by making registration more or less cumbersome or imposing compulsory voting, a rule that gives advantages to major parties, as shown by what happened in the Netherlands following the 1971 abrogation of compulsory voting).

received 23.4% of the votes and got less than 10% of the seats; in the next election it received only 7% of the votes and no seats, improving the proportionality of the outcome). What occurs under the proportional rule appears more controversial to scholars not acquainted with the voters' investment embodied in the strong party organization nurtured by that rule. As already mentioned, the advantage of lower costs of entry in the political arena is more than compensated by a monopolistic competition fostering the loyalty of better ideologically served supporters. Dissatisfied supporters, therefore, prefer staying home rather than voting for another party. In this way, they help the major contenders to get a higher share of seats: Put simply, those who abstain can be viewed as voting for a "phantom party," which gets no seat, thus making the eventual outcome less proportional. An interesting implication of that opposite impact is that the time-honored divergence of the seats/votes ratio occurring under the two rules tends to shrink, and that asymmetric impact of the abstention from the vote is consistent with our analysis of the forces at work in increasing the costs of entry for new challengers, thus favoring the incumbents.[25]

Summing up, we can say that the circumstantial evidence referred to does not contradict the incumbent representatives' ability to develop in time tactics apt to trap their supporters. If that is the case – no voting rule is good at keeping incumbents' uncertainty high enough to reduce the space for their opportunistic behavior – is it inevitable that the voters have to pay more, in terms of waves of inefficiency, for the services of senior and skilful representatives? Should we conclude that a change of rules is better than stable rules in order to keep incumbents' uncertainty at its efficient level? Conversely, how can a constitutional order combine stability and change without causing political traumas or painful discontinuities? Before replying, let us consider the role played by uncertainty at the moment expressing the triumph of political partisanship, the gerrymandering that has been defined one of the most conflictive forms of regular politics short of violence.

EFFICIENT UNCERTAINTY AND POLITICAL RESPONSIVENESS

Although redistricting is needed when demographic changes engender malapportionment, the pathology takes hold when redistricting is accomplished in the pursuit of partisan aims. Views are divided, however, on whether gerrymandering reduces the competitiveness of the electoral game or not. The traditional view underlines its partisan and anticompetitive effects,[26] but other

---

[25] We are not aware of any comparative historical testing of that implication, although Taagepera and Shugart (1989, p. 128) seem to support it when they observe that "over the long run, most plurality systems are not as unrepresentative as their detractors say, and most PR systems are not as unstable as their detractors say."

[26] Without reviewing a quite extensive literature, let us only mention Niemi and Winsky (1992) and Cox and Katz (1999), who find strong evidence that "both partisan control and reversionary

research-works[27] found that gerrymandering supplies short-term advantages susceptible to backfiring in the long run, because what it does is to trade current district security for more seats. Along that view, Gelman and King (1994) find that redistricting reduces partisan bias in an indirect and unexpected way because it increases *the level of uncertainty* on the eventual outcome. In other words, an apparent minor change of constituency boundaries fulfils the conditions of uncertainty featuring our previous combination C.

That result is worthy of further reflection on how to handle the constitutional quandary of combining stability and change of voting rules. To keep political competition vital, the solution cannot be left to casual external shocks – not void of dangers – to term limits impoverishing the logic of the political proxy or to the waves of mistrust previously described. If coping with re-election uncertainty is incumbents' main target, and if they succeed in reducing it under different voting rules, to search for the best – or the less worse – rule is a fruitless exercise. The starting point of a new reflection invests the very stability of any voting rule as the factor that allows those devices to succeed. Some kind of built-in device inserting the uncertainty necessary to discipline incumbents within a stable system would be needed. Without indulging in fancy proposals that are not easy to implement,[28] let us work – by way of example – a manageable reinterpretation of a proposal put forward by Henry Theil.

A Modest Proposal

The degree of representativeness of an electoral system depends upon the geographic distribution of votes, the rate of turnout, the number of contestants (when not upon the proper working of the machine reading the ballots). Those more or less casual factors are easily accepted, but we can inquire whether that degree could not result out of a choice made by voters themselves, not once for ever but on the occasion of each election. That was the aim of a proposal put forward by Henry Theil in a paper in 1969, in which he wondered whether citizens could not "have the right [on the occasion of each election] to vote on the degree to which they will be politically divided in their own parliament." More precisely, Theil suggested to give the voting procedure a two dimensional character, allowing each citizen to vote on one hand for the party he prefers

---

outcomes systematically affect the nature of a redistricting plan and the subsequent elections held under it."

[27] From Gopoian and West (1984) to Ostidiek (1995).

[28] To illustrate what we mean by *built-in device*, let us mention that under the proportional rule the number of seats of the legislative assembly could be reduced in proportion to the rate of turnout: An unpredictable number of seats would make political parties' tactics more difficult. For the same purpose, under plurality incumbents could be confirmed only if they get a predetermined threshold of percentage points over their best challenger, thus giving more weight to dissent than to routine consent.

and on the other hand on a number expressing the degree of preferred proportionality. Theil's proposal as such is not easy to implement,[29] but it could be reformulated in more manageable ways. For example, the country could be divided in single member constituencies, and each voter asked to express, besides the party choice, his preference for pure plurality or proportional representation. The constituencies where the majority of the voters opt for the first solution get the first winner. When the majority opts for the proportional solution, all constituencies sharing that choice could have their votes summed up and the seats distributed according to some version of the proportional rule.[30] Constituencies of unpredictable size would make incumbents' calculus more complex without destroying the incentives to political responsiveness, thus supporting a time consistent fiduciary exchange. Besides, such a solution would internalize the fact that voters' marginal rate of substitution between majority stability and representativeness can be different as economic and social circumstances change. The risk of partisan maneuvering cannot be excluded, but the costs of its implementation would be higher.

THE QUANDARY OF STABILITY VERSUS CHANGE OF RULES

Taagepera and Shugart (1989) praise the stability of voting rules allowing parties, candidates and voters to learn new strategies, but they underestimate the price paid for that learning in undermining the basic representative proxy. Our reflection on the voting rules began by maintaining their constitutional status and ended with a dilemma on whether their stability is apt or not to control the opportunism of the representatives. Along the way, we recast the difficulties raised by Anthony Downs – asymmetric information costs and the irrationality of political delegation in presence of goals dissonance – and stressed the latent conflict between voters and incumbents, with the latter better equipped to exploit the bond useful to stabilize the process of political decision-making in order to emasculate the threat of dismissal, the main control tool in the hand of the voters. Under any voting rule stable in time what encourages voters' loyalty loses representatives' discipline, by making the threat of dismissal less credible. In this way we have a benchmark to assess the devices apt to increase the expected goals congruence: how much they increase or reduce the impact of that threat. Hence the dilemma at the heart of the constitutional design of the voting rules in combining stability and change of those rules. A dilemma which

---

[29] Starting with the formula $q_i = p_i^\alpha / \Sigma p_j^\alpha$ – where p_i is the ratio of votes and q_i the ratio of seats going to party i – Theil's proposal requires a vote on the value of α, with the related problem of devising its most preferred value. Theil submitted that his proposal would stimulate each voter to take a broader view of the political structure as a whole, while making his or her own party choice.

[30] The summing up could occur at national level, or within states or regions of predetermined size, since there is no reason why the same rule should apply to the whole country (as a matter of fact, it never happens today because of the factors distorting the logic of either system).

reveals the implicit rationale of the apparently incongruent critics of either rule when advocating the introduction of the opposite one (too easily dismissed in terms of an "others' gardens are always greener" effect).

The problems posited by the governance of the citizens/representatives relationship has a more general bearing since it affects all the situations (think of the bureaucracy) where the agents are able "to respond to new constraints by making various adjustments on margin they still control" (Thrainn Eggertsson, 1995). Here, the very elapsing of time comes to affect the working of permanent rules superintending principal/agent relationships. The time dimension of those relationship cannot be neglected because that permanency can encourage investment in devices apt to bypass the rules, leading to a zero- or negative-sum outcome. It is with time that the agents learn how to adjust to the constraints they face, so that a change of rules can at times be better than the best of rules to keep the proper set of incentives. That makes for an important difference between the private or market setting and the public or political one. In the former, well defined and stable rights are the prerequisites of efficient exchanges, but in politics stability provides an asymmetric advantage to those better equipped to learn how to bypass the constraints imposed on them. Whenever the agents are in a better position to apply the terms of the incomplete contract supposedly defining the limits of their action – that is, to control and to influence with time the contents of their "property rights" – changes or periodic redefinition of those rights are prerequisite to keeping the set of incentives consistent with efficient outcomes (the alternative being that the agents come to define *de facto* the terms of their own contract).

In the electoral case the agents' self-regulation is of a more immediate evidence. In this case, we would need built-in devices apt to make incumbents electoral success more uncertain thus making the bite of competitive elections credible in a ordinary way. Until we find out a workable solution, we can only register the limits of constitutional binds on political control, just as the market registers daily the limits of corporate control.

REFERENCES

Acemoglu, Daron, and James Robinson, 2000, "Why did the West extend the franchise? Democracy, inequality, and growth in historical perspective," *Quarterly Journal of Economics* 116, 1167–1199.

Alghion, Philippe, and Jean Tirole, 1997, "Formal and real authority in organization," *Journal of Political Economy* 105, 1–29.

Barro, Robert, 1973, "The control of politicians: an economic model," *Public Choice* 14, 19–42.

Bartolini, Stefano, and Peter Mair, 1990, *Identity, Competition and Electoral Availability: The Stabilization of European Electorates 1885–1985*, Cambridge University Press.

Berg, Jooyce, John Dickhaut, and Kevin McCabe, 1995, "Trust, reciprocity and social history," *Games and Economic Behavior* 10, 122–142.

Blaustein, Albert P., and Gispert H. Flanz, 1984 (and successive updating), *Constitutions of the Countries of the World*, Dobbs Ferry, New York: Oceana Publications Inc.

Boix, Charles, 1999, "Setting the Rules of the Game: the Choice of Electoral Systems in Advanced Democracies," *American Political Science Review* 93, 604–624.

Brennan, Geoffrey, and Loren Lomasky, 1993, *Democracy and Decision: The Pure Theory of Electoral Preference*, New York: Cambridge University Press.

Breton, Albert, 1996, *Competitive Governments*, New York: Cambridge University Press.

Breton, Albert, and Gianluigi Galeotti, 1985, "Is proportional representation always the best electoral rule?," *Public Finance – Finance Publique* 40, 1–16.

Buchanan, James, and Gordon Tullock, 1962, *The Calculus of Consent*, Ann Arbor, MI: The University of Michigan Press.

Buruma, Ian, 2001, "The Japanese Berlusconi?," *New York Review of Books* 48 (12), 42–44.

Calvert, Randall, 1995, "The rational choice theory of social institutions: Cooperation, coordination and communication," in Jeffrey Banks and Eric Hanushek (eds.), *Modern Political Economy*, New York: Cambridge University Press, 216–267.

Congleton, Roger, 1984, "Committees and rent-seeking effort," *Journal of Public Economics* 25, 197–209.

Cooter, Robert, and Thomas Ulen, 1998, *Law and Economics*, Glenview, Ill.: Scott, Foresman and Company.

Cox, Gary, and Jonathan Katz, 1999, "The reapportionement revolution and bias in U.S. Congressinal elections," *The American Journal of Political Science* 34, 903–935.

Dick, A., and J. Lott, 1993, "Reconciling voters' behavior with legislative term limits," *Journal of Public Economics* 50, 1–14.

Downs, Anthony, 1957, *An Economic Theory of Democracy*, New York: Harper and Row.

Edlin, Aaron, and Joseph Stiglitz, 1995, "Discouraging rivals: Managerial rent-seeking and economic inefficiencies," *American Economic Review* 85, 1301–1312.

Eggertsson, Thrainn, 1995, "On the Economics of Economics," *Kyklos* 48, 201–210.

Finer, S. E., 1997, *The History of Government from the Earliest Time*, New York: Oxford University Press.

Friedman, Daniel, and Donald Wittman, 1995, "Why voters vote for incumbents but against incumbency: A rational choice explanation," *Journal of Public Economics* 57, 67–83.

Galeotti, Gianluigi, 1994, "On proportional non-representation," *Public Choice* 80, 359–370

Galeotti, Gianluigi, 2000, "Founding fathers vs. rotten kids: A positive approach to constitutional politics," in G. Galeotti, P. Salmon and R. Wintrobe (eds.), *Competition and Structure: The Political Economy of Collective Decisions: Essays in Honor of Albert Breton*, New York: Cambridge University Press, 104–125.

Galeotti, Gianluigi, and Albert Breton, 1986, "An economic theory of political parties," *Kyklos* 39, 47–65.

Gelman, Andrew, and Gary King, 1994, "Enhancing democracy through legislative redistricting," *The American Political Science Review* 88, 541–559.

Gopoian, David, and Darrell West, 1984, "Trading security for seats: Strategic considerations in the redistricting process," *The Journal of Politics* 46, 1080–1096.

Grillo, Michele, 1997, "Democracy, competition and the principle of *Isonomia*: An economic analysis of the political exchange as an incomplete contract, in A. Breton, G. Galeotti, P. Salmon, and R. Wintrobe (eds.), *Understanding Democracy: Economic and Political Perspectives*, New York: Cambridge University Press, 47–63.

Grofman, Bernard (ed.), 1996, *Legislative Term Limits: Public Choice Perspectives*, Dordrecht: Kluwer Nijhoff.

Hardin, Russell, 1989, "Why a constitution?" in B. Grofman and D. Wittman (eds.), *The Federalist Papers and the New Institutionalism*, Agathon Press, 100–123.

Kreps, David, 1990, "Corporate culture and economic theory," in J. Alt and K. Shepsle (eds.), *Perspectives on Political Economy,* New York: Cambridge University Press, 90–143.

Kishlansky, Mark A., 1986, *Parliamentary Selection: Social and Political Choices in Early Modern England*, New York: Cambridge University Press.

McKelvey, Richard, and Peter Ordeshook, 1985, "Elections with limited information: A fulfilled expectation model using contemporaneous poll and endorsement data as information sources," *The Journal of Economic Theory* 36, 55–85.

McNutt Patrick, 1997, "Rent-seeking and political tenure: First estimates," *Public Choice* 92, 369–385.

Mueller, Dennis C., 1988, *Public Choice II*, New York: Cambridge University Press.

Mueller, Dennis C., 1996, *Constitutional Democracy*, Oxford: Oxford University Press.

Myerson, Roger B., 1999, "Theoretical comparisons of electoral systems," *European Economic Review* 43, 671–697.

Niemi, Richard, and Laura Winsky, 1992, "The persistence of partisan redistricting effects in Congressional elections in the 1970s and 1980s," *The Journal of Politics* 54, 565–572.

Ordeshook, Peter C., 1992, "Constitutional stability," *Constitutional Political Economy* 3, 137–175.

Ostidiek, Donald, 1995, "Congressional redistricting and district typology," *The Journal of Politics* 57, 533–543.

Palfrey, Tomas, and Howard Rosenthal, 1985, "Voter participation and strategic uncertainty," *American Political Science Review* 79, 62–78.

Persson Torsten and Guido Tabellini, 2000, *Political Economics: Explaining Economic Policy*, Cambridge, Mass.: The MIT Press.

Powell, G.B., 1981, "Party systems and political systems performance," *The American Political Science Review* 75, 861–879.

Riker, William, and Peter Ordeshook, 1968, "A theory of the calculus of voting," *American Political Science Review* 1968, 25–42.

Rokkan, S., 1970, *Citizens, Elections, Parties: Approaches to the Comparative Study of the Process of Development*, Oslo: Univeristetdforlaget.

Shleifer, Andrei, and Robert Wishny, 1989, "Management entrenchment," *Journal of Financial Economics* 25, 123–139.

Taagepera, Rein, and Matthew Soberg Shugart, 1989, *Seats and Votes*, New Haven, CT: Yale University Press.

Theil, Henry, 1969, "The desired level of political entropy," *The American Political Science Review* 63, 521–525.

Weingast, Barry, and William Marshall, 1988, "The industrial organization of Congress; or, why legislatures, like firms, are not organized as markets," *Journal of Political Economy* 96, 132–163.

Wintrobe, Ronald, 1987, "The market for corporate control and the market for political control," *Journal of Law, Economics, and Organization* 3, 435–448.

Wintrobe, Ronald, 1998, *The Political Economy of Dictatorship*, New York: Cambridge University Press.

Wittman, Donald, 1995, *The Myth of Democratic Failure,* Chicago: University of Chicago Press.

Wohlgemuth, Michael, 1999, "Entry barriers in politics; or, why politics, like natural monopoly, is not organized as an ongoing market process," *Review of Austrian Economics* 12, 175–200.

11

Citizens' Sovereignty, Constitutional Commitments, and Renegotiation: Original versus Continuing Agreement

Viktor J. Vanberg

INTRODUCTION

It is often argued that democratic polities, being founded on the principle of the sovereignty of the people, are inherently limited in their capacity to make binding commitments. Because a present parliament cannot effectively bind future parliaments, the argument goes, a commitment made at some point in time "in the name of the people" may be overturned by a parliament representing the respective constituency at a later time.[1] In his "Distinguished Lecture on Economics in Government" the former chairman of the Council of Economic Advisors, Joseph Stiglitz, identifies this as a principal source of government failure when he notes: "The problem of commitment stems from the inherent nature of government itself. Government is the primary enforcer of contracts. It uses its monopoly on the legal use of force to create the possibility of private commitment. There is no one, however, whose job it is to guard the guardian. The government cannot make commitments because it always has the possibility of changing its mind, and earlier 'agreements' cannot be enforced."[2]

To be sure, to the argument that by contrast to private contracting parties within an established legal order the constituents of self-organized democratic polities have no external enforcing apparatus to which they could turn to give binding force to their commitments, one might respond that democratic politics operates at various levels (e.g., the level of local communes, of states or *Länder* within a federal union, of nation-states, up to the level of multinational arrangements), and that constituencies at any one level may choose to use an arrangement at the next higher level to give binding force to commitments that

---

[1] For example, A. Breton and A. Frascini (p. 62) note: "It is formally impossible for a democratic parliament to bind successor parliaments. The laws put in place by one parliament can be modified or even repealed by another. That is one implication of popular sovereignty. That fact would seem to make commitments to any particular long-term course of action by a succession of governments next to impossible."

[2] J. Stiglitz (1998: 9f.)

they wish to make. Thus, for instance, states within a federal union can commit to certain principles through contracts at the federal level, or nation-states can choose to bind themselves through international agreements (such as, for instance, GATT/WTO), thereby raising the costs of revoking the respective commitments in the future.

This would, however, not answer the fundamental question of the ability of democratic polities to commit, and it is, in any case, not the line of argument that I wish to pursue here. Instead, the purpose of this chapter is to examine some of the more general conceptual and theoretical aspects of the problem of commitment in democratic polities. Approaching the issue from a constitutional economics perspective, I shall look at such commitments as *social contracts* that the citizens-constituents of polities enter into between each other in order to realise mutual gains.[3] The guiding idea is that, just as individuals can realise mutual "gains from trade" through ordinary voluntary exchange-contracts, citizens can use the instrument of *social contracts* to realise mutual gains from *joint commitment*. Benefits from joint commitment can obviously be captured only where, and to the extent that, the ability to commit exists. And it is with the ability to commit that, according to the above noted argument, the principle of the sovereignty of the people seems to be in conflict. The question, therefore, that I shall seek to explore in this chapter is whether democratic polities, as self-governing entities, are, indeed, condemned to forego the kinds of gains that a capacity to commit might promise.

The focus of the discussion will be on what may be called *internal* as opposed to *external* commitments, because the *ability to commit* appears to raise less fundamental issues in regard to the latter than in regard to the former. Internal commitments, in the sense the term is used here, are commitments that constituents of democratic polities make among themselves, while external commitments are those that constituencies of democratic polities make vis-à-vis third parties.[4] The sovereignty of the people is normally not considered a legitimate excuse for a parliament to revoke commitments to third parties made by previous parliaments. This may, of course, not prevent parliaments from doing so. Yet, theoretical reflection as well as empirical evidence suggest that in international affairs there are often prudential reasons for later constituencies to honor earlier made commitments even if, factually, they could repudiate

---

[3] D. C. North and B. R. Weingast (1996) in their study on the evolution of constitutional provisions in early modern England also deal with the issue of the "ability of government to commit" (ibid.:139). They are concerned, however, with the question of how the emergence of the institutions of representative government served to make the Crown's commitments credible rather than with the issue of the ability of popular governments to commit.

[4] To say that the issue of the ability to commit is more significant with regard to *internal* than to *external* commitments is not meant to imply, of course, that the latter do not raise serious problems.

them.[5] In any case, it is surely with regard to internal commitments that the *ability to commit* poses a more challenging issue.

DEMOCRACY AS A COOPERATIVE ENTERPRISE: THE NOTION OF CITIZEN SOVEREIGNTY

The starting point of my inquiry is the notion that a democratic polity can be viewed "as a cooperative venture for mutual advantage" (Rawls 1971: 84). From this outlook the fundamental defining criterion of a democratic polity is seen not in particular institutional-procedural features, such as general elections or representative governmental institutions, but in the fact that its members or citizens are the principals, or owners, or sovereigns of the collective enterprise. It is their common interests that the enterprise is meant to serve, and institutional-procedural provisions are instrumental to that purpose. Accordingly, institutional provisions in a democratic polity are to be ultimately judged in terms of their suitability to serve that purpose.[6]

In the most general sense, the fundamental problem that people have to solve in their dealings with each other – or, in grander terms, the fundamental problem of social order – is how to improve the prospects for realising mutual gains, and how to avoid the mutual harm that too easily results from the ever-present temptation to seek one's own advantage at the expense of others. Economics as the science of gains from trade traditionally focuses on how people can realise mutual gains through voluntary exchange of ordinary goods and services in markets. Yet, as James M. Buchanan has persistently emphasised, the economist's "gains-from-trade paradigm" can be generalized from its traditional domain, market exchange, to all kinds of social arrangements,[7] including the realm of political action and of constitutional choice (Buchanan 1979: 27ff.). The general idea is that decentralized market transactions, in their typical form of bilateral exchange, are a most important but not the only kind of social transactions through which participants can realize mutual gains. Rather, the realm of politics can also be looked at from a "voluntary exchange perspective," as an arena where mutual gains can be realised through politically

---

[5] For instance, most often governments continue to serve foreign debts, even in cases, such as, e.g., the People's Republic of China, where a revolutionary government denies the legitimacy of the antecedent governments that incurred the debt.

[6] Note that from this perspective the question of what are suitable "democratic institutions" cannot be answered in terms of some predefined notion of what is "democratic" (e.g., majority rule), but only in tems of the suitability of institutions in serving the common interest of the citizens.

[7] Buchanan (1977:136): "Economists . . . are specialists in exchange. . . . When they observe a social interaction, they interpret the results in exchange terms, as possibly emerging from voluntary action. To the extent that results can be fitted into the exchange pattern, economists can infer that *all* parties secure gains, as these gains are measured in terms of the participants' preferences and not those of the observer. . . . This explanatory-evaluative task for the economist may be extended from the simplest to the most complex institutional structures."

coordinated collective action (Brennan and Buchanan 1985: 25ff.; Buchanan and Congleton 1998: 16ff.).

In light of a generalized gains-from-trade paradigm, political organization is seen as a potential instrument for securing mutual benefits. Organizing themselves in polities at various levels (communes, states, nations, and supra-national formations) is one way in which people can seek to capture mutual gains that could not be secured at all, or not as effectively, by other means, be it through decentralized market transactions or through privately organized collective action, that is, by organizing themselves in "clubs" (Buchanan 1987a). The term *public goods* may be used to identify benefits of this kind, benefits that can only be internalised by means of political organization.

If a democratic polity can be looked at "as a cooperative venture for mutual advantage" (Rawls 1971), the rules and institutions of democratic politics can, in the sense noted, be looked at as organizational devices that may help citizens-members-constituents to realize mutual benefits. Just as *cooperatives*, as *member-owned* enterprises are there to promote the interests of their members, democratic polities, as *citizens cooperatives*, are there to serve the common interests of their members, the citizens. And just as the organizational rules of ordinary cooperatives can be judged in terms of their capacity to promote the common interests of their respective members, the rules and institutions of democratic politics can be analyzed, and compared with each other, with regard to their capacity to enable citizens to realise mutual gains, and to protect them from being exploited, through the political process, by fellow-citizens or by political agents.

The criterion for desirability or *efficiency* implied in such an understanding of democratic institutions may be called *citizen sovereignty,* in analogy to *consumer sovereignty*. *Consumer sovereignty*, as a criterion for judging the efficiency of market institutions, means that the market process should be institutionally framed in such a way that consumer preferences are the principal controlling variable governing producer choices. In other words, *consumer sovereignty* requires markets to be institutionally framed in a way that make producers most responsive to consumer wants. By comparison, *citizen sovereignty* means that the political process should be institutionally framed in such a way that citizen preferences are its principal controlling variable, that the producers of politics, such as politicians and government bureaucrats, are made most responsive to citizens' common interests. Like consumer sovereignty, citizen sovereignty is a *procedural* criterion. It cannot be applied to outcomes directly, but only to the processes from which outcomes result. Not by looking at market *outcomes per se* but only by looking at the nature of the *choice processes* that have generated them can we judge whether these outcomes may be presumed to satisfy consumer sovereignty. Equally, not by looking at policy outcomes as such, but only by looking at how policy outcomes are arrived at, can one judge whether the criterion of citizen sovereignty is satisfied. The extent to which democratic polities satisfy the criterion of citizen sovereignty depends on how well their organizational structure or constitutional provisions can be expected to enable citizens to realize common benefits and to protect them from being exploited by other citizens or political agents.

The principle of citizen sovereignty means that the individual citizens who, at any given time, constitute a democratic polity are the ultimate sovereigns in whose common interests the polity should be operated. At any given time the ultimate decision-making authority rests with the *current* members or constituents, and it is in terms of *their* common interests that the working properties of a democratic polity are to be justified. Accordingly, the issue to be addressed in this chapter can also be stated in terms of the question of whether the principle of citizen sovereignty limits citizens in their capacity to realise potential gains from commitments. The next two sections serve to clarify some preliminary questions relevant to this issue.

MUTUAL ADVANTAGE AND VOLUNTARY AGREEMENT IN POLITICS

According to the *gains-from-trade paradigm* of ordinary economics, it is the parties' voluntary agreement to market exchanges that allows us to classify such transactions as *mutually advantageous*. The economist's standard notion of the *efficiency* of market outcomes is, ultimately, based on nothing other than the presumption that they result from voluntarily agreed-on transactions. In its generalized application to the political realm, the gains-from-trade paradigm equally implies that voluntary agreement is, ultimately, the only conclusive proof of mutual advantage.[8] Only from voluntary agreement on the part of all participants can we safely conclude that politically orchestrated choices are, indeed, advantageous to everybody involved.

The logic of the generalized gains-from-trade paradigm implies that the criterion of mutual advantage and voluntary agreement is extended from market transactions to political action. It is often questioned that such extension can be meaningful. Critics note that even though mutual advantage and voluntary agreement may be the relevant criterion of efficiency for market transactions, applied to the realm of politics they appear too restrictive to be of any practical significance. In essence, a market can be defined as an institutionally framed

---

[8] Buchanan (1960: 122): "In a sense, the political economist is concerned with discovering 'what people want.' The content of his efforts may be . . . summed up in the familiar statement: *There exist mutual gains from trade.* His task is that of locating possible flaws in the existing social structure and in presenting possible 'improvements.' His specific hypothesis is that mutual gains do, in fact, exist as a result of possible changes (trades). This hypothesis is tested by the behavior of private people in response to the suggested alternatives. Since 'social' values do not exist apart from individual values in a free society, consensus or unanimity (mutuality of gain) is the only test which can insure that a change is beneficial."

social arena in which, ideally, voluntary contracting is the only method of interpersonal dealings. The principal function of the institutions that constitute markets is to ensure that only such transactions take place, and only such cooperative arrangements are formed, that are based on voluntary agreement of all parties involved. By contrast, the institutions of democratic politics are clearly not designed to allow only for measures to which all citizens voluntarily agree. Instead, political actions are regularly taken without unanimous approval, by majority vote, and those in disagreement are forced to accept whatever the majority decides. Indeed, it is difficult to see how effective politics should be possible at all if it were restricted to choices voluntarily agreed to by all participants. If this has to be acknowledged, how can the criterion of mutual advantage and voluntary agreement be applicable at all to the realm of politics?

A way out of this seeming dilemma can be found in the distinction between unanimity as the ultimate *legitimizing principle* for political action and unanimity as a *decision rule* in practical politics. The essential argument on this matter is, of course, the one developed by J. M. Buchanan and G. Tullock in their Public Choice classic *The Calculus of Consent* (1962). Unanimity as the ultimate legitimizing principle reflects the normative standard that in a "cooperative venture for mutual advantage" ideally only such collective decisions should be taken that benefit everybody in the group and that can, therefore, command everybody's consent. As Buchanan and Tullock show, the difficulty with using unanimity as a decision rule within a defined group, such as the constituents of a polity, results from decision-making costs, in particular – but not only – due to the temptation for strategic bargaining. Independent of whether or not a citizen would benefit from a proposed policy measure or rule-change, he or she may seek to extract additional advantages from "selling" his or her agreement at the highest possible price. The temptation to seek such strategic gains may prevent projects from being implemented, even though – in the absence of such obstacles – they promise gains for everybody. Recognizing this impediment to their prospects of realising mutual benefits through concerted political action, citizens may, with good reasons, voluntarily agree to adopt a less-than-unanimity rule for deciding political matters. For prudential reasons, because of their mutual interest in securing the prospects of realising potential mutual gains through concerted political action, they may also voluntarily agree to adopt institutions of indirect democracy, delegating decision-making authority to political agents. It is the voluntary agreement at the *constitutional* level that legitimises the application of non-unanimous choice procedures at the sub-constitutional level.

Such transitions from unanimity to majority decisions and from direct to indirect democracy imply, of course, the possibility that political decisions will be made that are de facto not to everybody's benefit and that would never find the voluntary agreement of all members of the polity if they were decided upon separately and independently. Yet, this does not mean at all that the ultimate normative standard – mutual advantage and voluntary agreement – has been replaced by some other criterion. It simply means that, given the inevitable facts of organized political action, the adopted decision-making rules allowing for non-unanimous decisions provide overall the best prospects for citizens to advance their common interests. What legitimizes the institutions of democratic politics is, in this sense, nothing other than that – among feasible alternatives – they offer the best balance between prospects for mutual gains and risks of being harmed. As noted earlier, the proper normative standard against which democratic institutions are to be judged, is whether in their overall working properties they serve the common interests of the respective constituency better than any feasible alternative arrangement. If, as we have to assume, an institutional arrangement that would require *unanimity as decision-rule* for all in-period choices is less attractive to citizens in its overall working properties than one that allows for non-unanimous choices, it has to be judged inferior in terms of the underlying criterion, that is, *unanimity as a legitimising principle*. It is the application of the criterion of mutual advantage and voluntary agreement at the *constitutional level* that carries overriding power here.

Note that, in the context of markets as well as in the political arena, the criterion of mutual advantage and voluntary agreement is properly applied in a comparative sense, not as an ideal, absolute standard. To say that the market is to be viewed as an arena for voluntary contracting is not to say that all existing arrangements which we may call *markets* do in fact provide an absolute guarantee that coercion and fraud are perfectly excluded and no transactions are carried out, or cooperative arrangements are formed, except they are based on perfectly voluntary agreement of all parties concerned. To be sure, the ideal image of the market as an arena of such perfect voluntariness would be far from what we observe in the real world, where market participants are often severely constrained in their "freedom to choose," by lack of economic power, lack of knowledge, lack of available alternatives, and so on. Yet, the finding that existing markets fall short of such an ideal standard is irrelevant for the issue of practical institutional choices. Relevant for this issue is only the comparison between *feasible alternative arrangements*. In this sense, the criterion of mutual advantage and voluntary agreement should not be interpreted as describing an ideal, frictionless world, irrespective of what is attainable in the world in which we live. It is to be applied in a comparative sense, comparing existing market institutions with potential, feasible alternatives in regard to their *relative* capacity to ensure voluntariness in within-market transactions.

The same is true for the institutions of democratic politics. Here as well, the criterion of mutual advantage and voluntary agreement is not to be interpreted in the sense of an unattainable ideal in comparison to which every existing institutional arrangement must inevitably look deficient. It ought to be applied in a comparative sense, as a criterion that allows us to say what counts as an improvement in democratic institutions. Among feasible alternative institutional arrangements those qualify as preferable that offer better prospects to citizens for the realization of mutual gains and/or better protection against exploitation from other citizens or from political agents.

COMPLEX EXCHANGE TRANSACTIONS AND CONSTITUTIONAL COMMITMENTS

For the purposes of this chapter it is useful to subdivide the mutual benefits that democratic constituencies may realise through the political process into two kinds, namely, gains from *complex exchange transactions* and gains from *constitutional commitments*.

By complex exchange transactions, I mean organized collective actions that serve to coordinate the contributions of constituents to the production of a good that benefits all members of the polity, but that free-rider problems prevent from being produced privately. Such collective action can be interpreted as *complex exchange* in the sense that, in light of the benefits to be had, the costs of contributing to the production of the good are worthwhile for all members of the constituency, provided everybody else shares in the burden. Under such conditions all parties can benefit from an arrangement that requires everybody to contribute. They *exchange*, so to speak, conditional commitments to contribute – that is, promises to pay one's share on the condition that all others do so as well – and political organization is the instrument to implement such a complex transaction that generates benefits to all parties involved. The transaction is similar to an ordinary market exchange in that each participant receives a benefit in return for a contribution. Its difference lies in the fact that the give and take occurs not in decentralized bilateral transactions between trading parties, but requires simultaneous coordination of the contributions of all members of the benefiting group.

By constitutional commitments I mean organized political action that serves to define and enforce the *rules of the game* to which the members of a polity are subject. By jointly committing to suitable rules, that is, by mutually agreeing to submit to the discipline of such rules, all members of a polity may be able to realize gains that could not be had if they were not so constrained. The typical instances of such cases are social-dilemma situations in which individually rational, unconstrained choices generate a pattern of outcomes inferior to what would result if all participants were appropriately constrained in their choices. Unlike the previously described complex exchange transactions, constitutional commitments are not about orchestrating citizens' separate contributions to a specific joint project. Instead, they are about defining the general terms, the rules of the game, under which the members of a polity are to operate in the future. And the benefits participants expect from such constitutional commitments are not derived from specific anticipated outcomes, but are the *overall benefits* that result *over time* from having the continuing process of interaction and cooperation bound by suitable constraints.

Constitutional commitments, in the sense the term is used here, can be said to be always concerned with defining rules of the game. They can be distinguished, though, in terms of the kinds of rules they are about. In particular, along with the familiar distinction between private and public law, one can distinguish between commitments to rules that are to govern the interaction and cooperation of citizens in their private capacities and commitments to rules that are to govern their interrelations as members of the organized polity. The latter are constitutional rules in the more narrow, everyday sense of the term *constitutional*. They are the rules that define the terms of membership in a polity. As members of a polity, citizens may seek to realize mutual gains from constitutional commitments in both spheres, by agreeing to changes in the rules for the private arena as well as by agreeing to changes in the rules for the public arena. And the political process is the vehicle through which both kinds of commitments must be orchestrated.

Stated in terms of the game-metaphor, there are two principal ways in which people can realise mutual gains. They can seek to exploit opportunities for mutual advantage in playing a given game, that is, a game defined by given rules. And they can seek to realize mutual gains from playing a better game, better for all parties involved, by adopting more adequate rules. The gains from trade that ordinary economics is concerned with are the mutual gains that people can realise in playing the *market game*, through voluntary transactions in which they engage in their private capacities. What I referred to earlier as the mutual gains from complex exchange, are the gains that citizens can realise in playing the *game of politics*, by concerted action aimed at producing common benefits. The gains from *constitutional* commitment are the mutual gains that people can realise by managing to play a *better game*, be it by defining and enforcing more conducive rules for the private realm or be it by improving the rules of politics.

The distinction, emphasized here, between two ways in which people can use the political process to realize mutual gains, namely through complex exchange transactions on the one side and constitutional commitments on the other, is implicit in, but not clearly recognized in Buchanan's notion of "politics as exchange" (Brennan and Buchanan 1985: 25ff.; Buchanan 1987b: 307f.; Buchanan and Congleton 1998: 16ff.), a notion that, otherwise, provides the essential inspiration for the thoughts developed in this chapter. In fact, Buchanan's emphasis on the analogy between exchange-transactions in markets and *exchanges* concluded through the political process,[9] is apt to gloss over the very distinction that I seek to describe here. As far as "collective action project(s)" (Buchanan and Congleton 1998: 17) that involve the sharing among all citizens of the costs of commonly desired benefits are concerned, there is indeed a direct analogy between ordinary, bilateral market exchange and its

---

[9] Buchanan emphasizes that "political exchange is no different from market exchange, except for the number of direct participants" (Buchanan and Congleton 1998:16).

more complex multilateral counterpart in politics. With regard to this kind of political exchange, that is, what I refer to as complex exchange transactions, it can indeed be said: "In the market, individuals exchange apples for oranges; in politics, individuals exchange agreed-on shares in contributions toward the costs of that which is commonly desired, from the services of the local fire station to that of the judge" (Buchanan 1987b: 308). This is, however, not so for what Buchanan refers to as "constitutional 'exchange'" (308) and what I call *constitutional commitments*. The relevant difference between constitutional commitments and ordinary exchange transactions in markets is not a matter of the "number of direct participants." Instead, it is a matter of the *nature of the contract*. As noted before, constitutional contracts are not about specifying the terms of a *transaction* that is to be carried out between the contracting parties, whether their number is two or more. Instead, they are about defining the rules of the game which the parties to the contract promise to respect in their future dealings with each other. One may, of course, decide to subsume such contracts under the rubric of *exchange* by describing them as *exchange of commitments*. This should, however, not distract from the difference in substance that separates *exchange transactions*, be they bi- or multilateral, from *constitutional commitments*, be they bi- or multilateral.[10]

In order to see in what ways the distinction between the two kinds of *political agreements*, namely, complex exchange transactions and constitutional commitments, is of relevance to the theme of this chapter, it is useful to look at the role of original agreement in the social contract model of politics.

ORIGINAL AND CONTINUING AGREEMENT

In the tradition of social contract theory, the models of constitutional choice behind a veil of uncertainty or ignorance, as advanced in James M. Buchanan's and Gordon Tullock's *Calculus of Consent* (1962) and John Rawls's *Theory of Justice* (1971), are based on the premise that what legitimizes a constitutional regime is the voluntary agreement of all parties involved. There are two aspects of the veil-model that are noteworthy.

Its primary function is to specify conditions of constitutional choice that foster impartiality, conditions that induce the parties involved to compare alternative rules in terms of their general working properties, unbiased by partial interests. In other words, the veil-model is meant to describe general conditions under which potential interests in privileges are filtered out (because the

---

[10] It should be noted that the distinction between exchange transactions and constitutional commitments applies to the market realm as well as to politics. Contracts concluded among private parties can also be classified in either of the two categories. Ordinary market transactions fall, of course, into the "exchange transaction" category, while, e.g., marriage contracts or contracts establishing business partnerships or corporations fall into the "constitutional commitment" category.

parties cannot predict with sufficient reliability whether they will be among the beneficiaries or not), and under which self-interested actors are, instead, motivated to opt for rules that are in their *common constitutional interests*. In fact, the veil-model can be said to specify, in a stylized way, conditions that help constituents to find out what their common constitutional interests are. To utilize the lessons of the model for practical purposes would mean to submit the process of constitutional choice to procedural constraints that promise to serve that very purpose: to increase the prospects for constituents' common constitutional interests to prevail.

In addition to its primary function the veil-model tends, however, also to focus attention on the *original* agreement on which rule-regimes are based, thereby suggesting that the issue of legitimacy is essentially a matter of original voluntary consent. It is this latter aspect that is of particular significance in the present context since the issue of whether there is a conflict between the *sovereignty of the people* and the ability of democratic constituencies to commit has obviously to do with the ability of later constituencies (or parliaments) to revoke *original agreements* entered into by earlier constituencies (parliaments).

The critical question of whether the focus on *original* agreement can provide an adequate answer to the issue of the legitimacy of ongoing political arrangements has often been raised in discussions on the social contract tradition, at least since David Hume's essay "Of the Original Contract" (1963 [1741/42]). Hume's critique focused on the issue of whether for established polities the notion of an original contract, voluntarily entered into by their founding members, is more than a myth, and whether an original agreement, even if there ever was one, can bind future generations. Apart from these classical objections, there are, however, other reasons to doubt whether original voluntary consent can provide sufficient legitimacy to an ongoing political regime, even in cases where such original agreement can safely be assumed, and where current members and original contractors are identical.

What is of relevance, here, is a critical difference – corresponding to the previously drawn distinction between *complex exchange transactions* and *constitutional commitments* – between *transaction-agreements* on the one side and *constitutional agreements* on the other.[11] As noted earlier, political organization can provide citizens with these two instruments for realising mutual advantages. Like ordinary, bilateral exchange transactions in markets, the complex exchange transactions in politics can be looked at as contractual schemes that specify in

---

[11] The following analysis has in many respects affinities to the literature on the "economics of contracts," associated, among others, with the name of O. E. Williamson (e.g., 1985). Though relating this literature to the issue discussed in this chapter would be, in itself, an interesting undertaking, it would not only go beyond the scope of the present analysis but would also distract from its main concern. I shall, therefore, disregard this literature here, except for a brief reference below (fn. 18).

advance the contributions that the contracting parties promise each other to make, expecting to reap a net benefit from the inclusive arrangement. In the case of such transactions, whether they occur as trades in markets or as complex exchanges in politics, it is the initial agreement, based on expected payoffs, that legitimises the transaction as *mutually advantageous*. In such cases the nature of the deal requires that the original agreement keeps its binding force until the transaction is completed. Where the give and take in ordinary exchange, or the multilateral contributions in complex political exchange are *simultaneous*, no problem arises.[12] Where trade – either simple or complex – is not carried out simultaneously, but where the nature of things requires some parties to move first while others contribute their share later, problems may arise because the latter may be tempted to renege on the original agreement. For obvious reasons, if transaction-agreements are to serve their purpose, the binding force of the original agreement must be protected against such opportunistic reneging. Otherwise, nobody would be willing to be the first mover in non-simultaneous exchange transactions, making it impossible to realise any potential gains that such transactions promise.[13]

Matters are significantly different, though, in case of constitutional agreements. The purpose of such agreements is not to specify the respective contributions that the parties to a simple or complex exchange transaction promise to make. It is, instead, to define the terms of an ongoing relationship, the rules of a continuing cooperative arrangement. As in the case of exchange transactions, the original agreement of the contracting parties to constitutional contracts is motivated by expectations of future gains. But such gains are not expected from the completion of a particular project. They are expected from the different quality that the mutual commitment to constraining rules provides to the ongoing cooperative venture. By contrast to transaction-agreements, the point of constitutional commitments is not a mutual promise to contribute one's share

---

[12] Parties to a transaction may, ex-post, regret to have agreed to it, after they find their expectations disappointed. Yet, such ex-post regret cannot undo the ex ante legitimacy of the transaction. There is a constitutional rationale for treating voluntarily entered transaction-commitments as binding, irrespective of ex-post regret: Playing a game that does not allow ex-post regret to undo previously agreed-on transactions is more advantageous to all players involved than playing according to rules that would entitle dissatisfied parties to return to the status quo. Or, stated in a less apodictic manner: To provide a constitutional rationale for not allowing ex-post regret to invalidate previous transaction-commitments would mean to show that it is in the common constitutional interest of the members of the respective constituency to insist on the binding force of "original agreements," because the working properties of the game so defined are overall more attractive than the working properties of the alternative game.

[13] Again, stated in constitutional terms, playing a game that would allow for such reneging would be less attractive for all players involved than playing according to rules that make original agreements to non-simultaneous exchanges binding until the transaction is completed, because only under the latter condition certain "gains from trade" can be realized that could not be achieved otherwise.

to a common project, *it is a mutual promise to submit to certain rules in ones' ongoing dealings with each other.*

My principal conjecture is that, because of the differences between transaction-agreements and constitutional agreements, in case of the latter it is not the *original* agreement alone that can carry the burden of providing legitimacy to the ongoing constitutional arrangement. Instead, normative significance must be assigned to the *continuing, ongoing* agreement to the terms of the arrangement. Only such ongoing agreement can count as a relevant indicator of whether the terms of the *ongoing arrangement* are, indeed, mutually advantageous to all parties involved. In the case of transaction commitments, the original agreement by which the respective obligations of the contracting parties are specified is all that counts. It is only the inclusive package of obligations that makes the deal advantageous to all parties involved, and it is only their trust in the completion of the package that can motivate parties to non-simultaneous trades to move first. Continuing agreement, as opposed to original agreement, can, in such cases, not play a meaningful normative role. By contrast, constitutional commitments are based on the expectation that an ongoing relationship can be more advantageous to all parties involved if all respect certain agreed-on rules of the game. The original agreement reflects the parties' anticipation that they will, indeed, benefit from the arrangement. It can, however, not be meant as an unconditional promise to submit indefinitely to a rule-regime, even if it should turn out not to be to one's advantage. As I shall argue in more detail, it must be viewed as a promise to comply with the agreed-on rules as long as the other parties are equally willing to submit to them, and as long as the game defined by these rules is, indeed, advantageous to all parties involved. Yet, parties who no longer consider the rule-regime advantageous must be allowed to opt out or to ask for re-negotiation. By contrast to transaction agreements, the case of constitutional agreements to allow for re-negotiation or cancellation of the contract does not undermine the very purpose of such agreements, namely to allow parties to realize mutual gains from joint commitment to rule-constraints. Such *mutual* gains can only be made *as long as* the joint commitment is in fact advantageous to everybody involved.

Requiring that commitments be honored that were originally made in transaction-agreements is a necessary precondition for realizing gains from non-simultaneous trade. Requiring persons to comply with rules that they have agreed to, *as long as they play the game*, is a necessary condition for realising the mutual gains that can be had from joint commitments to suitable rules. This is quite different, though, from requiring persons to continue to play a game the rules of which they no longer consider advantageous, because they do no longer expect to benefit from the pattern of outcomes that result under these rules. To be sure, disagreement with rules that were originally agreed to cannot be allowed to serve as an excuse for cheating on the rules, that is, for non-compliance. But, original agreement cannot be claimed to continue to provide legitimacy to a constitutional arrangement that is no longer considered advantageous by parts of the constituency.

OPPORTUNISM AND RENEGOTIATION

For the reasons discussed earlier, at the operational, sub-constitutional level the decision-making procedures in democratic polities must allow for non-unanimous choices, even though democratic polities are to be seen as cooperative ventures for mutual advantage, and even though voluntary agreement is the only conclusive indicator of mutual advantage and, therefore, the ultimate criterion of legitimacy. That is to say, feasible democratic institutions will inevitably fall short of guaranteeing that only those decisions are generated by the political process that promise advantages for all parties involved.[14] Such inevitable *imperfections* of democratic politics as an enterprise for mutual advantage might of course be a reason for suspecting that the ability to commit is not a feature of democratic politics. Shifting majority coalitions could cause commitments made by one parliament to be overturned by a later parliament. Likewise, other shortcomings of actual processes of collective decision making that prevent citizens' common interests from being reliably implemented could be responsible for such reneging on earlier commitments. This is, however, not the aspect of the issue that I want to examine here. Instead, I shall concentrate on the question of whether the *sovereignty of the people* – that is, the fact that constituencies at any particular time are *sovereign*, and can turn over commitments made by previous constituencies – is in and by itself the reason for the presumed inability to commit. Leaving aside problems that may be generated by the above mentioned imperfections in collective choice procedures, my focus is exclusively on the issue of whether an inability to commit follows, indeed, as an inevitable consequence from the permanent option to re-negotiate that is implied in such sovereignty. In other words, my concern here is only with the question of whether the power of parliaments to revise previously made commitments would render democratic constituencies incapable of realizing mutual benefits from workable (internal) commitments, even if there were no imperfections in collective choice procedures that prevent parliamentary choices from reliably reflecting the genuine common interests of the citizenry.

Joint commitments, whether they come in the form of transaction agreements or as constitutional agreements, are instruments by which citizens can realize mutual advantages. The benefits from such commitments are made possible by the fact that the parties involved simultaneously accept constraints on their behavior. Imposing such constraints on one's own behavior is a price one is

---

[14] Within the open set of feasible democratic institutions we will, of course, find differences in regard to the risk of decisions being made that run against the interests of parts of the constituency, and we can compare different institutions in terms of their capacity to promote those interests that all citizens have genuinely in common.

willing to pay if the advantages from doing so exceed the costs. At the time parties voluntarily enter a joint commitment, they all expect to gain from the arrangement. Yet, in an uncertain and changing world committing to constraints on one's future behavior involves the risk that what initially looked like an advantageous arrangement may later on, in the light of new information or under changed circumstances, turn out different.[15] Parties to such commitments may, therefore, wish to be protected against ex-post regret by requiring a re-negotiation option and to make their continued cooperation contingent on their *continuing* agreement to the terms of the arrangement. Because such interest in being protected against ex-post regret appears to be quite natural, it can only be because of the expected costs or disadvantages of such protection that contracting parties may prefer to forgo the option to re-negotiate and to be bound by their original agreement alone.

In this context it is important clearly to distinguish between two separate issues, namely the *re-negotiation issue* that is presently at stake and the *opportunism issue* that has been the main theme of the previous section. Re-negotiation is a matter of changed perceptions of the advantages that the original agreement promises. Opportunism, that is, the temptation to cheat on an agreement, is about exploiting opportunities to escape one's obligations in a joint commitment, irrespective of whether there is any reason to re-evaluate the terms of the agreement itself. Re-negotiation is about the ex-post wish to have entered a different agreement, opportunism is about incentives to cheat on an existing agreement. In any agreement involving non-simultaneous contributions there are incentives for parties who are to contribute later to take advantage of those who had to move first. These incentives have nothing to do with a re-evaluation of the terms of the agreement in light of new information. They can already be anticipated at the time the original agreement is made, and they are entirely independent of whether or not the agreed-on arrangement as such continues to be advantageous for all parties involved.

To allow for opportunistic behavior is obviously in fundamental conflict with the very purpose of entering into any joint commitments. It is the mutuality of obligations that makes the arrangement mutually advantageous, and no party can be allowed to escape its obligations without offsetting the balance of costs and benefits. If the incentives for opportunism cannot be sufficiently controlled, such commitment will not be workable and may, therefore, not be concluded in the first place. By contrast, the interest in taking precautions against ex-post regret, and the wish to be able to re-negotiate an agreement in light of relevant new information or significant changes in circumstances, are perfectly

---

[15] For certain kinds of commitments, such as mutual insurance schemes, dealing with an uncertain future is the very purpose of the arrangement. In order to serve the purpose of the original agreement, such commitments must, of course, be binding in a sense demanded by this purpose. See footnote 17.

legitimate concerns that are not *per se* in conflict with the purpose of seeking to realise mutual gains through joint commitments. The relevant question is whether and how such concerns can be accounted for without defeating the very purpose that a joint commitment is meant to serve. In this regard, there is again a critical difference between transaction-agreements and constitutional agreements.

RE-NEGOTIATION IN TRANSACTION-COMMITMENTS AND CONSTITUTIONAL COMMITMENTS

Even though the wish to be able to re-negotiate a commitment in light of unanticipated new information or changes in relevant circumstances is a legitimate concern, in case of *transaction-agreements* it is apparently difficult to separate such legitimate concern from opportunistic attempts to escape the obligation to fulfil one's part of the bargain. In non-simultaneous complex exchange transactions illegitimate opportunism can easily be camouflaged as a legitimate interest in re-negotiation, and in the absence of a reliable method for telling them apart, allowing for ex-post re-negotiation could easily render transaction-agreements unworkable. Furthermore, even if they could be separated, allowing for legitimate re-negotiation would introduce uncertainties that may deter parties who have to move first from entering into joint commitments that would be mutually beneficial in the absence of such uncertainty. For these reasons, in order to secure the prospects of realising potential gains from transaction-agreements, all parties may well find it in their common constitutional interest to operate under a rule that excludes re-negotiation options from such agreements, even though they anticipate that there will be occasions where they would, for legitimate reasons, wish to have that option.

The same reasoning does, however, not apply to *constitutional agreements*. Such agreements are not about promises to make specified contributions to a joint project. They are about joint commitments to submit to common rules of the game, rules that are expected to constrain the participants' behavior in mutually beneficial ways. One may describe a constitutional agreement as an *exchange of commitments* in the sense that accepting rule-constraints on his own behavior is the price each participant is willing to pay in exchange for the benefits he expects from the fact that all others are willing to be likewise constrained. Yet, the reasons discussed earlier for excluding re-negotiation in case of non-simultaneous transactions do not apply in the case of such *exchange of commitments*. Problems of opportunism, in the sense of *cheating*, are present, of course. But while in transaction-agreements the principal opportunism-problem arises from the temptation to exploit the vulnerability of parties who had to move first with their contributions, in constitutional arrangements the principal opportunism-problem arises from the temptation to take advantage of the continuing rule-compliance of other participants while allowing oneself to act unconstrained. Here, opportunism is primarily not a matter of non-simultaneity, it is about violating rules while others continue to comply.[16]

Because of their noted differences from transaction-agreements, and by contrast to the latter, in constitutional agreements the opportunism-issue and the re-negotiation-issue can be systematically separated. Opportunism is about cheating on obligations that *have arisen* within agreed-on rules. Re-negotiation is about changing these rules with regard to *future* dealings. In non-simultaneous exchange transactions an attempt to evade one's obligations to contribute can be camouflaged as a desire to re-negotiate the terms of the deal. In constitutional commitments such ambiguity need not arise. More precisely, in constitutional arrangements issues of meeting one's current obligations within a given set of rules can be unambiguously separated from the issue of whether participants may wish to change these rules with regard to their future dealings. Obviously, re-negotiation cannot be allowed to be used as an instrument for escaping *current obligations* that arose within an existing, agreed-on set of rules. Otherwise, the incentive to camouflage opportunistic cheating as re-negotiation would make constitutional agreements unworkable in that critical inter-temporal imbalances in benefits and costs must be expected to arise among participants.[17] This does not imply, however, that re-negotiation may not be legitimately used to avoid *future obligations* that would arise if the existing constitutional contract were to remain in force.

The different role that re-negotiation can be allowed to play in constitutional commitments as opposed to transaction-commitments accounts for the previously noted difference in the significance that must be attributed, respectively, to ongoing agreement and to original agreement in the two kinds of commitment. Due to the difficulties in separating opportunistic behavior from legitimate re-negotiation, transaction-agreements could hardly serve their purpose if re-negotiation were allowed. It is in the common constitutional interest of potential contractors to regard the original agreement to a transaction as binding until the deal is concluded, and not to allow ex-post regret or lacking ongoing agreement to provide an excuse for re-negotiation. The rationale for

---

[16] This is not to say that non-simultaneity of contributions *within* constitutional arrangements may not raise significant problems. As I shall note (fn. 17 and fn. 18) such problems arise, in particular, for mutual insurance arrangements and in cases of relation-specific investments. Constitutional contracts must address such problems, and if they do not provide adequate solutions they may invite opportunistic misuse of re-negotiation options. The issue of inadequate constitutional provisions for non-simultaneous contributions within constitutional arrangements should, however, be separated from the re-negotiation issue *per se*.

[17] This is, for instance, the case for constitutional arrangements that have insurance characteristics. Where participants promise each other to mutually insure certain risks, the wish to renegotiate cannot be allowed to serve as an excuse for not meeting one's obligation to pay when the need arises. This does not mean, however, that the participants may not legitimately seek to renegotiate the terms of the insurance arrangement prospectively, with regard to future periods.

this is that potential contractors have good reasons to assume that the prospective costs of allowing for re-negotiation, namely the foregone mutual gains from transaction-commitments that are not made because of the risks of re-negotiation, most likely exceed the expected benefits.

By contrast, the purpose of constitutional commitments is not obstructed by allowing for re-negotiation. Potential contractors can very well realise the mutual benefits to be had from joint commitments to constraining rules, and at the same time seek protection against ex-post regret by allowing for prospective re-negotiation of the terms of the arrangement. To be sure, what has to be excluded is that re-negotiation can be used as an instrument to escape obligations that already arose under agreed-on rules. But to require that such obligations be honored is different from requiring that participants continue to accept rules that they no longer consider to their advantage. The benefits expected from joint constitutional commitments are the *ongoing* benefits that participants expect to realise from the fact that they are all bound by common rule-constraints. These benefits are generated continuously, and the arrangement qualifies as mutually advantageous only so long as all parties continue to benefit. (This is in contrast to transaction-agreements where only the inclusive package of contributions, from the first move to the concluding act, is to be judged advantageous by all parties, and where stages in between need not at all meet that standard.) When parties to an open-ended constitutional agreement come to the conclusion that, counter to their initial expectation, the agreed-on arrangement is no longer beneficial to them, there is no reason why they should not seek to re-negotiate the terms for their future dealings with the other parties, or, if re-negotiation is not a promising option, why they should not terminate the contract. The purpose of constitutional commitments, namely to capture the ongoing benefits from mutual constraints, is compatible with allowing participants to re-negotiate the rules for future periods or to exit from the arrangement (provided, of course, obligations previously incurred under the arrangement have been met).[18]

---

[18] The arguments above imply that with regard to the re-negotiation issue it is not only important to distinguish between transaction-agreements and constitutional agreements, but also between constitutional agreements as such and the transactions that are carried out *within* constitutional arrangements. Paying attention to these distinctions may help, for instance, to clarify the role of re-negotiation in the context of long-term contracts that involve relation-specific investments, an issue that has been addressed in a number of recent contributions to the incomplete contract literature (see e.g., O. Hart 1995: 24ff.; E. Maskin and J. Tirole 1999; U. Schweizer 2000; I. Segal 1999). While this literature appears to conclude that the hold-up problem in case of relation-specific investments renders re-negotiation *in general* problematic, the present analysis suggests that the noted distinctions should be of relevance. If, and to the extent that, re-negotiation can be used to expropriate relation-specific investments, allowing for re-negotiation would obviously deter such investments. Yet, as noted above (fn. 16), the issue of how constitutional contracts protect relation-specific investments, and what the respective provisions imply for investments already made, should be separated from the issue of whether these provisions may be re-negotiated prospectively.

What does the above argument imply for the issue of whether the ability to commit is a feature of democratic politics? It is useful to consider this issue separately for the two kinds of commitments that have been contrasted here. As far as *transaction*-commitments are concerned, the fact that a future parliament may revoke commitments made by a present parliament would seem to jeopardize the ability to commit. Yet, even for such commitments, closer inspection suggests that for internal transaction-commitments, that is, commitments that constituents have made among themselves, the sovereignty of future constituencies *per se* need not pose a problem. If, as noted above, for our present purposes we disregard potential deficiencies of the political process in implementing citizens' common interests and, instead, assume that these interests are properly reflected in policy choices, it is not obvious why the sovereignty of future constituencies should come into conflict with the ability of constituents to enter into effective transaction-commitments among themselves. If a later parliamentary decision, revoking or reneging the original commitment, were to be used by part of the constituency in order to escape its own obligations and to exploit the first-mover disadvantage of other citizens, the latter will find their interests violated and will object. Such a decision can pass only if the political process allows for decisions to be made that do not reflect common interests of all citizens, but advance the interests of some at the expense of others. To the extent that this is so, the ability to commit is obviously limited. But this is not because future constituencies are sovereign in their decisions, but because the political decision making process allows parts of the constituency to exploit others. The proper remedy for this problem would be to install institutional provisions that minimize the risk of decisions being generated by the political process that violate the interests of parts of the constituency.

As far as *constitutional* commitments are concerned, the fact that future parliaments can revoke past parliamentary choices – again: disregarding potential deficiencies of the political process in reflecting citizens' common interests – does pose even less of a problem. For constitutional commitments, *ongoing* agreement is the relevant criterion of mutual advantage and legitimacy. Accordingly, current constituencies are the proper judges on whether or not an existing constitutional arrangement can still be said to be mutually advantageous to all parties involved, and lacking agreement on this issue signals that reforms may be necessary in order to justify the claim that everyone benefits. Parties to a constitutional agreement who find that their interests are no longer sufficiently accounted for can legitimately ask for re-negotiation or, if that does not appear promising, decide to terminate the contract or to opt out of the arrangement.[19]

---

[19] This seems to me to be the legitimate claim of the conceptualization of constitutions as self-enforcing coordination devices (P. C. Ordeshook 1992; S. Voigt 1999). In this interpretation, "self-enforcing" would mean that the rules of a stable constitution are in the common interest of all parties, in the sense that they all wish the constitution to remain in force. "Self-enforcing"

CONSTITUTIONAL ARRANGEMENTS: ONGOING AGREEMENT AND STRATEGIC BARGAINING

The foregoing discussion has focused on one particular reason why contracting parties may wish to exclude a re-negotiation option, namely the difficulty to reliably separate between cheating on obligations arising from a commitment and legitimate re-negotiation of the terms of the commitment. As was argued, such separation is particularly difficult in transaction-agreements, but much less so for constitutional agreements. In case of the latter, the issue of honoring current obligations that arose within previously agreed-on rules, such as obligations resulting from an insurance contract, can be clearly separated from the issue of re-negotiating the terms for future dealings. The cheating-issue therefore, cannot be used as an argument against relying on *ongoing* agreement rather than original agreement as the relevant criterion of legitimacy in constitutional contracts. This does not mean, of course, that allowing for re-negotiation and relying on continuing agreement may not interfere in other respects with the purposes of constitutional agreements. In fact, even if the cheating issue is not of significance, problems may arise because of difficulties to reliably separate legitimate interests in re-negotiation from strategic bargaining.

Joint constitutional commitments are mutually advantageous if all parties to the contract expect payoffs in excess of their expected costs. A constitutional arrangement is mutually beneficial if all parties realise gains from participating that exceed their opportunity costs. The ultimate test of expected mutual advantage in joint commitments is voluntary original agreement. The ultimate test of mutual benefits in constitutional arrangements is continued voluntary agreement to the terms of the contract. If it were not for reasons of strategic bargaining, all constitutional commitments that promise gains for all participants should be able to find voluntary approval, and all constitutional arrangements that generate positive net-payoffs for everybody involved should enjoy continued voluntary consent. Yet, the interest in *selling* their agreement at the highest possible price may induce parties to strategically withhold or withdraw their consent, even though the terms of the respective constitutional commitment or arrangement are beneficial to them. Such strategic behavior may prevent potential mutually advantageous commitments from being concluded, and it may threaten the stability of mutually beneficial constitutional arrangements.

To be sure, the likelihood of strategic bargaining to occur and to obstruct mutually beneficial agreements varies with certain contingencies. Two aspects appear to be of particular significance, namely, first, that *original* agreements are

---

need not mean that all parties have an interest in complying with the rules of the constitution in the absence of appropriate enforcement mechanisms. *Constitutional interests* are a different matter from *compliance interests*.

less threatened by strategic bargaining in *self-selected* as opposed to *pre-defined* groups, and, second, that *ongoing* agreement is less vulnerable to strategic behavior in arrangements from which participants can easily opt out. It is instructive to compare democratic polities to private voluntary associations along both dimensions.

The distinction between self-selected and pre-defined groups concerns the question of whether the principal beneficiaries of a prospective commitment can be defined independently from their actual participation in the commitment. If a group of beneficiaries can be identified prior to the reaching of an agreement, it is, in the terminology adopted here, pre-defined. For example, residents around a lake can be considered a pre-defined group with regard to commitments that are intended to provide for a cleaner lake. In such groups, parties may be tempted to withhold their agreement for strategic purposes, in the hope of negotiating more advantageous terms. By contrast, a group is self-selected, in the sense the term is used here, if there are no pre-defined beneficiaries, if only those who join the commitment can expect to benefit. For example, participants in an economic venture, recruited from an open pool of potential candidates, can be regarded as a self-selected group with regard to commitments that promise to make the joint venture economically successful. In such groups there is much less opportunity for strategic bargaining since any party seeking privileged treatment can be substituted by some other candidate from the pool. Compared with private voluntary associations, the constituencies of polities are, obviously, much more of the nature of pre-defined groups. Potential mutually beneficial commitments are, therefore, more likely to be obstructed by strategic bargaining in politics than in the private arena.

The difference between self-selected and pre-defined groups is of relevance with regard to the issue of initial or *original* agreement to a joint enterprise. Strategic bargaining is less of an obstacle to reaching an agreement the more the group of prospective contractors shares the characteristics of a self-selected group. With regard to the issue of *ongoing* agreement within constitutional arrangements the critical factor is to be found in the second of the previously mentioned aspects, that is, the ease with which parties can exit from the arrangement. Ongoing agreement is less likely to be obstructed by strategic bargaining in constitutional arrangements where the greater the ease with which participants can opt out from such arrangements or, in other words, the more the respective group of contractors shares in the characteristics of a voluntary association.

Ongoing agreement to a constitutional arrangement can be expressed in two ways, by continued participation (non-exit) and by *voice*, that is, verbal approval (Hirschman 1970). Correspondingly, disagreement can be expressed by exit and by voiced disapproval. There is an interesting asymmetry involved here: Voiced approval can ordinarily be considered a reliable indicator of voluntary agreement, except for cases where, because of intimidation or other special circumstances, incentives for "preference-falsification" (Kuran 1995) may be present. Voiced disapproval, however, cannot ordinarily be trusted to be a reliable indicator of factual disagreement, in the sense of reflecting a legitimate re-negotiation interest, because it may be used for strategic purposes. However, by contrast to voiced approval, continued participation cannot be generally considered a sufficient indicator of voluntary agreement, because with high exit costs continued participation may not indicate much more than a lack of accessible alternatives. Exit, however, can obviously be regarded as a truthful indicator of disagreement since it cannot be used for strategic purposes. To be sure, the *threat of exit* may be used to bargain for better terms within a constitutional arrangement. Yet, threatening with exit means to use *voice*. Actual exit obviously means to give up any ambition to improve one's position *within* the constitutional arrangement one exits from.

In private voluntary associations continued participation can be viewed as a reliable indicator of ongoing agreement to the terms of the arrangement, the more so the easier it is for participants to opt out. As long as parties continue to participate in the presence of easily accessible alternatives, they can be presumed to consider the arrangement advantageous to them, even if they voice dissatisfaction. To be sure, exit of dissatisfied (and entry of new) participants cannot be the only mechanism for voluntary associations to deal with dissent and to maintain ongoing agreement. Because in a changing world parties may legitimately wish to re-negotiate the *social contract* of a common enterprise of which they want to remain a part, voluntary associations must be able to respond to such interests if they are to be able to adapt and to survive. And participants in voluntary associations may, of course, be tempted to use the re-negotiation option for strategic purposes, to seek to achieve privileged terms for themselves. Yet, under conditions of low-cost exit, re-negotiation is of limited effectiveness as a tool for strategic bargaining. To the extent that attractive alternatives are easily available to them, other participants will be unwilling to make unwarranted concessions and will resist strategic re-negotiations. Such conditions are favorable for separating legitimate re-negotiation from strategic bargaining.

Compared with private voluntary associations, opting out is typically more costly in the case of polities. Accordingly, there is much more room for re-negotiation to be used for strategic purposes. And, securing ongoing agreement is a much more delicate matter in politics. Yet, even if their differences to voluntary associations are in part inherent to the very nature of political entities and, therefore, unavoidable, there is considerable room for giving polities more of the qualities of voluntary associations by suitable institutional and organizational reforms that make for lower exit costs. Without going into details here, it may suffice to mention that competitive federalism, in its territorial and functional forms, is an important instrument for that purpose (Frey and Eichenberger 1999; Vanberg 2000).

CONCLUSION: CITIZENS SOVEREIGNTY AND
THE ABILITY TO COMMIT

To function ideally as "cooperative ventures for mutual advantage" democratic polities would have to be able to reliably identify and implement measures that promise benefits to all citizens, and exclude measures that harm the interests of some or all citizens. Practically feasible institutions of political decision making fall necessarily short of that unattainable ideal. They err, more or less, on both sides: They miss out on implementing measures that would be beneficial to all citizens, and they allow for measures to be taken that violate the interests of citizens. Alternative political institutions can be compared in terms of the risks with which they allow the two *errors* to occur, and from the citizens' perspective those institutions are preferable that bring the two risks in the most favorable balance.

The focus of this chapter has been on the issue of whether the sovereignty of democratic constituencies limits their ability to commit. Since there are obvious benefits to be had from workable commitments, an inability to commit would mean that democratic constituencies were inherently incapable of realizing such benefits. And, short of giving up the principle of citizens sovereignty, there would hardly seem to be an institutional remedy available for this inherent defect. I have sought to argue that there is no reason for such pessimistic conclusion to be drawn. The principle of citizen sovereignty and the ability to commit are, I submit, compatible. In particular, the requirement, implied in the principle of citizen sovereignty, that *ongoing* agreement is to be regarded as the relevant standard of legitimacy of constitutional arrangements is perfectly compatible with the ability to commit. What is necessary for ongoing agreements to be a workable foundation for constitutional commitments is that legitimate re-negotiation can be separated from cheating on commitments and from strategic bargaining. In democratic polities such separation should be possible, and to the extent that constitutional provisions provide for effective separation, the principle of the sovereignty of the people need not compromise their ability to commit.

REFERENCES

Brennan, Geoffrey, and James M. Buchanan 1985: *The Reason of Rules – Constitutional Political Economy*, Cambridge: Cambridge University Press.
Breton, A., and A. Frasahini, "Vertical Competition in Federal States: The Case of Italy," *Public Choice*, Vol. 114 (1–2), 57–77.
Buchanan, James M. 1960: *Fiscal Theory and Political Economy*, Chapel Hill: University of North Carolina Press.
Buchanan, James M. 1977: *Freedom in Constitutional Contract*, College Station: Texas A&M University Press.
Buchanan, James M. 1979: *What Should Economists Do?* Indianapolis: Liberty Press.

Buchanan, James M. 1987a: "An Economic Theory of Clubs," in: *Economics –
Between Predictive Science and Moral Philosophy*, compiled and with a preface by
Robert D. Tollison and Viktor J. Vanberg, College Station: Texas A&M University
Press, 207–221.

Buchanan, James M. 1987b: "The Constitution of Economic Policy," in: *Economics –
Between Predictive Science and Moral Philosophy*, compiled and with a preface by
Robert D. Tollison and Viktor J. Vanberg, College Station: Texas A&M University
Press, 303–314.

Buchanan, James M., and Gordon Tullock 1962: *The Calculus of Consent – Logical
Foundations of Constitutional Democracy*, Ann Arbor: University of Michigan Press.

Buchanan, James M., and Roger D. Congleton 1998: *Politics by Principle, not Interest –
Towards Nondiscriminatory Democracy*, Cambridge: Cambridge University Press.

Frey, Bruno S., and Reiner Eichenberger 1999: *The New Democratic Federalism
for Europe – Functional, Overlapping and Competing Jurisdictions*, Cheltenham,
UK/Northampton, MA: Edward Elgar.

Hart, Oliver 1995: *Firms, Contracts, and Financial Structure*, Oxford: Clarendon Press.

Hirschman, Albert O. 1970: *Exit, Voice and Loyalty. Responses to Decline in Firms,
Organizations and States*, Cambridge, MA: Harvard University Press.

Hume, David 1963 [1741/42]: "Of the Original Contract," in: *Essays – Moral, Political
and Literary*, London: Oxford University Press, 452–473.

Kuran, Timur 1995: *Private Truths, Public Lies – The Social Consequences/ of Preference Falsification*, Cambridge, MA: Harvard University Press.

Maskin, Eric, and Jean Tirole 1999: "Unforseen Contingencies and Incomplete
Contracts," *Review of Economic Studies*, Vol. 66, 83–114.

North, Douglass C., and Barry R. Weingast 1996: "Constitutions and Commitments: The
Evolution of Institutions Governing Public Choice in Seventeenth-century England,
in: L. J. Alston, T. Eggertsson and D. C. North, eds., *Empirical Studies in Institutional
Change*, Cambridge: Cambridge University Press, 134–165.

Ordeshook, Peter C. 1992: "Constitutional Stability," *Constitutional Political Economy*,
Vol. 3, 137–175.

Rawls, John 1971: *A Theory of Justice*, Cambridge, MA: Harvard University Press.

Schweizer, Urs 2000: "An Elementary Approach to the Hold-Up Problem with
Renegotiation," Department of Economics, University of Bonn, Germany.

Segal, Ilya 1999: "Complexity and Renegotiation: A Foundation for Incomplete
Contracts," *Review of Economic Studies*, Vol. 66, 57–82.

Stiglitz, Joseph 1998: "The Private Uses of Public Interests: Incentives and Institutions,"
The Journal of Economic Perspectives, 12 (2), 3–22.

Vanberg, Viktor J. 2000: "Functional Federalism: Communal or Individual Rights?
On B.S. Frey's and R. Eichenberger's Proposal for a 'New Federalism'," *Kyklos* 53,
363–386.

Voigt, Stephan 1999: "Breaking with the Notion of Social Contract: Constitutions
as Based on Spontaneously Arisen Institutions," *Constitutional Political Economy*,
Vol 10, 283–300.

Williamson, Oliver E. 1985: *The Economic Institutions of Capitalism*, New York: The
Free Press.

12

Constitutional Rules and Competitive Politics: Their Effects on Secessionism

Albert Breton and Pierre Salmon

INTRODUCTION

Constitutional rules (or, more generally, constitutional variables) must be ana-lyzed in competitive settings. These rules can constrain the behavior of public sector actors and ensure that political competition remains active and vigorous. Political competition, in turn, can affect the capacity of constitutions to constrain political action. Among the different ways of modeling political competition in the case of democratic societies, we retain two: a) electoral competition, as understood in the probabilistic voting model; and b) competition among centers of power in compound governments (Breton, 1996).

In that framework, the preferences and opinions of citizens in their capacity as voters or demanders of public policies necessarily count. In the literature, these preferences are usually restricted to goods and services; in what follows, they are defined over constitutional variables as well.[1] Moreover, we assume that there will necessarily be trade-offs or compensations between goods and services on the one hand and constitutional variables on the other. This is often the case at the level of individual citizens, but it will obtain at the collective level as a matter of necessity. By itself, this creates a first strong linkage among all issues, including the constitutional ones. In addition, a second linkage derives from the fact that decision-makers in the public sector normally function in institutional settings – parliaments, cabinets, political parties, for instance – that make it natural and easy to bring together apparently unconnected issues.[2] Thus, pushed by competition, decision-makers will not ignore the possibilities of trade-offs or compensations and therefore can be expected to engage in

---

[1] See Salmon (2001a).

[2] This aspect of politics or policy-making is stressed in recent books by Tullock (1998) and Cooter (2000). In the latter, we read (p. 120): "Broad jurisdiction *splices* independent issues together like the strands of a rope. In contrast, narrow jurisdiction *factors* politics into independent issues like a mathematician dividing a large number into prime numbers . . . Splicing widens the scope for bargaining by lowering the transaction costs of political trades" (italics in the original).

various kinds of trades, exchanges, or bargains, involving objects of all kinds, constitutional or other.

In the following section, we provide illustrations of the variables we assume enter the preference functions of citizens as constitutional rules. We also stress some of their characteristics, such as continuity, that are not usually considered in the literature. The discussion makes clear that constitutional variables are numerous and varied. However, to obtain precise results, the trade-off between them and goods and services has to be restricted to a subset of these variables. To give focus to the models of the next two sections – concerned respectively with electoral competition and competition in compound governments – we limit ourselves to the subset of rules that define the degree of autonomy (the limit value being secession) of the constituent units of larger jurisdictions – a province in a federation for example. In addition, we distinguish between this subset of rules and exogenous rules, identified as meta-rules, that pertain to the procedure governing the implementation of the constitutional rules that control changes in the degree of autonomy. We therefore have two types of constitutional rules, one endogenous and the other exogenous. To economize on space and without loss of generality, we limit ourselves to the analysis of one comparative disturbance, namely a change in average incomes. The effects of that disturbance depend on the content of the meta-rules. The penultimate section offers a comparison of the outcomes of the compensation mechanisms in the two models of political competition. A conclusion section completes the chapter.

PREFERENCES

We assume that citizens can be represented by utility functions defined over: (a) goods and services (including redistribution), (b) the services derived from the set of rules and other variables that define the constitutional set-up (the particular case of meta-rule being discussed at the end of this section), and (c) the services derived from the institutions that define economic regimes. The goods and services that enter the utility functions of individual citizens are the stuff of microeconomics and public sector economics and are well-known. The set of variables that define the constitutional set-up are, however, less familiar. For purpose of illustration, we mention the nature and the extent of the separation of the executive, legislative, and judicial branches of government, the type and degree of the division of powers among levels of government, the character of the rules governing parliamentary debates, legal procedures governing changes to the constitutional set-up, the specificity of the rules regulating the civil service, the method of cabinet formation and so on. This constitutional set-up also includes whether the governmental system is congressional or parliamentary and whether governments within the system are unicameral or bicameral, the character of the electoral system, the rules pertaining to how judges, commissions of inquiry, and heads of departments (ministries) are appointed, how political parties are financed, the degree of autonomy of central banks, regulatory and administrative tribunals, and other like bodies, the status of the military and constabulary forces, the relations between church and state, and so on. Finally, the constitutional set-up includes compliance to the rule of law, to rights (civil, human, and political), to the principle of equality before the law – a principle sometimes labeled *isonomy* that was associated to the democratic constitution of Athens, as early as the 6th century B.C. (see Grillo, 1997; Mueller, 2001) – and so on.

The set of institutions which constitutes economic regimes includes elements such as whether the economy is largely market oriented or planned, whether price, wage, rent, and exchange controls are extensively used, whether minimum wage legislation exists, as well as the extent of protectionism, the strength of anti-trust legislation, the definition and enforcement of property rights, the conditions on the use of takings, and others. We therefore accept the point made by Vanberg (1998) that the institutions of economic regimes are elements of overall constitutional set-ups and call all of them – the components of constitutional set-ups and the institutions of the economic regimes – constitutional variables.

We wish to underline five features of the variables just listed (and others like them) and of the utility functions in which they enter as arguments. First, though our illustrations often refer to stocks – the existing electoral rules, the character of the separation of executive, legislative, and judicial powers, the rules governing parliamentary debates, the bicameral or unicameral nature of governments – what enters the utility functions of citizens are services that flow from these stocks. Constitutional variables are genuine capital assets in that they are costly to design, implement, and alter and because the stream of services they yield are reaped over time.

Second, contrary to what one might be tempted to think, the arguments of utility functions are, in most cases, continuous. That is the case for all those we have listed earlier. Consider electoral rules, unicameralism and bicameralism, and the autonomy of public nonelected bodies. Discussions of electoral rules – simple majority and proportional representation, for example – are often conducted in a framework that can lead one to think that the choice is between one or the other. A casual look at the real world soon reveals, however, that the two rules are combined in a sufficient number of ways to warrant treating the variable as continuous. Governments can be unicameral or bicameral. The relative powers of the two houses under bicameralism can, however, vary enormously, so much so that a system is more or less bicameral. Finally, the degree of autonomy of public nonelected bodies – the extent to which they operate at arm's length from elected politicians – does, as a matter of observable fact, vary a great deal.

Third, some of the goods and services provided and most, probably all, constitutional variables are pure Samuelsonian public goods. To put it differently, a particular electoral system, a given degree of bicameralism, the degree of autonomy of public bodies, the extent of reliance on markets, once selected will be the same for all citizens, whether that is what they desire or not.

Fourth, the goods and services as well as the constitutional variables can be independent of each other, complement each other, or substitute for each other. To put it differently, if a constitutional variable is reduced by one unit, an individual can be made to remain on the same indifference curve by an increase in the amount of a good such as police protection, unemployment insurance, public broadcasting, or a combination of all of these. Conversely, because constitutional variables are as a rule continuous, an individual can be made to remain at the same level of utility following a decrease in (say) police protection by a change in a constitutional variable.

Even though preferences are genuine, the demands for goods, services, and constitutional variables are initially latent or potential – they are activated by entrepreneurs (as is always the case) and/or by the observation of what obtains in other jurisdictions.

We note also that individual preference orderings may be dominated and shaped by what are, in effect, meta-preferences or basic beliefs. These can include an overriding commitment to democracy, to principles such as popular sovereignty, a respect for the constitution, and/or to the belief, well expressed in the American Declaration of Independence, that "all men are created equal" in respect of "certain unalienable rights, among which are life, liberty, and the pursuit of happiness." We need not add that the basic beliefs of some individuals may refer to the absolute opposite of those just mentioned.

In our framework of analysis, meta-rules have a particular status. Their function is to regulate the trade-offs and the associated compensations between constitutional rules and between these rules and other variables. As already noted, we treat the meta-rules as exogenous.[3] We also often take them as discontinuous.

ELECTORAL COMPETITION

In this section, we concentrate on voting and disregard the existence of competition among different centers of power which will be examined in the next section. Here, compensation operates within political sets-ups that may vary a lot but have in common their reliance on electoral competition, itself animated by the dominant desire of office-holders and their challengers to be elected or re-elected.

The General Framework

To study the way compensation operates, we consider exchanges between two legislators each elected according to a majority rule. We assume that, in each

---

[3] We make this assumption well aware that in the world of experience meta-rules cannot be fully exogenous. See Voigt (1999) for the view that all constitutional rules evolve.

legislator's district, the incumbent legislator is competing with a single opponent. Both the incumbent legislator and his or her opponent perceive electoral competition as it is conceived in the theory of probabilistic voting: What they are concerned with is the effect of what they do or say – that is, of their platform or program – on the probability of winning, or the expected share of the votes, at the next contest. We stress that the difference between the probabilistic voting and the median voter models is not limited to different ways of conceiving democracy. The probabilistic voting model allows for the possibility that only subgroups of voters have preferences over constitutional rules and for the possibility that these subgroups can make these preferences count in the final equilibrium. Those possibilities, ubiquitous features of the real world, have no place in the median voter model.[4]

In such setting, the logic of the Cournot-Nash equilibrium will normally lead to convergence (meaning identity) of the two platforms (Mueller, 1989; Coughlin, 1992; Lafay, 1992).[5] For our purpose, this means that if, as a consequence of some change in an exogenous variable, the maximization of expected votes by the incumbent candidate X dictates that she adopts a new policy Q, this also applies to her challenger Y. The electoral prospect of X (or, for that matter, Y) is not improved compared with the situation before the exogenous change; it is improved only compared with what would have obtained if she had not decided policy Q, and thus had conceded an advantage to her opponent. In other words, because of the intensity of competition between office-holders and their challengers, the behavior of the former is determined (the behavior of challengers also, but this is of no enduring interest to us).

When, as we will see, the decisions of an office-holder are the outcome of a negotiation with some third party (a decision-maker other than his or her challenger), the logic of convergence extends to this situation and remains compelling: were X not attempting to get the most favorable outcome, this would immediately be exploited by her challenger Y. The need to maximize votes just for the purpose of remaining afloat dictates X's conduct.

We now turn to the exchange between two legislators L_A and L_B. In each of the two districts (D_A and D_B), L_A or L_B competes with a single opponent or challenger in the perspective of the next election. As noted, the incumbents as well as the challengers are exclusively concerned with winning the election. The voters are concerned with two things: the value taken by a continuous constitutional characteristic (R) and the total net amount of goods and services – G_A or G_B – available in their district. Legislator L_A will exchange some items with, say, legislator L_B inasmuch as not doing so would decrease

---

[4] For discussions of some limitations of the probabilistic voting model which are not, however, contrasted to limitations of the median voter model, see Usher (1994) and Kirchgässner (2000).

[5] Whatever theoretical framework or model one adopts, platform convergence is a source of problems for what one may expect from constitutions (see Salmon, 2001b).

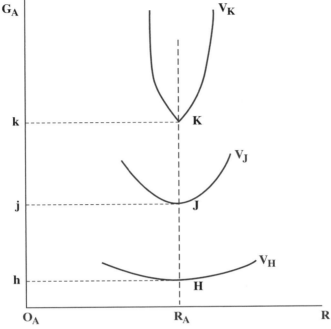

Figure 12.1. Legislator L_A

his or her probability of winning the next election, and the same is true of
Legislator L_B.

An important consideration in this setting is whether the total net quantity
of goods and services available to the inhabitants of the district – say, G_A –
is conditional or not on the stand taken by the representative of that district
with regard to the constitutional rule. If G_A is available unconditionally, it
is reasonable to assume that its amount will not affect the value (R_A) of the
constitutional rule that is electorally optimal for our incumbent legislator (the
value of the rule whose endorsement maximizes the probability that he will
win the election), as well as for his challenger. In Figure 12.1, the vertical
line passing through R_A reflects this orthogonality assumption: whether G_A is
measured by h, j, or k, the electorally optimal value of R remains equal to R_A.

Now, suppose that the amount of goods and services available in the district is conditional on the position adopted by the legislator with regard to the
constitutional rule. More precisely, the district can rely on an unconditional
(exogenous) amount of G_A equal to $O_A h$ but will receive more provided that
L_A changes his stand on R. Curve V_H in Figure 12.1 indicates, for each considered value of R, the minimal amount of G_A that L_A is compelled by electoral
competition within district D_A to demand for accepting that offer – that is, the

amount necessary to ensure, if no bargaining is involved (see Fig. 12.1), that L_A would receive at least as many votes, or would have at least the same probability of winning, than if he had not departed from his stand at R_A. It is reasonable to assume that the larger the departure from R_A (in either direction), the larger the necessary marginal compensation in terms of G_A – hence, the shape of the curve.

If instead of being grafted on an unconditional amount of G_A corresponding to h, the offer is grafted on an unconditional amount that is larger, for instance j, the corresponding curve will be V_J. If he is given the choice between the two curves, the legislator will always chose curve V_J. Even though being on one curve rather than on another entails at equilibrium no difference in the probability of winning the election, electoral competition imposes the choice of the higher one. This is a straightforward implication of the assumptions.

What does not follow from the assumptions is that, in Figure 12.1, V_J has more curvature than V_H. This property reflects the supposition that the degree of attachment of voters to their preferred value of R, that is, to R_A, is akin to a superior good. When G_A is small, that is, when the district is relatively poor, a small supplement in G_A will *buy* a large departure from R_A but when G_A is large (the district is richer), a large supplement in it will be necessary to get only a small departure from R_A. If the unconditional amount of G_A is increased further, equal for instance to $O_A k$ in Figure 12.1, V_K will have even more curvature than V_J. The same reasoning holds for curves higher than V_K. We willingly admit that this assumption, although plausible in some contexts, is not always compelling: It may be the case that the poorer the district the more stubborn or uncompromising its voters in their preference for R_A. In fact, we will also use the assumption that the curves are vertically identical (corresponding to quasi-linearity in the function underlying them).

To bring into the analysis the second incumbent legislator (L_B), who is also competing electorally with a single opponent in her own district (D_B), we make use of Figure 12.2 in which R is measured vertically instead of horizontally as in Figure 12.1 and G_A, horizontally instead of vertically. This imparts to the V-curves and to the straight line R_A the position shown in the diagram. Figure 12.2 is constructed so that the data relating to that second legislator must be read from right to left and upward starting from origin O_B. This applies to G_B, the amount of goods and services available to the inhabitants of the district of this second legislator, to R_B, the electorally optimal endorsed value of the constitutional rule in the case of unconditional amounts of G_B, and to the U-curves we provide the second legislator with, that are the equivalent of the first legislator's V-curves and, as the former, are convex with respect to their relevant axis. The distance between O_A and O_B measures the total amount (G_T) of goods and services available in the two districts (that is: $G_T = G_A + G_B$).

R_A and R_B are different but, because the two legislators live in (the two districts are part of) the same country and there may be only one value of R

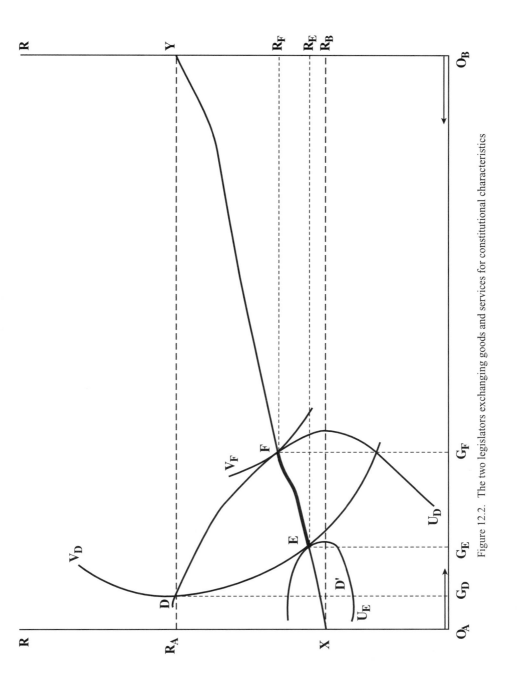

Figure 12.2. The two legislators exchanging goods and services for constitutional characteristics

in the country (it is a public good), the exact rule, that is, the value of R, that prevails must be the same. We suppose that it is enough that the two incumbent legislators agree on a value of R for that value to prevail. We also suppose that whatever distribution of G_T they agree on will be implemented costlessly. This opens up the possibility of reaching an agreement on the value of R by the way of a variation in, or a redistribution of, goods and services.

For expositional purposes, let us choose an out-of-equilibrium point such as D as the original situation. At point D, amounts G_A and G_B are measured by distances $O_A G_D$ and $G_D O_B$, respectively, and the prevailing value of the constitutional rule, read on the vertical axis, is R_A (the rule preferred by L_A). Legislator L_A is willing to depart from R_A provided his district receives a larger amount of G_A. The degree of this willingness (in the absence of bargaining, see next paragraph) is indicated by curve V_D. Now turn to Legislator L_B. She would accept that her district D_B receives a smaller amount of G_B provided that rule R takes a value closer to R_B. The degree to which she would want this (in the absence of bargaining) is indicated by curve U_D, which passes through D. For an equilibrium to obtain, – that is, for no unexploited possibility of reaching a higher curve to remain – a V-curve and a U-curve must be tangent, the locus of equilibrium points being thus the traditional contract curve. Depending on how the exchange situation is specified, equilibrium will necessarily lie somewhere on that contract curve between E and F.

Our repeated insistence, in the course of defining the V-curves and the U-curves, that there be no bargaining is now readily understood. Loosely speaking, there is a gain to trade, or surplus. However, whatever the equilibrium outcome of the negotiation about that surplus, the probabilities of an electoral victory of L_A and L_B against their respective challengers are, at equilibrium, constant. Nonetheless, each of the two legislators is compelled by the electoral competition he or she is submitted to in their respective districts to strive for the best bargain possible. Failing to do so would immediately be exploited by their challengers. Thus we do face the typical problem of two-player bargaining for the distribution of a gain to trade or surplus and cannot say where the equilibrium will stand on the contract curve between E and F.

In Figure 12.2, the contract curve is extended on the two sides of E and F to show the locus of equilibria whatever the initial situation. Making the plausible assumption that V-curves and U-curves tend to become straight vertical lines when the amounts of G_A and G_B respectively tend to zero, the contract curve goes from X (on the R_B line) to Y (on the R_A line). Suppose that the initial situation had been point D' on the R_B line instead of D – that is, the same distribution of goods and services but a constitutional rule fitting the rich district D_B instead of the poor one D_A. Then, although we have not drawn the corresponding U- and V-curves, it is clear from the geometry that the exchange would have been very limited, leading to a point on the contract curve XY very close to D' (a little above and on the left). This particular result is, of course, a consequence of our assumption that the richer the district the less likely it is to change its constitutional preferences in exchange for more goods and services. But the more general lesson is that the choice of a rule depends on where we start from – on where exactly is the status quo. When a constitutional characteristic is exchanged against goods and services, this result seems plausible. We will see, however, that, at least in the provincial autonomy context to which we turn now as a specification of the more general framework, this result is not independent of the meta-rules that govern political exchanges.

Meta-Rules

Because we define the meta-rules for the particular provincial setting just mentioned we must make some adjustments in the basic framework discussed so far. First, one of the two electoral districts, D_P, is now a province or region of a country and the other electoral district, D_{ROC}, is the rest of the country; we suppose L_P and L_{ROC} to have been elected to represent these two districts in the same conditions than those spelled out above.[6] Second, the constitutional variable is interpreted now as the degree of autonomy of D_P. The maximum value that this variable can take is 1, corresponding to complete independence following secession. Third, the value of the degree of autonomy which, in the absence of any compensation in terms of goods and services, maximizes the expected votes obtained by L_P and L_{ROC} – R_P and R_{ROC}, respectively – is 1 for L_P and a relatively low value for L_{ROC}, as indicated in Figure 12.3. That figure should be read in the same way as Figure 12.2 (the origins, however, now being called O_P and O_{ROC}). Fourth, the resources in goods and services available to the inhabitants of D_P and D_{ROC} are respectively G_P and G_{ROC}. They are measured horizontally exactly in the same way as resources were measured in Figure 12.2.

We distinguish between two possible meta-rules. One says that secession, that is, the change from a degree of provincial autonomy different from one to a degree equal to one, is exactly like any other change in the degree of autonomy in that it must receive the agreement of both L_P and L_{ROC}. The other possible meta-rule says that the secession of the province by the way of a unilateral decision of L_P is possible. In other words, it says that all changes must be agreed on by both legislators except secession. As we show, the effects of exogenous disturbances depend on which of the two meta-rules applies.

Comparative Statics

Assume that the meta-rule in force is the first one, that the exogenous disturbance is an increase in income in D_P, and that the original situation corresponds to

---

[6] Because we assume relations between L_P and L_{ROC} to be shaped by the calculus of the probabilistic voting model, we conceive of secession and secessionism in a way which is quite different from the approaches that model democracy using the median voter model. See for example Alesina and Spolaere (1997), Bolton, Roland, and Spolaore (1996), and Rota Graziosi (2001).

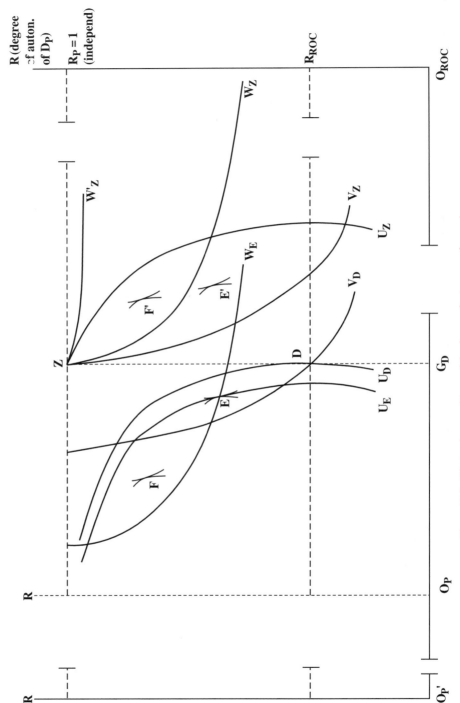

Figure 12.3. Electoral competition and the degree of autonomy of a province

point D in Figure 12.3. Legislator L_{ROC} is willing to depart from R_{ROC} provided her district receives a larger amount of goods and services. This willingness is reflected by U-curves, one of which, U_D, passes through D. Similarly, before the exogenous income increase in province D_P, V-curves express the willingness of legislator L_P to exchange variations in the degree of autonomy of his province for changes in the distribution of goods and services. One of these curves is V_D, which passes through point D.

Point D is not an equilibrium. One possible equilibrium point (at which a U-curve, at least as "high" as U_D, and a V-curve, at least as "high" as V_D, are tangent) is E. The position of E expresses the fact that it was electorally optimal for both L_P and L_{ROC} to have some redistribution of goods and services in favor of D_{ROC} in exchange for a degree of autonomy of the province higher than the one electorally preferable (in the absolute) in D_{ROC}. In other words, it is as if the province had paid in goods and services for an augmented degree of autonomy.

Suppose now that the income of D_P increases. The effect of that, as reflected in Figure 12.3, is a translation to the left of both the left vertical axis (origin O_P moves left to $O_{P'}$) and the whole family of V-curves, which (because we consider only the part of the set which can be depicted within the limits of the diagram) we relabel W-curves. By contrast, U-curves are not affected (in addition, because D_{ROC} is much larger than D_P, the U-curves that can be represented in Figure 12.3 should, reflecting quasi-linearity, be assumed to be identical, with constant curvature). One of the W-curves is curve W_E, which passes through point E. Assuming, as in Figure 12.1, that the degree of attachment of voters to their electorally preferred value of the constitutional rule (here the degree of autonomy) is a superior good, curve W_E has more curvature (with respect to the vertical axis on the left) than the V-curve passing through E. As a consequence, E is not an equilibrium any more. The new equilibrium is, say, point F. Again a higher degree of autonomy for D_P has been exchanged for more redistribution in favor of D_{ROC}. If the windfall to the province had occurred when the initial position D was still prevailing, the relevant W-curve would, like the relevant U-curve, have passed through D and a position different from F would have been agreed upon. This shows that, under this first meta-rule, the exact time sequence of constitutional adjustments and increases in the exogenous income of D_P – the exact *history* of the relationship and exogenous events – counts, even though there is no transaction cost or imperfect information.

Suppose now that the meta-rule is the second one: The secession of the province by the way of a unilateral decision of L_P becomes possible. In other words, now all changes must be agreed on by both legislators except secession. Under the first meta-rule, the reasoning concerned only the part of the diagram on the left of vertical line $G_D Z$. Under the second meta-rule, starting again from D, the whole left part of the diagram becomes irrelevant. What counts is the initial distribution of goods and services G_D. To simplify the analysis, we assume that initial distribution to apply also when the province is independent, that is at point Z. Curve V_Z, which passes through Z, expresses the willingness of L_P to give up some degree of autonomy of the province against a redistribution of goods and services in its favor. If there is no such redistribution, secession obtains. Curve U_Z expresses the willingness of L_{ROC} to accept a redistribution of goods and services in favor of the province to avoid its secession. Equilibrium is, say, at point E'.

We introduce now the income increase in the province. For the same reasons as before, V-curves are replaced by W-curves, and in particular curve V_Z by curve W_Z. Equilibrium is now at point F'. If there was a second income increase in D_P, and consequently W-curves had to be replaced by W'-curves endowed with even more curvature (as seen from the left axis), the position of curve W'_Z on the diagram shows that it could be the case in the model that both legislators agree on secession.

If we compare the stories under the two meta-rules, the one with unilaterally decided secession impossible and the other where it is possible, two points emerge that are worth stressing. First, whereas the history of the relationship counts in the first case, it does not in the second. Second, the actual level of autonomy is not very different in the two cases but the redistribution of goods and services is dramatically reversed.[7] If we compare point E' with point E – which prevailed when secession by unilateral decision of the province was precluded – we observe that there is no variation, or not much variation, in the degree of autonomy but that the redistribution of goods and services is now in favor of the province. After the income increase, the same is true when we compare points F and F'. In other words, in this model, the right to secede unilaterally is highly valuable in terms of goods and services. We might want to derive from this the prediction that even voters of the province who do not favor secession have good reasons to value the right for the province to secede unilaterally (whereas, conversely, voters in the rest of the country who do not really care about secession have nonetheless tangible reasons to be hostile to that right).[8]

COMPETITION IN COMPOUND GOVERNMENTS

The organization of this section is the same as that of the preceding one. We present first the general framework of analysis, followed by a description of the meta-rules, and by some comparative statical exercises.

The General Framework

Given the preferences of citizens, the response of suppliers to these preferences will depend on the mechanisms in place on the supply side. One such mechanism

---

[7] The result is akin to that generated by the Coase Theorem.

[8] For a completely different approach to the pre-secession effects of explicit secession rules, see Bordignon and Brusco (2001).

derives from the assumption that governmental systems are competitive as in Breton (1996). Three building-blocks are needed to make that assumption operational. A first one pertains to the character and structure of governmental systems; a second to the relationship between the centers of power that constitute governmental systems and the citizenry; and a third to the nature of the competitive interaction among centers of power.

Democratic governmental systems are made up of a multiplicity of centers of power, some of which are elected, others not. Which centers of power are elected varies a great deal from country to country. In parliamentary systems like those found in Canada, France, Italy, and the United Kingdom, the executive is typically elected. In a congressional system like that in the United States, the head of the executive is elected, but other members of the cabinet are not. In certain bicameral systems, both houses are elected; in others, only one is. In general, the judiciary is not elected, but there are important exceptions.

There is a great variety of nonelected centers of power. Among them, one finds government departments or ministries, public enterprises, military and constabulary forces, central banks, intelligence bureaus, granting bodies, commissions of inquiry, and tribunals of all sorts.

To understand the nature of the relationship between citizens and centers of power, assume that the particular constitutional variable on which we focus is a pure public good. If the citizens to whom the variable is provided differ in their preferences, the quantity supplied may satisfy some individuals, but of necessity, if exactly the same quantity of the good is made available to all, some citizens will be off their demand curves and suffer utility losses. This idea can be given diagrammatic representation. In Figure 12.4, let the constitutional variable R be provided at an exogenously set taxprice τ^*. At that price, a given individual will demand R^* of R. If the quantity of R actually supplied is either larger or smaller than R^*, the individual will suffer a loss in welfare equal to abc ($= \lambda_1$) or aef ($= \lambda_2$) depending on whether the quantity provided is larger or smaller than the quantity demanded.

It is possible to compensate the individual for utility losses by changing the quantity supplied of a substitute commodity that will shift the d-curve in Figure 12.4 and, at the limit, eliminate the λ_1 or λ_2 welfare loss. If R has a complement, the response will be more complicated – it will usually call for variation in the quantity of more than one substitute – but the underlying logic is the same.

We now assume that all centers of power maximize expected consent, which for elected centers we take to be strictly proportional to expected electoral support or votes.[9] We define expected consent (EC_a) as the probability that

---

[9] The best empirical proxy for consent is public opinion – dimensions of which are regularly measured by opinion polls.

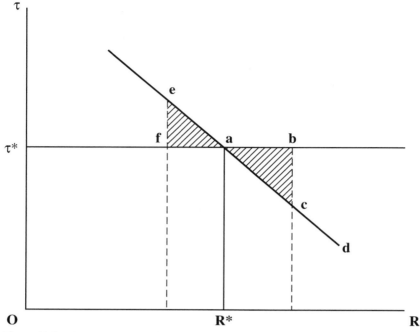

Figure 12.4. Measures of utility loss when the demand for a constitutional variable differs between citizens

citizen j will grant her consent to center of power a. Formally, we have:

$$EC_a = \Sigma_{1,2,\ldots,J} \phi^j_a \qquad 1 \geq \phi^j_a \geq 0 \qquad (4.1)$$

in which ϕ^j_a is the subjective probability of center of power a that j will grant it her consent.

We now borrow from the probabilistic theory of voting (see Calvert, 1986) the notion that the probabilities of consent (ϕ^j_a) are continuous and twice differentiable functions of the actions of centers of power, which in the present context means that they are functions of utility losses (λ). To be specific, we assume that there are N elected and nonelected centers of power, indexed n (= $1, 2, \ldots, N$), and that the probability that citizen j will grant her consent to one of them, let us say center a, is a function of the utility losses which that center and the others impose on j. We then have:

$$\phi^j_a = \phi^j_a(\lambda^j_a, \lambda^j_n) \qquad \forall j, n \neq a \qquad (4.2)$$

with $\partial\phi^j_a/\partial\lambda^j_a < 0$ for all j's and $\partial\phi^j_a/\partial\lambda^j_n > 0$ for all j's and all $n \neq a$. We also borrow from the probabilistic theory of voting the assumptions that the λ^j_n functions are strictly concave in λ_a and strictly convex in λ_n (with $n \neq a$).

A consideration of equation (4.2) reveals that centers of power necessarily compete with each other. In other words, equation (4.2) tells us that the probability that citizen *j* will give her consent to center of power *a* depends on what *a* does, but also on what all other $N - 1$ centers of power do. Since these last centers must be assumed to be seeking their own advantage and not that of *a*, it follows that they will, of necessity, be competing with *a* and, incidentally, with each other. It also discloses that the electoral success of an elected center of power depends on the actions of other centers of power, including nonelected ones. To put it differently, the expected vote of an elected governing party can be adversely affected not only by the actions of opposition parties, but also by the actions of nonelected centers of power such as a supreme court, a commission of inquiry, or a central bank.

The interaction among centers of power is best described by the colloquial expression *checks and balances*. To be balanced – *equipoised* in an older language (see Panagopoulos, 1985) – centers of power must possess sufficient freedom of action and power to stand their ground and defend their interests in competitive struggles with other centers of power. Checking, standing one's ground and defending one's interests, does not always, indeed does not usually, mean using instruments to block particular outcomes by force or coercion, but refers instead to engaging in the sort of behavior that is associated with another felicitous political colloquialism that holds that "politics is the art of compromise."[10] Compromising must not, however, be conceived as pertaining *primarily* to the negative actions of giving up on, backing down from, or renouncing an initial position. Instead, it should be thought as belonging to the class of positive activities associated with creative and innovative Schumpeterian entrepreneurship.

We formalize the "checking or compromise process" by assuming that more than one center of power is involved, at some point in time $t = 0$, in the design and production of bundles (B_0) of goods, services, and constitutional variables that are fully described by a vector of Lancasterian (1966) characteristics $Z_{w0}(w = 1, 2, \ldots, W)$. For any one bundle ($i$) in the set of bundles, we have

$$B_0 = (Z_{wi0}) \qquad \forall w \qquad (4.3)$$

We also assume that the demand for each Z_{wi0} is a function of the availability (provision) of all other characteristics $Z_{v0}(v = 1, 2, \ldots w - 1, w + 1, \ldots V)$, and of the taxprices of all Z_{w0}, as well as of the $m(= 1, 2, \ldots M)$ prices of market goods and services:

$$Z_{wi0} = \varphi(Z_v, \tau_{v0}, p_{m0}) \qquad (4.4)$$

---

[10] The Canadian diplomat Lester B. Pearson, Nobel Peace Laureate and later prime minister, is said to have remarked that "diplomacy is letting someone else have your way." (*Vancouver Sun*, March 18, 1965)

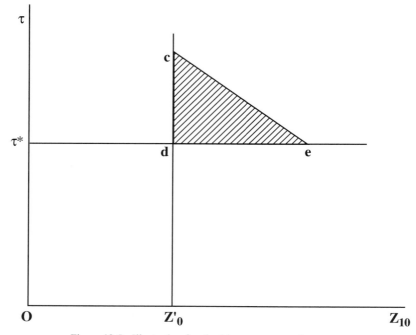

Figure 12.5. Illustration for checking or compromise process

with φ_1, φ_2, and φ_3 all ≥ 0; where $\varphi_1 = \partial\varphi/\partial Z_\mathrm{v}$, and so on. In other words, given τ_{i0}, the position of the demand curve for characteristic Z_{i0} in bundle (i) will shift as the volume supplied, the taxprices of other characteristics, and the prices of market goods and services are varied.

The checking or compromise process can be illustrated by examining the behavior of two centers of power – a and b – to each of which is attached a homogenous constituency – c_1 and c_2. To describe the process in the simplest way possible, assume that initially the situation is as portrayed in Figure 12.5. There, the exogenously given taxprice is τ^* and the volume of a constitutional characteristic Z_{10}, which b proposes to implement, is Z'_0. At point d, c_2 experiences zero utility loss and is, therefore, on its demand curve, whereas c_1 is off its demand curve (a section of which is shown as ce) and suffers a utility loss equal to cde. As a consequence a will check b. Let us assume that the checking is successful in the sense that it shifts c_1's demand curve in such a way that it now goes through point d. That will happen if the concessions made by b lead to a compromise that causes a change of the *right* magnitude in the design and production of one or more other characteristics of the constitutional variables and/or of the goods and services to which Z_{10} belongs, a change in the design and production of characteristics of other constitutional variables and/or goods and services, and/or a change in the position of supply and demand curves for market goods and services through changes in the relevant taxes and subsidies, while the position of c_2's demand curve was made to continue to run through point d. In general, of course, c_2's demand curve will shift. However, if perfect information is available to centers of power, a *tâtonnement* mechanism defined by the competitive checking or compromise process will lead to the complete elimination of utility losses. If information is imperfect – the position of demand curves not well known – some utility losses will remain in equilibrium, but it will be by an amount consistent with the cost of acquiring more information.

When the checking process has worked itself through, all constitutional variables and the flows of all goods and services in any one bundle will be in equilibrium. In other words, even if the actual implementation of the compensation principle is drawn out and complicated, it will lead to an equilibrium vector of goods, services, and constitutional variables. In the absence of disturbances, at $t = 0$ the equilibrium will be stationary, and the flows of goods and services made available to citizens – the volume of police protection, of law and order and of justice, the size of family allowances, the level of international diplomacy, and all the others – will be observable and, in principle, measurable. However, in regards to the flow of services derived from the stock of constitutional variables, nothing is observable. The electoral rules in place are equilibrium rules and, by definition, receive the assent of citizens. The same will be true for the degree of separation of the executive, legislative, and judicial branches, the level of bicameralism, the extent of interjurisdictional decentralization, the relative size of the market sector, and so on.

The foregoing is an obvious point, but to the extent that the implementation of the compensation principle leads to outcomes that are at or near to equilibrium outcomes, it may help understand why a large body of opinion holds to the view that citizens in general do not have preferences over the characteristics of constitutional variables. Indeed, only when citizens find themselves significantly away from equilibrium will they reveal these preferences.

Running the process for different taxprices will trace a complete demand curve for the services of the constitutional characteristic Z_{10}. Checking processes are therefore true revelation mechanisms. The processes and mechanisms do not, however, generate a unique bundle (B_t) made of a given volume of goods and services and a given value of constitutional variables. It will, indeed, have been constructed by combining a subset of characteristics from the set of all available characteristics. There are a great many such subsets. The one constructed at a particular moment of time will depend on chance events such as the number and identity of the centers of power admitted to participate in the checking process, the order of intervention of centers of power in checking, the control over characteristics exercised by different centers of power, the differences in the personalities of those engaged in the checking processes, and so on. As a consequence, checking processes generate a multiplicity of equilibrium states or $B_t s$.

The Meta-Rules

The foregoing brief description of the workings of competition in compound governments has made no reference to the role of meta-rules in the determination of equilibrium outcomes. In this subsection, we introduce some relevant meta-rules before observing how they influence outcomes in the discussion of the next subsection.

The constitutional variable we have chosen to illustrate our basic position is still the degree of autonomy of a province (P) in a given country, a variable which, once normalized, continues to take values between zero and one, with one representing secession. In the preceding section, the meta-rule concerning secession affected all negotiations even when secession was not the issue. With the right to secede unilaterally in the background, we saw that the direction of transfers between P and the rest of the country (ROC) could be the reverse of what obtains under the meta-rule that unilateral secession cannot occur. In this section, meta-rules serve to differentiate changes in the demand for autonomy when these changes do not entail secession and independence from those changes which do. In the case in which the marginal change in autonomy does not lead to secession, the outcome depends on the nature of the exogenous disturbance, on the set of centers of power that would participate in the checking process, and on the particular characteristics of the autonomy variable over which the checking is to take place. In the case in which a marginal increment in autonomy would lead to secession and independence of P, the meta-rules conditioning the outcome would include the extent to which the ability of the province to secede as well as its ability to make a successful break can be affected by ROC. We examine both instances in the next section.

Some Comparative Statics

Let us assume that in the bundle of goods, services, and constitutional variables produced in the initial equilibrium, one constitutional variable is a given degree of autonomy for a province in a given country, namely A_{P0}. To appreciate what happens when that equilibrium is disturbed, it is necessary to understand that A_{P0} is constituted of a set of characteristics which, in effect, define what the word *autonomy* means. Some of these characteristics pertain to the role (formal and informal) of the province in influencing (say) monetary, fiscal, health care, and immigration policies in ROC; the weight of the province in the appointment of persons to different boards, tribunals, and councils in ROC; the capacity of the province to act without coordinating with other governments in matters such as labor mobility, subsidies to capital investment, the promotion of exports that affect ROC generally; and so on.

The checking process that produces A_P – that assembles the characteristics that define a particular level of A_P – requires the participation of many centers

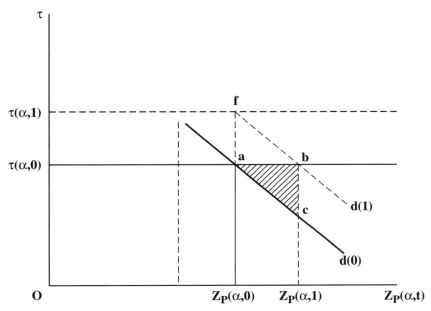

Figure 12.6. Utility loss as a consequence of an income induced shift in the demand for a characteristic

of power housed in the central government of the country and in the provincial and territorial governments.

Let us now consider an exogenous disturbance that takes the form of an increase in the average income of P's population. Let us further assume that this exogenous increase in income leads to an increase in the demand for A_P – the size of which depends on the income elasticity of the demand for A_P, whose size, in turn, we suppose, depends on the ratio of the number of federalists to secessionists in the province, being smaller the larger the ratio. However, the increase in the demand for autonomy, in this first case, falls short of being a demand for secession. The government of P knows that A_P is crafted by the centers of power listed earlier and it, consequently, knows that the increment in demand for A_P cannot be for an across-the-board increase in all the characteristics that define A_{P0}. An across-the-board increase in all characteristics would, indeed, jam or block the checking process and lead to zero increase in A_P, simply because the give and take associated with the checking process could not take place. P must therefore select one or a few characteristics as the object or objects of its increased demand for A_P. Let us call that characteristic or set of characteristics at time $t = 1$, $Z_P(\alpha,1)$, which is greater than $Z_P(\alpha,0)$, the flow of the set of characteristics α prevailing at $t = 0$. This is shown in Figure 12.6, which also portrays the utility loss (abc) suffered by P – given $Z_P(\alpha, 0)$ – as a consequence of the income induced shift in d from $d(0)$ to $d(1)$.

Will P get what it wants? In the absence of information problems, the answer to that question depends on the checking process operating to make utility losses for the constituents of all centers of power equal to zero. If one focuses on P alone as represented in Figure 12.6, as long as the $Z_P(\alpha, 0)$ determined in $t = 0$ persists, the new demand curve $d(1)$ implies a utility loss of *abc*. That loss can be reduced to zero in a number of ways. For example, P can be granted $Z_P(\alpha, 1)$. Or it can be provided with a substitute to $Z_P(\alpha, 1)$ that will return $d(1)$ to $d(0)$. The shift in $d(1)$ need not, however, be complete, in which case *abc* can be reduced to zero by granting some $Z_P(\alpha, 1')$ intermediate between $Z_P(\alpha, 0)$ and $Z_P(\alpha, 1)$ depending on how perfect the substitute is.

The substitute that shifts $d(1)$ is in the nature of a transfer from the other centers of power to P and will create a utility loss for the constituents of these centers. Adjustments therefore have to take place elsewhere. We assume, as we did earlier, that these adjustments will be governed by a *tâtonnement* process that leads to an overall equilibrium.

Consider now an exogenous increase in average incomes in P that leads to an increased demand for autonomy sufficiently large to be, in effect, a demand for secession and independence. We have to this point assumed the taxprice of $Z_P(\alpha, t)$ to be given and the checking process to be carried out at that price. We must now recognize that the taxprice of autonomy, and therefore of secession, can change as a consequence of variations in *technological* or *institutional* factors – in the meta-rules – that will bring about changes in the position of the supply curve. In Figure 12.6, the displacement of the supply curve raises the unit prize of autonomy to P from $\tau(\alpha, 0)$ to $\tau(\alpha, 1)$. The utility loss of *abc*, caused by the exogenous increase in average incomes has been wiped out.

An example of such a technological-institutional meta-rule change is the bill, informally known as the Clarity Bill, which was recently enacted in Canada. That Act of the Canadian Parliament does not affect the right of the Government of Quebec to make unilateral decisions regarding the referendums on secession, although it does affect other meta-rules. In particular, it specifies that unless the referendum question is "clear"[11] and unless the fraction of the Quebec population voting in favor of secession is "sufficiently large," the centers of power in the governments of *ROC* would not be obligated to negotiate with Quebec – would not have to enter into a checking process – even if the government of the province declared that it had "won" the referendum.[12]

The Clarity Act, it would appear, reduced the supply of $Z_P(\alpha, t)$ and thus raised its taxprice. If the increase in $\tau(\alpha, t)$ had happened to be equal to

[11] In 1982 and again in 1995, the referendum questions crafted by the Quebec government were paragons of obscurity.
[12] The Clarity Act applies to all provinces. We write Quebec because that is the province with the strongest secessionist population at this moment. For factual information on the economic aspects of secessions and secessionism in a large number of countries, see Bookman (1993).

$\tau(\alpha, 1) - \tau(\alpha, 0) = af$, then the quantity of $Z_P(\alpha, t)$ demanded by Quebec – even with a larger average income – would continue to be $Z_P(\alpha, 0)$ and the utility loss in Quebec would have been wiped out completely, as can be seen in Figure 12.6. If the increase in the taxprice happened to be less than af, the utility loss could still have been made equal to zero either by a judicious increase in $Z_P(\alpha, t)$, or in one or more of its substitutes, or by a combination of both.

We possess no information on the size of the increase in $\tau(\alpha, t)$ following the enactment of the Clarity Bill and, *a fortiori*, on the reduction in utility losses that the increase in the demand for A_P on the part of the Quebec government has created. It is remarkable, however, that notwithstanding the serious efforts of the Parti Québécois government – Quebec's secessionist government – to mobilize public opinion in Quebec against the bill, polls indicate that the bill received the overwhelming support of Quebeckers. The increase in the taxprice of $Z_P(\alpha, t)$ must have been nearly equal to af. In other words, it would appear that the Clarity Act, though it in no way affected the right of Quebec to act unilaterally in matters related to the holding of referenda on secession and independence, did reduce the demand for autonomy, and therefore secession, by increasing its supply price.

COMPARING THE OUTCOME OF COMPENSATION IN THE TWO MODELS

The model of this chapter's section on electoral competition places in center stage negotiations between incumbent legislators – negotiations in which compensations play a central role. The model of the chapter's section on compound governments gives the same place to a checking and compromise process in which compensations also play a basic role. In the remainder of this section, we point to a difference between the two models that has so far not been mentioned.

In the case of electoral competition, the fact that there is a "gain from trade" (recall the reservations to the use of that term formulated in that section) for legislators does not translate directly into one for voters. Within one district, the compensation between what is gained on one side of the transaction and what is lost on the other takes place within the maximization of an aggregate variable: the sum of the probabilities that individuals will vote for the incumbent. In turn, these probabilities depend not only on the individual utilities derived from the platforms of the incumbent and his or her opponent but also on the responsiveness of these probabilities to variations in the platforms. Thus, as a result of the transaction between the two incumbent legislators, some voters in both districts receive a benefit and partake in a cost, other voters receive benefits without paying anything, others still contribute to costs without receiving benefits. To illustrate, if the representative of the first jurisdiction accepts an increase in the value of the constitutional rule R in exchange for more subsidies given to his or her district, and if the subsidies benefit to various degrees all the voters in the district, this constitutes an *undeserved* benefit for the voters who in any case were in favor of an increase in R. Conversely, in the other district, there are voters who pay extra taxes although they are displeased by the change in R. They clearly lose from the transaction. Should we expect the legislators to attempt to compensate losers by the way of taxes imposed on winners? This would be very detrimental to the objective of vote maximization. Moreover, because sensitiveness may play as large a role as utility in the maximization formula, it is not even sure that such compensation would, even in principle, be possible. As a consequence, there can be no general presumption that the exchanges undertaken by the legislators are welfare enhancing and it is certainly improper to say that a district as a whole gains or loses from a transaction struck by its representative.

The matter is different in the case of the competitive compound government model. There, the assumption of perfect competition among a large number of centers of power on the supply side justifies multiform checking processes that, at the limit (that is when stationary equilibrium is reached) eliminate all utility losses at the level of individual citizens or, more generally, at the level of all individuals who are in some sense empowered. The compensations that underlie these processes are highly disaggregated whereas constitutional rules and the exact values that they take are on the contrary highly aggregated, being almost always in the nature of pure public goods. In that framework, compensation involving only constitutional rules would be difficult to achieve. But, under our approach, this means that compensation between constitutional characteristics and goods and services, which are in most cases private goods, apportionable at the level of individuals, is highly relevant to the understanding of constitutional change. It should also be noted that, inasmuch as compensation is complete, and contrary to the electoral model, the notion of a gain achieved by the change of a constitutional rule is necessarily defined at the level of individuals, and there must be a presumption that the exchanges are in a sense welfare enhancing.

CONCLUSION

The effect of constitutional rules, we have argued, depends on the nature of political competition and on the content of exogenous meta-rules that embody the procedures regulating the application and the modification of constitutional rules. Two models of competition – electoral competition and compound government competition – were outlined and the nature of the transactions between the parties involved described. In the two models, the transactions are over constitutional rules and ordinary goods and services, all of which are arguments in the utility functions of possibly all citizens but, in general, of only a subset of citizens who, however, will have an impact on outcomes given the assumption regarding the probabilistic nature of political competition.

Because the implementation of constitutional rules is always affected by procedural meta-rules, it is necessary to select a particular constitutional rule to examine the impact of a given meta-rule. We have chosen to focus on the constitutional rule associated with the demand for political autonomy, a variable which, at the limit, becomes a demand for secession and independence. A concentration on this phenomenon allows us to give a precise meaning to the effects of a procedural meta-rule. We found that relatively small differences in the content of the meta-rules led to large differences in equilibrium outcomes. Whether that conclusion can be generalized to all constitutional rules for which meta-rules are significant is a question we cannot answer. It is certainly one deserving further attention.

REFERENCES

Alesina, Alberto, & Spolaore, Enrico (1997), "On the number and size of nations," *Quarterly Journal of Economics*, Vol. 112, No. 4, 1027–1056.

Bolton, Patrick, Roland, Gérard, & Spolaore, Enrico (1996), "Economic theories of the break-up and integration of nations," *European Economic Review*, Vol. 40, nos. 3–5, 697–705.

Bookman, Milica Zarcovic (1993), *The Economics of Secession* (London: Macmillan).

Bordignon, Massimo, & Brusco, Sandro (2000), "Optimal secession rules," *European Economic Review*, Vol. 45, No. 10, 1811–1834.

Breton, Albert (1996), *Competitive Governments. An Economic Theory of Politics and Public Finance* (New York: Cambridge University Press).

Calvert, Randall L. (1986), *Models of Imperfect Information in Politics* (Chur, Switzerland: Harwood Academic Publishers).

Cooter, Robert C. (2000), *The Strategic Constitution* (Princeton: Princeton University Press).

Coughlin, Peter J. (1992), *Probabilistic Voting Theory* (Cambridge & New York: Cambridge University Press).

Grillo, Michele (1997), "Democracy, competition, and the principle of *Isonomia*: An economic analysis of the political exchange as an incomplete contract," in Albert Breton, Gianluigi Galeotti, Pierre Salmon, and Ronald Wintrobe, eds., *Understanding Democracy* (New York: Cambridge University Press), 47–63.

Kirchgässner, Gebhard (2000), "Probabilistic voting and equilibrium: An impossibility result," *Public Choice*, Vol. 103, Nos. 1–2, 35–48.

Lafay, Jean-Dominique (1992), "La théorie probabiliste du vote," *Revue d'Economie Politique*, Vol. 102, No. 4, July–August, 487–518.

Lancaster, Kelvin J. (1966), "A new approach to consumer theory," *Journal of Political Economy*, Vol. 74, No. 2, April, 132–157.

Mueller, Dennis C. (1989), *Public Choice II* (New York: Cambridge University Press).

Mueller, Dennis C. (2001), "On writing a constitution," in Ram Mudambi, Pietro Navarra, and Giuseppe Sobbrio, eds., *Rules and Reason: Perspectives on Constitutional Political Economy* (Cambridge & New York: Cambridge University Press), 9–32.

Panagopoulos, Epaminondas P. (1985), *Essays on the History and Meaning of Checks and Balances* (Lanham: University Press of America).

Rota Graziosi, Grégoire (2001). "Une analyse économique de la sécession," *Recherches Economiques de Louvain*, Vol. 67, No. 3, 315–348.

Salmon, Pierre (2001a), "Ordinary elections and constitutional arrangements," in Ram Mudambi, Pietro Navarra, and Giuseppe Sobbrio, eds., *Rules and Reasons: Perspectives on Constitutional Political Economy* (Cambridge & New York: Cambridge University Press), 165–180.

Salmon, Pierre (2001b), "Constitutional implications of electoral assumptions," *Constitutional Political Economy*, Vol. 12, No. 4, 333–349.

Tullock, Gordon (1998), *On Voting: A Public Choice Approach* (Cheltenham, UK: Edward Elgar).

Usher, Dan (1994), "The significance of the probabilistic voting theorem," *Canadian Journal of Economics*, Vol. 27, No. 2, May, 433–445.

Vanberg, Viktor J. (1998), "Freiburg School of Law and Economics," in Peter Newman, ed., *The New Palgrave Dictionary of Economics and the Law*, Vol. 2 (London: Macmillan), 172–179.

Voigt, Stefan (1999), *Explaining Constitutional Change: A Positive Economics Approach* (Cheltenham, UK: Edward Elgar).

Index

virtue (*cont.*)
    role of, 101–4
    screening mechanism and, 112–13
    stock of, 109
    two-tier representation of, 115–21
Vishny, Robert W., 170n24, 185
voice, 80–2, 82n23, 218–19
Voigt, Stefan, 7, 10, 165, 225n3
voter(s), 2, 120, 181, 192–94
    altruism and, 9, 94–7, 95n1, 96n2,
        97n3, 98n4
    communication and, 17–18
    controlling power, 183–85, 183n12
    delegation and, 182–85, 182n7
    entrapment, 188–90
    expressive, 150n2
    income of, 55n11
    inferences/mappings of, 19, 21
    majority of, 55, 55n11, 96, 96n2
    median, 51–4, 53f, 58, 96n2
    negative advertising and, 16–18, 26–8
    principals'/agents' goals and, 7, 185,
        194
    reliance, support of, 185–88, 186f,
        186nn15–16
    solidarity and, 10
    utility, 26–7
voter preferences, 18–19, 20f, 21–6, 22f.
    See also policy(ies), agendas
    cyclic majorities and, 49–51
votes, 15, 31, 188–89, 189n22, 192–94,
    192n28

wages, 34n7
Ward, Benjamin, 93
Washington, 15
wealth, 51
    assets and, 55, 55n9
    distribution of, 48

material, 9
median voter and, 52–4, 53f
redistribution of, 54, 93
Weber, Max, 158
Weingast, Barry R., 49, 189, 199n3
welfare
    economic growth and maximized, 37
    function, 95, 95n1
    individual, 32, 36
    personal, 51n7
    states, 7, 10, 148, 167–68
    technological growth and, 40
West, 5, 34n7
"When Discourse Also Matters for
    Growth," 32, 41–2
Whyte, William, 139–40
will
    General, 125, 137–38
    weakness of, 151n3
Williams, B., 107n5
Williamson, O. E., 208n11
Wilson, Woodrow, 61n19
Winsky, Laura, 191n26
Wintrobe, Ronald, 6, 11, 127–28, 130–31
    on solidarity, 127–28, 130–31, 133n3
Wittman, Donald, 6, 9–10, 44, 189
Wohlgemuth, Michael, 188n20
work
    ethic, 55n12
    hours for individuals, 34n7
    symposia and, 36–7, 39
    voluntary, 83, 99
World Values Survey, 160
World War I (WWI), 181
World War II (WW II), 5

Yugoslavia, 165n20

Zak, P., 157